The Master Chefs Cookbook

Also by Sandy Lesberg

THE SINGLE CHEF'S COOKBOOK
SPECIALTY OF THE HOUSE
GREAT CLASSIC RECIPES OF EUROPE
GREAT CLASSIC RECIPES OF THE WORLD
A SHORT DRIVE IN THE COUNTRY
AT THE TABLE OF ISRAEL
THE ART OF AFRICAN COOKING
SAUCY LADIES
THE ART OF THE DESSERT

The Master Chefs Cookbook

SANDY LESBERG

Recipes from the finest restaurants compiled
with the cooperation of Carte Blanche ®

THE McGRAW-HILL BOOK COMPANY

NEW YORK   ST. LOUIS   SAN FRANCISCO   TORONTO

First Edition

Library of Congress Cataloging in Publication Data

Lesberg, Sandy
  The Master Chefs Cookbook

  Includes index.
  1.   Cookery, International.   2.   Restaurants
  I.   Title
TX 725.A1L44   641.59   80-10284
ISBN 0-07-037333-7

This book is dedicated to friends John Bertram,
Al Freedman, Eugene Clarence Braun-Munk, Brian Ridgway,
Andre Sauzeau, *above all to my father*, Myer Lesberg

CONTENTS

INTRODUCTION

This book will hopefully contribute to the demystification of the art of preparing fine foods. Cooking and cookery have recently fallen victim to a great deal of folderol and nonsense involving the deification of individuals and institutions of some particular fad or fancy, all in the name of good taste (most of which it isn't). Stars and star makers abound in the culinary heavens and much ado is made of practically nothing new under those heavens. It's time to get back to earth.

If there is to be a star, a real virtuoso of the kitchen, a genuine leader and innovator to be acknowledged as such, then at the very least let us proclaim the rightful one—the WORKING CHEF!

The real creative wellsprings of the culinary arts are the chefs who day in and day out prepare their specialty dishes (together with quite a few others), and are put to the test of having their expertise tried on an ongoing basis by the public who may be friendly and sympathetic to the cause, but are also prone to fickleness when their palate is not well served. Most chefs are modest albeit prideful about their work. Certainly, most chefs, no matter how proficient and artful about their craft, even those who are genuine wellsprings of the art as a whole, are all really CHEFS and not public relations managers.

This book is therefore the voice of those chefs who perform their magic daily, assessing trends and passing fancies and judging the worth of all such fripperies in the light of their own instincts and experience. Theirs is, in great part, a dedication to consistency.

In this collection of signature recipes each carries the name of the restaurant of origination and most carry the name of the senior chef. You will find many great, classic dishes as well as much innovation. Each recipe represents a very generous gesture for which I am grateful. With the assistance of the Carte Blanche organization we have here, many for the first time in print, specialty dishes from some of the finest restaurants in the United States (and some from abroad). In many ways this represents a very unusual gift from them. Receiving a recipe from a master chef is like being invited to listen to a private concert by a great musician, or seeing for the first time a hitherto unknown painting by a master.

These are works of art and should be so considered. THE MASTER CHEFS COOKBOOK acknowledges the role of the chef as teacher and friend—and here is the best of many of them. In the past the pleasures contained here have been available only to those who were fortunate enough to be geographically able to visit each of the premises, but now the feast is truly moveable.

Each dish in this volume has a pedigree. Many recipes you will find challenging, some may be old friends with a new approach. In all instances I urge you, at least for the first time, to follow the directions as precisely as possible. The chefs have been very careful in presenting their works with great detail, and I suspect, given their expertise, not without reason.

Here, then, are over three hundred and fifty recipes from some of the great MASTER CHEFS both here and abroad. A wonderful experience awaits you, and now—it's time to begin!

SANDY LESBERG

SECTION ONE

Appetizers   *Soups*   *Salads*

The Mansion
Atlanta, Georgia
Proprietor: William S. Swearingen
Chef: Hans Bertram

BAKED OYSTERS BEACH HOUSE

1/4	stick butter
1/4	cup chopped green onions
1/8	cup chopped white onions
1/2	cup sliced fresh mushrooms
1/8	cup diced, peeled tomatoes
1/2	cup flour
2	cups milk
1	cup fish stock *(see index)*
1	cup white wine
1	touch garlic salt
1	touch white pepper
2	bay leaves
1	touch tabasco sauce
1	teaspoon Worcestershire sauce
2	egg yolks
1/2	cup cream
36	Long Island oysters, cooked on the half-shell
	Hollandaise sauce *(see index)*
	grated Parmesan cheese
	bread crumbs

Melt butter in casserole. Add chopped green and white onions and sliced mushrooms and sauté for about 3 minutes. Add tomatoes and mix well.

In a separate saucepan, mix flour in milk while heating. Add heated milk mixture, fish stock, and white wine to onions and mushrooms. Bring to a boil and stir until thick and creamy.

Add garlic salt, pepper, bay leaves, tabasco and Worcestershire. Mix egg yolks and cream together and stir into sauce, bringing to another boil. Remove from heat and cool.

Remove oysters from shells. Dip the sauce into the empty shells and put oysters on top of sauce. Bake at 350° for about 3–4 minutes. Remove from oven, cover with Hollandaise sauce, sprinkle with Parmesan cheese and bread crumbs. Broil until browned to perfection.

Serves: 6

Northstar Inn
Rosewood Room
Minneapolis, Minnesota
Chef: Pierre-Jean Laupies

MOULES ROCHELAISES

4	pounds fresh mussels, tightly closed
	white wine, as needed
	salted water, as needed
	herb butter *(see recipe below)*
1	cup bread crumbs

Wash mussels in a colander in running water. In a kettle, mix salted water and a little bit of white wine to cover mussels. Bring to a boil. Place mussels in boiling water and bring back to boil. Cook for 3–4 minutes and strain. Open mussels completely and break off 1 shell so they are in half-shells. Put some herb butter on each mussel and sprinkle with bread crumbs. Put in snail dish and bake at 350° for 10 minutes.

Herb Butter

10 ounces butter
2 ounces minced garlic
1 ounce finely chopped parsley
1 dash cognac
  salt and pepper, to taste

Mix all ingredients together.

Serves: 8–10

Red Onion
Metairie, Louisiana
Proprietors: Frank Grimoskas
and Frank Occhipinti, Jr.
Chefs: Muce Benjamin, Gary Mitchell,
and Alfred Stewart

RED ONION OYSTERS AMANDINE

36 oysters
   flour, to dust
   cooking oil, to fry
1 stick butter
2 tablespoons flour
1 tablespoon chicken base
2 cups water
2 tablespoons Lea & Perrins Sauce
  juice of 1/2 lemon
  sliced almonds

To prepare oysters: lightly roll oysters in plain white flour. Fry until golden brown in cooking oil. Prepare sauce while oysters are cooking.

To prepare Meunière sauce: melt butter in large saucepan. Remove pan from heat and add 2 tablespoons flour, chicken base, water, Lea & Perrins Sauce, and lemon juice to melted butter. Cook over medium-high heat until sauce comes to a boil, stirring often.

Place fried oysters in casserole dish.

Sprinkle almonds on top of oysters. Ladle Meunière sauce over oysters and serve.

Serves: 6

WINE: *Italian Frascati*
or French Chablis

Carlos N' Charlies
La Jolla, California
Chef: Francisco Arzaluz

OYSTERS MADRAZO

6 blue point oysters, shelled
  rock salt, as needed
3 teaspoons cooked and spiced spinach
3 teaspoons sour cream
6 dashes chile chipotle
  grated Monterey Jack cheese, as
  needed
  lemon and parsley, to garnish

Place oysters back into shells. On a small plate, place a bed of rock salt (so oysters won't turn over and spill) and place oysters on it. Add 1/2 teaspoon cooked spinach to each oyster, then add 1/2 teaspoon sour cream to each. Top each with a dash of chile chipotle. Cover oysters with grated cheese until all other ingredients are totally covered. Place oysters in a salamander (upright broiler) until cheese turns golden brown. Remove and garnish with slices of lemon and parsley.

Serves: 1–2

Hotel Dorset
New York, New York
Chef: William J. Spry

CLAMS CASINO

1 1/2	pounds butter
2	tablespoons chopped shallots
1	tablespoon chopped fresh parsley
1	clove garlic, chopped
	juice of 2 lemons
36	fresh cherrystone clams
1	pound sliced bacon, uncooked
	rock salt

Soften the butter to room temperature and mix well with all the chopped ingredients and lemon juice. Wash the clams well, open, and leave on half shell. Place a teaspoon of the savory butter on each clam. Cut bacon into 1″ pieces. Place a piece of bacon on the butter. Put 6 clams per person on an ovenproof dish with a bed of rock salt. Bake in a warm oven for about 15 minutes. Serve at once.

Serves: 6

Hampshire House
Boston, Massachusetts
Proprietor: Thomas A. Kershaw
Chef: Nicholas Francisco

MOULES MARINIER

4	shallots
3	cloves garlic
1/2	cup butter
1/2	cup white wine
1	bay leaf
2	tablespoons dry thyme
4	quarts bearded mussels
1/2	cup heavy cream
1/4	cup chopped parsley

Sauté shallots and garlic in butter until golden. Add wine, bay leaf, thyme, and mussels. Cook closely covered. Agitate the pan sufficiently to cook mussels evenly. Add heavy cream and chopped parsley and cook until mussels open. Pour the mussels and sauce in coquilles and serve over a seaweed bed.

Serves: 6–8

Albion's
Sherman Oaks, California
Proprietor: Claude Gobet
Chef: Guy Birster

FEUILLETÉ D'HUITRES AU SAFRON
(Oysters with Saffron Sauce in Pastry)

1/2	cup dry white wine
2	tablespoons finely chopped shallots
1/4	teaspoon saffron powder
4	medium-sized mushrooms, thinly sliced
4	large scallops, sliced
1	cup freshly-opened oysters, cut in small pieces
	salt and pepper, to taste
4	cooked pastry shells
1/3	cup whipping cream
2	ounces butter

Put white wine, shallots, and saffron into a saucepan. Boil and reduce to 1/2 original volume. Add mushrooms, scallops, and oysters. Season with salt and pepper. Simmer for 3 minutes, but do not boil.

Using a slotted spoon, remove scallops, oysters, and mushrooms and place them into warm pastry shells. Add cream to the saucepan. Boil and reduce for a few minutes. Remove from heat, add the butter, and swirl pan until butter is totally melted. Correct seasoning with salt and pepper. Pour into the pastry shells over the oysters, scallops and mushrooms and serve.

Serves: 4

WINE: *Chablis or Sylvaner*

Grenadier's Restaurant
Milwaukee, Wisconsin
Proprietor: Robert Jordan
Chef: Knut Apitz

OYSTERS À LA GRENADIER

- 24 large spinach leaves
- 1 teaspoon Pernod
- 24 bearded, cleaned, fresh oysters
- 2 cups fish velouté *(see recipe below)*

Blanch spinach rapidly, flatten out, and brush with Pernod. Roll each oyster into a leaf. Put into empty oyster shell. Lightly cover oysters with fish velouté. Bake at 350° for 10–15 minutes.

Fish Velouté

- 1/2 pound fish bones, coarsely chopped
  cold water, as needed
- 1/4 medium-sized onion
- 1/2 bay leaf
- 4 peppercorns
- 6 sprigs parsley
- 1/2 sprig celery
  pinch of salt
  roux *(see index)*
- 2 tablespoons heavy cream
- 2 egg yolks
- 1/2 cup dry white wine

To prepare fish velouté: in a pot, cover fish bones with water and add onion, bay leaf, peppercorns, parsley, celery, and salt. Bring slowly to a boil and simmer 5 minutes. Stand, strain through cheesecloth.

Bring to a boil again and thicken with beurre roux or beurre manié. Add heavy cream and egg yolks. *Do not boil.* Add white wine and strain sauce through a fine strainer.

Serves: 4

WINE: *Chablis*

Broussard's Restaurant
New Orleans, Louisiana
Proprietors: Joseph C. Marcello,
Joseph Marcello, Jr., Clarence Greco,
& Joseph Segreto

CRABMEAT AND OYSTERS CASSEROLE

- 4 ounces cream cheese, at room temperature
- 1/4 cup green peppers, cut finely
- 1/4 cup pimientos, dried
  salt and pepper, to taste
- 1 pound lump crabmeat
- 1 pint cream sauce, prepared
- 1 quart oysters, drained
- 2 ounces butter
- 4 green onions, cut finely
- 1 cup cream sauce, prepared
- 1/4 cup beef stock
- 2 dashes Lea & Perrins Sauce
  bread crumbs, as needed

To prepare crabmeat: put cream cheese in a bowl, then add green peppers, pimientos, salt and pepper and blend. Add crabmeat and sauce and set aside.

To prepare oysters: brown oysters on hot grill. In another pan, sauté green onions in butter for 3–4 minutes. Add browned oysters, cream sauce, and beef stock. Blend and cook about 5 minutes. Add Lea & Perrins Sauce and mix.

Put oyster mixture in center of casserole and lay crabmeat mixture around it. Sprinkle with bread crumbs and bake at 400° for at least 10 minutes.

Serves: 6–8

WINE: *White*

CRAB DANTÉ

1 1/4	sticks butter, and as needed
1/2	cup chopped onion
1/2	cup flour
1	pint milk (approximately)
1	cup stock or bouillon
3	bay leaves
	touch *each* salt, pepper, Worcestershire sauce, and tabasco sauce
1/2	pint cream
4	egg yolks
2	ounces white wine
1 1/2	pounds lump crabmeat
48	fresh mushroom caps
1/2	pint Hollandaise sauce *(see index)*
1/4	cup bread crumbs
1/4	cup grated Parmesan cheese

To prepare crab meat sauce: melt 1 stick butter, add chopped onion and cook for 5 minutes, then add flour and mix well. In a separate saucepan, heat milk and stock together, then mix with flour and butter, stir well. Add bay leaves, salt, pepper, Worcestershire sauce, and tabasco and boil slowly for about 30 minutes. During this time, add 1/4 stick butter and mix in thoroughly. Strain sauce. Mix cream and egg yolks with wine in a bowl, then slowly stir into sauce. *Do not boil sauce again.*

Mix crabmeat and sauce together. Sauté button mushrooms in butter in a separate skillet. Fill mushroom caps with crabmeat sauce, top with Hollandaise sauce, sprinkle bread crumbs and cheese on top, and bake under salamander or broiler until golden brown.

Serves: 8

CRABMEAT RENAISSANCE

6	ounces clarified butter
2/3	cup finely chopped shallots
18	ounces Alaskan King Crab meat
1 1/2	ounces dry sherry
2	ounces cognac
12	ounces lobster sauce *(see index)*
8	ounces heavy cream
	salt and pepper, to taste
2	cups cooked white rice
1	teaspoon chopped parsley

Heat a heavy-duty crepe pan. Place 2 ounces butter in pan and cook shallots lightly. Add crabmeat. Sauté crabmeat lightly, being careful not to bruise it. Add sherry, cook 1 minute. During this time, turn crabmeat over once. Add cognac and flame. Baste crabmeat with butter and sherry mixture. Add remaining butter. Lower heat and move crabmeat to one side of pan to make room for sauce preparation.

Add lobster sauce to pan and blend with butter until totally smooth. Add heavy cream, continue to cook and blend for 1 minute. Baste sauce over crabmeat. Allow to simmer for 5 minutes on low heat. Salt and pepper to taste.

Place cooked rice on dinner plate, forming a ring. Place crabmeat in center of rice. Sprinkle with chopped parsley.

Serves: 4

WINE: *Puligny-Montrachet*

Emily Shaws Inn
Pound Ridge, New York
Proprietor: John Shaw

JOHN SHAW APPETIZER

8 slices white bread
1 cup mayonnaise
1 teaspoon curry powder
14 ounces lump crabmeat (fresh or frozen)
 salt and pepper, to taste
1 cup grated cheddar cheese

With a cookie cutter or glass rim, shape bread into rounds, then toast *one side only* under broiler. Combine mayonnaise and curry powder and spread combination on *untoasted side* of bread. Place crabmeat on top of each round. Salt and pepper to taste. Sprinkle grated cheese over all and toast under broiler until cheese melts.

Serves: 8

WINE: *Chablis*

Ristorante Orsi
San Francisco, California
Proprietors: Anna and Joe Orsi
Chef: Loreno Orsi

CRAB ORSI

1 pinch sage
1 pinch thyme
1 pinch Italian parsley
1 pinch Italian watercress
3 ounces butter
3 ounces cream
3 ounces milk
1 ounce Marcella wine
5 ounces crabmeat
 grated Parmesan cheese, as needed
 bread crumbs, as needed

Mix sage and thyme with parsley and watercress and grind them together. Melt butter, add cream and milk to make a sauce. Add wine. Place crabmeat in scallop shell and cover with the sauce. Mix Parmesan cheese and bread crumbs together and spread on top. Bake at 500° until brown, approximately 20 minutes.

Serves: 2

WINE: *Marcella wine*

Kaphan's
Houston, Texas
Proprietor: Peter Tomac
Chef: Arnold Tomac

CRAB IMPERIAL

1 tablespoon English mustard
1 tablespoon salt
1/2 tablespoon white pepper
2 eggs, lightly beaten
1 cup mayonnaise
1 tablespoon MSG
1 green pepper, diced finely
2 pimientos, diced finely
3 pounds lumb crabmeat
 mayonnaise and paprika, as needed for topping

Mix together English mustard, salt, pepper, eggs, mayonnaise, and Accent. Add diced pepper and pimientos. Add crabmeat and mix lightly.

Prepare eight crab shells by scrubbing and soaking them in baking soda water for 15 minutes to sterilize and deodorize them, or use 8 small casseroles. Fill each container with the mixture. Top with a light coating of mayonnaise and sprinkle with paprika. Bake in 350° oven for 15 minutes. Serve hot or cold.

Serves: 8

Sign of the Dove
New York, New York
Chef: Guy Gauthier

LES CHEVEUX D'ANGE GENERAL ROMULO

1/2	ounce unsalted butter
2	ounces chopped leeks
2	ounces Alaskan King Crab meat
1	ounce finely chopped black truffles
1	ounce brandy
2	ounces Chablis (or other dry white wine)
4	ounces fish stock *(see index)*
4	ounces capelli d'angelo (angel hair pasta)
	salt and pepper, to taste
1	teaspoon chopped parsley

Place butter, chopped leeks, crabmeat, and truffles into pan and cook for 2–3 minutes over low heat. Add brandy and Chablis and let flambé. Add fish stock and bring to boil. Remove from heat.

In another pot, cook the capelli d'angelo, stirring constantly. (Quality of pasta and taste determine cooking time.)

When pasta is cooked, strain and place into sauce. Salt and pepper to taste. Add chopped parsley and serve.

Serves: 2

WINE: *Bardolino, Bertani*

The Ponchartrain Hotel
Caribbean Room
New Orleans, Louisiana
Proprietor: Albert Aschaffenburg
Chef: Louis Evans

CRABMEAT REMICK

1	pound lump crabmeat
	Remick Sauce
6	small pieces cooked bacon

Divide the crabmeat into 6 portions, pile into individual ramekins. Heat in 400° oven until hot. While waiting for crabmeat to heat, prepare sauce:

Remick Sauce

1/2	teaspoon dry mustard
1/2	teaspoon paprika
1/2	teaspoon celery salt
1/2	teaspoon tabasco sauce
1/2	cup chili sauce
1	teaspoon tarragon vinegar
1/2	cup mayonnaise

Blend together all dry ingredients and tabasco sauce. Add chili sauce and tarragon vinegar. Mix well. Then blend in mayonnaise.

Place a piece of crisp bacon in the middle of each hot crabmeat-filled ramekin and spread the Remick Sauce over it, just enough to cover.

Return ramekins to oven for just a few seconds and serve immediately. (The Remick Sauce will separate if the dish is left inside the oven too long.)

Serves: 6

Chesapeake Restaurant
Baltimore, Maryland
Proprietor: Richard P. Friedman
Chef: Edward Sullivan

CRAB IMPERIAL CHESAPEAKE

1	green pepper, finely diced
2	pimientos, finely diced
1	tablespoon English mustard
1	tablespoon salt
1/2	teaspoon white pepper
2	eggs
1	cup mayonnaise
3	pounds lump crabmeat
	mayonnaise and paprika, for topping

Mix diced pepper and pimiento. Add mustard, salt, pepper, eggs, and mayonnaise; mix well. Add crabmeat and mix in with fingers so lumps are not broken. Divide mixture into 8 clam shells, or the like, heaping it in lightly. Top with a light coating of mayonnaise and sprinkle with paprika. Bake at 350° for 15 minutes. Serve hot or cold.

Serves: 8

The 57 Restaurant
Boston, Massachusetts
Proprietor: Louis N. Dadasis
Chef: Anthony Ancopoulos

SHRIMP ATHENIAN SHORE STYLE

2 cloves minced garlic
2 tablespoons minced onion
2 tablespoons olive oil
1 cup canned Italian peeled plum tomatoes
18 medium shrimp, raw, peeled, and deveined
2 tablespoons minced parsley
2 tablespoons sherry wine
2 pinches of oregano
salt and pepper, to taste
4 ounces Feta cheese

Sauté garlic and onion in oil until onion is transparent gold. Add tomatoes and simmer gently for about 15 minutes. Add shrimp and simmer about 10 minutes over medium heat until shrimp are not quite cooked through. Add parsley, sherry, oregano, salt and pepper and about 2 tablespoons of Feta cheese. Continue cooking until shrimp has cooked and cheese has melted and is thoroughly absorbed in sauce.

Turn out onto warm plate and sprinkle pieces of remaining Feta cheese over the dish. Put under broiler for a moment, but don't overdo it. The cheese is supposed to appear on this dish in little lumps, and it will completely dissolve if it gets too hot.

Serves: 4

WINE: *Greek white wine*

Sea N' Surf
Framingham, Massachusetts
Chef: Eric Peterson

SHRIMP SCAMPI

12 jumbo shrimp, peeled, deveined, and split lengthwise
3 eggs
1 cup flour
juice of 2 lemons
salt and pepper, to taste
1 1/2 teaspoons oregano
1 1/2 teaspoons garlic powder
2 teaspoons fresh chopped parsley
Worcestershire and tabasco sauce, to taste
1 cup olive oil
1/4 pound fresh butter
3 ounces Chablis wine

Combine shrimp, eggs, 1/4 cup flour, juice of 1 lemon, salt and pepper, 1 teaspoon garlic powder, 1 teaspoon parsley, 3 drops each of Worcestershire and tabasco sauce, and blend to form a batter. Flour each shrimp individually, using remaining 3/4 cup flour. Place olive oil in frying pan at medium heat. Cook shrimp in oil until golden brown. Remove shrimp and place on paper towel to absorb grease. Remove oil from pan and wipe clean.

Place butter in pan on low heat. Add shrimp, Chablis wine, juice of 1 lemon, 1/2 teaspoon garlic powder, salt and pepper, 1/2 teaspoon oregano, 1 teaspoon parsley. Blend thoroughly and serve.

Serves: 4

Olly Otten's Swiss Chalet
San Antonio, Texas
Proprietor/Chef: Olly Otten

SHRIMP ROTHSCHILDT

2 ounces butter
6 shallots, chopped
2 cloves fresh garlic
8 medium shrimp, peeled and
    deveined
  salt and fresh ground pepper, to
    taste
3 ounces sherry wine
2 ounces Korbel brandy
3 ounces tomato sauce

Melt butter over low heat and add shallots and garlic. Add shrimp, salt, and pepper. When shrimp turns pink (about 5 minutes), add wine and brandy and flambé. Add tomato sauce and serve.

Serves: 2

La Louisiane
New Orleans, Louisiana
Chef: Nick Mosca

SHRIMP MOSCA

2   ounces olive oil
2-3 pounds fresh shrimp
8   whole bay leaves
1   teaspoon crushed whole black
     pepper
6-8 garlic buds
1   teaspoon salt
1   pinch oregano
1   pinch rosemary
1   ounce white wine (Chablis or
     sauterne)

Heat oil in frying pan and add shrimp and spices. Sauté for 10–15 minutes or until garlic is a golden color. Add white wine and cook until wine is reduced 1/2. Total cooking time: 20–30 minutes.

Peel shrimp at the table and serve with hot crisp bread.

Serves: 4–6

Guido's Italian Cuisine
Los Angeles, California
Proprietor: Guido Perri
Chefs: Guido and Karin Perri

SPAGHETTI WITH SHRIMP SCAMPI

1   ounce sweet butter
1/2 pound peeled shrimp, chopped in
     small pieces
1   ounce capers
4   chopped shallots
2   ounces brandy
1   pint heavy cream
4   ounces ground pear tomatoes
1   pound round spaghetti, cooked "al
     dente"

In a saucepan, sauté the butter, shrimp, capers, and shallots. Before the butter turns brown, add brandy and flambé. Add heavy cream and tomatoes. Let the sauce reduce slowly until it reaches a creamy consistency. Drain the spaghetti, add to sauce, and toss.

Serves: 4

HOT CRUSTED SHRIMP IN ORANGE SAUCE

1	pound (about 15) jumbo shrimp, slit and cleaned
	cooking oil, as needed
8	ounces orange marmalade
2	ounces currant jelly
8	ounces white Chablis or sauterne
1/2	half ounce crushed red pepper
1/2	ounce garlic powder
1	egg, beaten
1/2	cup milk
1	teaspoon honey
1/2	cup bread crumbs

Sauté shrimp in oil for 2–3 minutes, then thoroughly dry on paper towels.

To prepare sauce: combine marmalade, currant jelly, wine, crushed red pepper, and garlic powder, and whip by hand in a bowl for 3 minutes or in a blender for 1 1/2 minutes.

To prepare batter:

In another container, blend egg, milk, honey, and bread crumbs. Adjust bread crumbs or milk to reach a smooth crepe-batter consistency.

Marinate sauteed shrimp for 5 minutes in sauce. Then, dip each shrimp into the batter and coat thoroughly. Bake battered shrimp in a cookie sheet in oven at 325–350° for 7–10 minutes or until crust turns golden brown. Serve with sauce.

Serves: 4–6

WINE: *Chablis Great Western or Soave*

SCALLOPS CONTINENTAL WITH WINE, LIME & THYME

12	fresh scallops
	butter, to sauté
	juice of 1 lime
	juice of 1 garlic clove
1	pinch each salt and white pepper
4	ounces Chablis wine
1	pinch sugar
1	teaspoon thyme

Sauté scallops in butter with lime juice, garlic juice, salt and white pepper for 3 minutes over medium heat. Remove scallops and put aside. Whip Chablis and sugar into sauce for 2 minutes over heat. Then add thyme. Pour sauce over scallops and serve.

Serves: 2–4

Siple's Garden Seat
Clearwater, Florida
Proprietor: Richard B. Siple
Chef: Louis Mantzanas

SHRIMP MOUTARDE

2   ounces mayonnaise
1   ounce Dijon mustard
1   ounce minced onion
6   ounces diced celery
18 large cooked shrimp, peeled and
    deveined
    croutons, as needed

Combine mayonnaise with mustard, then add onion and celery and mix to make sauce. Place 3 ounces of the sauce into 3 suitably-sized ramekins or gratin dishes and add 6 shrimps to each. Top with croutons and bake briefly until thoroughly hot. Serve immediately.

Serves: 3

WINE: *Trimbach Gewürztraminer*

Northstar Inn
Rosewood Room
Minneapolis, Minnesota
Chef: Pierre-Jean Laupies

COQUILLES ST. JACQUES AU BLEU

1   wedge bleu cheese
8   ounces white wine
1   ounce chopped shallots
2   pounds fresh scallops
    Hollandaise sauce (2 egg yolks, 1
    cup melted butter, salt and
    pepper, combined)

In a pan, scramble the bleu cheese, add wine and shallots, and bring to a boil. Put the scallops in the pan. Cover and let steam for a few minutes, making sure they do not overcook.

Drain the scallops and put on a shell or serving dish.

Reduce the cooking juices until they reach a creamy consistency. Add Hollandaise sauce. Pour over scallops and serve.

Serves: 4-6

Tango
Chicago, Illinois
Proprietor: George Badonsky
Chef: John J. Stoltzmann

SCALLOPS TANGO

2   pounds fresh sea scallops
1/2 cup lemon juice
1/2 cup lime juice
1/3 cup olive oil
1   teaspoon minced garlic
2   teaspoons salt
     white pepper, to taste
1   red onion, chopped
2   green peppers, diced
1   pint cherry tomatoes, halved
1/2 cup black olives, halved
     lettuce leaves
     chopped fresh parsley
     fresh limes

Cut scallops in half and place in shallow glass bowl. Add lemon juice, lime juice, olive oil, garlic, salt and pepper. Marinate overnight, making sure scallops are covered by marinade.

Add chopped onion, diced green pepper, cherry tomatoes, and black olives. Mix well and chill.

When ready to serve, place on lettuce leaves and sprinkle with chopped parsley. Serve with fresh lime.

Serves: 8

WINE: *Chablis*

Alameda Rooftop Restaurant
Alameda Plaza Hotel
Kansas City, Missouri
Chef: Jess Barbosa

LOBSTER AMERICAINE

8	tablespoons butter
1/4	cup finely chopped carrots
1/4	cup finely chopped onions
1/4	cup finely chopped celery
1/4	cup finely chopped shallots or scallions
2	tablespoons finely chopped fresh parsley
1/2	teaspoon saffron soaked in wine
4	4-ounce lobster tails
1	beaten egg mixed with 2 tablespoons milk
1	cup flour seasoned with 1 tablespoon Parmesan cheese
3	ounces tomato juice
1	cup dry white wine
3	cups peeled, seeded, coarsely chopped tomatoes
1/2	teaspoon lemon juice
	cornstarch, as needed

In a heavy saucepan, melt 4 tablespoons butter over moderate heat. When the foam subsides, stir in carrots, onions, and celery. Cook about 5 minutes, then add shallots. Continue cooking another 3 minutes. Add parsley, marinated saffron, and cook another 2 minutes. Set aside.

Split lobster tails lengthwise in half. Pull meat out. Dip in egg and milk mixture. Then dredge in flour. Shake off excess flour. In another skillet, cook tails on one side for 3-4 minutes at moderate heat in remaining butter. Then, turn and do the same on the other side until golden brown.

Pour contents of first pan over lobster. Add tomato juice, white wine, chopped tomatoes, and lemon juice. Blend careful-ly, heat, and correct seasoning. Add cornstarch as needed to thicken the sauce.

Serve when desired consistency is reached.

Serves: 4

Otto's Restaurant
Stockton, California
Proprietor: Joe Varni
Chef: Mike Boggiano

LOBSTER À LA BOURGOGNE

2	pounds butter
1/2	pound margarine
1/2	cup garlic, chopped finely
1	cup red onions, chopped finely
2	cups chopped parsley
	juice of 4 lemons
2	tablespoons Worcestershire sauce
1/3	teaspoon tabasco sauce
	salt and white pepper, to taste
4	lobsters, 1 pound each
	paprika, as needed

Allow butter and margarine to reach room temperature until semi-soft. Mix both in a large mixing bowl, blending well until creamy. Add garlic, onions, and parsley. Blend well again. Add juice of 2 lemons, worcestershire sauce, and tabasco sauce, and season to taste with salt. Chill for 1 hour.

With a knife, split the lobster in half, removing lobster from shell along with red film on top of lobster. Chop lobster into medium chunks, place in ovenproof escargot dish. Squeeze juice of remaining 2 lemons directly over lobster. Spoon chilled butter mixture over lobster. Sprinkle paprika over finished dish. Bake at 450° for 5–6 minutes or until bubbly.

Serves: 4–6

WINE: *Chablis*

CHICKEN AND MUSHROOM CREPES

        3 eggs
      1/4 teaspoon salt
        1 cup flour
      2/3 cup milk
      2/3 cup water
        1 tablespoon cooking oil
        2 tablespoons butter
        2 tablespoons flour
        1 cup chicken bouillon or broth
      1/4 teaspoon salt
      1/2 cup sliced fresh mushrooms
        1 egg yolk
        2 tablespoons cream
      1/4 cup cooked diced chicken or turkey

To prepare crepes: combine eggs and salt. Add flour, milk, and water, then add oil and stir. Using low flame, pour small amount of batter into an oiled crepe pan as you would a thin pancake. Turn over and remove. Makes 16 to 20 crepes.

To prepare filling: melt butter in a saucepan. Blend in flour, then add bouillon and salt. Stir and cook over moderate heat about 2 minutes or until thickened. Stir in mushrooms. Cook for 1 minute and remove from heat.

In a separate bowl, mix egg yolk and cream together, then stir a small amount of the hot mushroom mixture into it. Mix well, then combine both mixtures in the saucepan. Cook over low heat for another minute. Stir in chicken.

In a large, shallow baking dish, fill crepes with the mixture and bake in a moderate oven until heated through.

Serves: 8–10

WINE: *White*

CRAB CREPE MAXIM'S

      1/2 cup flour
      1/2 teaspoon salt
      1/2 cup half and half
        1 lightly beaten egg
        1 tablespoon cooking oil
        4 teaspoons butter
    1 1/2 cups Alaskan crabmeat chunks
        3 heaping tablespoons sour cream
        1 fresh lime
        1 tablespoon catsup
      1/2 teaspoon Dijon mustard
        4 drops tabasco sauce
      1/4 teaspoon salt
           paprika
        1 chopped boiled egg
        1 tablespoon chopped chives
        8 thin center slices of lemon
        8 bits of truffles or 8 olive halves

To prepare crepes: sift flour with salt, stir in half and half. Blend well. Add egg and oil, whisk only until blended. Batter should be thin enough to make crepes not over 1/8″ thick. Add flour or half and half as needed to correct. Heat a crepe or an 8–9″ omelette pan. Melt butter until bubbly but not brown. Make 4 crepes. Do not cook crepes on the top side. They should be lightly brown underside, glossy but firm on top. Place on wax paper.

To prepare crab filling: divide meat onto crepes. Squeeze 1/4 lime on each and add 1 heaping tablespoon sour cream. Roll lightly.

To prepare sauce: lightly blend remaining sour cream, catsup, mustard, tabasco and salt. Spoon over filled crepes. Gently sprinkle a little paprika over sauce, followed by chopped egg and chives.

Garnish each crepe with 2 slices of lemon which have been slit to the center, twisted and dotted with truffle bits or olive halves.

Can be prepared one or two hours before serving. Refrigerate up to 1/2 hour before serving. Best when not too cold.

Serves: 4

WINE: *Dry Champagne, Vouvray, or a dry Chenin Blanc*

The Inn at Turtle Creek
San Antonio, Texas

HOT CHEESE SOUFFLÉ

  1   large egg
1/8 teaspoon salt
1/8 teaspoon garlic or onion salt
1/2 pound freshly shredded firm
      processed American or cheddar
      cheese (use small shredder)
      two-day-old bread cut into either 20
      2″-rounds or 40 1 1/2″-rounds,
      thickly sliced
      soft butter, as needed

Beat egg slightly. Add seasonings and cheese, a little at a time, to egg, mixing well with a fork or spoon for about 1 minute, then with hand, until well blended and firm. Preparation must be very firm for best results and must not stick to hands when shaping rounds.

If using 2″-rounds, pick up 1 rounded standard measuring teaspoon of cheese preparation (about 2 level teaspoons) in palms of hands and shape into very smooth balls. Flatten balls and place them on lightly buttered bread rounds, leaving 1/4″ of bread free of cheese all around.

If using 1 1/2″-rounds, form small balls with 1 level measuring teaspoon cheese preparation.

About 5-6 minutes before serving, place prepared rounds on center of small baking sheet in preheated 425° broiler, 2″ from heat, until brown and puffed for about 5 minutes.

Soufflés may be broiled hours or even a day in advance, then kept in a covered container until shortly before ready to serve. To reheat, place them on a heat proof platter or baking sheet in oven (not broiler) preheated to 425° for about 5-6 minutes. An entire large platter or baking sheet may be reheated at one time and served immediately.

Serves: 10-20

The Farmer's Daughter
Orland Park, Illinois
Proprietor: Kandy Norton-Henely

QUICHE

    1   thinly rolled 8″-pastry shell
 1/3 cup finely chopped onion
    2   tablespoons butter
 1/3 cup chopped Swiss cheese
    6   slices bacon, fried and chopped
    2   tablespoons freshly chopped parsley
    1   tablespoon grated Parmesan cheese
    4   eggs, beaten
1 1/4 cups coffee cream
 1/4 teaspoon salt
 1/4 teaspoon white pepper
    1   teaspoon MSG
      paprika

Bake pastry shell in preheated oven at 400° just until it is light in color, about 15-20 minutes. Sauté onion in butter until transparent. Mix together all ingredients, except paprika, and pour into pastry shell. Bake on bottom rack of preheated 325° oven for 25-30 minutes or until custard is set in center when tested with tip of a knife. Cool 10 minutes and serve, or serve at room temperature or reheated in 350° oven for 15 minutes

Serves: 6-8

The Pantry
Portland, Oregon
Proprietor: Lee Hamblin
Chef: Ron Kern

CHEESE SPREAD

1 pound margarine
1/2 pound sharp cheddar cheese
1/4 pound grated Romano cheese
1 teaspoon Worcestershire sauce
1/4 teaspoon garlic powder
1/2 teaspoon paprika

Combine all ingredients at room temperature. Whip slowly together with mixer until fluffy.

Serving suggestion: spread on sourdough French bread and, under broiler.

Serves: 8–10

Sea Inn
Hallandale, Florida
Proprietor: Charles Lamanno
Chef: Joseph Bonomo

FRIED RICOTTA

2 ounces Impasata ricotta
flour, as needed
1 egg, beaten
oil, for frying

Make a patty with the ricotta, dip into flour, then in beaten egg. Fry in oil until golden brown.

Serving suggestion: marinara sauce on the side.

Serves: 1

The Abbey
Atlanta, Georgia
Proprietor: William S. Swearingen
Chef: Hans Bertram

PETITS ASPICS LUCULLUS

1 1/2 cups water
2 ounces Savoury Jelly (or substitute plain gelatin made with beef stock or consommé instead of water)
1 ounce butter
6 pieces fresh goose liver
salt and pepper
1/2 cup Madeira wine
1 truffle
2 sliced hard-boiled eggs
pickle slices, to garnish
chopped parsley
6 slices Goose Liver Pâté Strassbourg (pâté de foie gras)

Bring water to a boil. Stir jelly into water and bring to a boil again. Remove from heat to cool. Heat butter in a skillet. Season goose liver with salt and pepper. Cook goose liver slowly in skillet until done, then remove from heat. Cool in refrigerator. After jelly has cooled, add Madeira wine, then cover bottom of six individual molds with jelly and chill in refrigerator until set, about 1/2 hour.

Decorate each set mold with slice of truffle, slice of hard-boiled egg, pickle slice, etc. Put slice pâté carefully on top of decorations. Wipe off excess grease from goose liver and lay on top of the pâté. Sprinkle chopped parsley inside mold and fill mold with remaining jelly until everything is covered. Place in refrigerator for about 2 hours to chill well.

To unmold: turn mold upside down and run warm water over mold. Place aspic on plate and decorate top with eggs, tomatoes, parsley, pickle, etc.

Serves: 6

The Shalea Inn
Auburn Heights, Michigan
Proprietor: Patrick A. Elwell

SHALEA INN CHEESE SPREAD

1/2 pound sharp cheddar cheese, ground finely
2 ounces cream cheese
1 green onion, chopped finely
sprig of parsley
3 ounces bleu cheese dressing
2 ounces light beer
2 ounces dark beer
2 tablespoons horseradish
1 teaspoon Lea & Perrins Sauce

Mix cheeses, onion, parsley, and dressing until smooth. Add beer, horseradish and Worcestershire sauce. Refrigerate. Bring to room temperature before serving with crackers.

Serves: 8

Wine: *White*

Rinaldo's
Guilford, Connecticut
Proprietor: Ronald Baia
Chef: Carlo Valdisarra

PANE COTTO

crushed fresh garlic, as needed
1 loaf Italian bread, 2–3 days old, cut in pieces
4 tablespoons olive oil
1 pinch crushed hot pepper
1 pinch salt
1 pinch white pepper
1 bunch escarole, cut in half
1 can cannellini beans with juice

Rub garlic on bread. In a saucepan, mix together oil, hot pepper, salt, and white pepper. Fry the escarole, beans, and bean juice in the seasoned oil. When oil boils, add pieces of bread and soak 2–3 minutes until all juice is absorbed. Serve.

Serves: 4

The Toast of the Town Restaurant
North Miami Beach, Florida
Proprietor: Ethyl Spector
Chef: Toby S. Spector

HOME STYLE CHICKEN LIVERS SAUTÉ

4 tablespoons butter
5 ounces chicken livers
1 clove garlic, crushed
1/4 teaspoon tarragon
1/2 teaspoon prepared mustard
1 medium onion, thinly sliced and sautéed
juice of 1/2 lemon
salt and pepper, to taste

Melt butter in an 8" skillet on medium heat. When hot, add chicken livers. When cooked on one side (approximately 2–3 minutes), turn over and add remaining ingredients. Cover tightly and cook until done (livers should be slightly pink). Correct seasoning and serve.

Serves: 4

Wine: *White Burgundy*

GRAVLAKS WITH MUSTARD DILL SAUCE

   3   pounds fillet of salmon with skin on bottom side
       salt and sugar, to taste
       crushed white peppercorns, to taste
   2   bunches fresh dill, cut up
1/4   cup aquavit, or more, to taste
   1   cup vegetable oil
       Mustard Dill Sauce (*see recipe below*)

Place the salmon in an ovenproof dish, skin side down. Sprinkle with salt, sugar, and peppercorns. Place dill over all. Sprinkle with aquavit and place oil on top. (If aquavit is too strong for your taste, use light Danish beer instead.) Lay a piece of waxed paper over the fish and press with a weight. Let marinate for 48 hours, turning once, if desired.

To serve: slice thinly on the diagonal and cover with Mustard Dill Sauce.

Mustard Dill Sauce

1/4   cup brown sugar
1 1/2 teaspoons rock salt
   2   tablespoons granulated white sugar
1/4   cup freshly chopped dill
1/4   cup red wine vinegar
1/2   cup salad mustard
3/4   cup salad oil
       salt and pepper, to taste
       tabasco sauce, to taste

Combine together all ingredients and serve over marinated salmon.

                  Serves: 4–6

MUSHROOMS DAVID

 17   ounces snow crab meat
3/4   cup shredded Swiss cheese
1/4   cup melted butter
  1   teaspoon Italian seasoning
  1   teaspoon lemon juice
  1   teaspoon grated Parmesan cheese
      medium-sized mushroom caps, as needed
      butter, as needed

Combine first six ingredients and place on mushroom caps. Brush with butter and broil for 5 minutes.

                  Serves: 4–6
      Wine: *Chardonnay*

PÂTÉ MAISON

  3   pounds veal shoulder
  1   pound fresh pork butt
  1   quart white wine, for marinade
      cooking oil, as needed
  2   eggs
1/2   pound cooked, smoked beef tongue, diced
  3   ounces pistachios, chopped
  2   ounces brandy
1/8   teaspoon *each* cloves, ginger, pepper, and nutmeg, all ground
1/8   teaspoon *each* paprika, basil, thyme, marjoram, and rosemary
1/2   teaspoon salt

Marinate veal and pork in white wine. Dice 1 pound veal into 1/4" cubes and sauté in oil. Grind remaining veal finely and pork coarsely. Combine with other ingredients and seasonings. Mix well. Pack firmly into form and bake in 350° oven for about 1 1/2 hours.

Serves: 15–20

Great Escape Restaurant
North Miami Beach, Florida
Proprietor: Richard Laibson
Chef: Alan Laibson

CHICKEN LITTLE DELIGHTS

1	12-ounce can of beer
2	eggs
1/4	teaspoon white pepper
1/4	teaspoon salt
1	cup milk
2	tablespoons baking powder
2	cups flour (approximately) cooking oil, to sauté
4	medium Spanish onions sliced 1/4"-thick
2	pounds fresh split chicken livers

In a bowl, mix together beer, eggs, pepper, salt, milk, and baking powder. Add flour until mixture is the consistency of pancake batter. Refrigerate 2 hours.

Place oil in skillet and heat to 350°. Drop in onions and fry until translucent. Dip livers in refrigerated batter, covering completely with batter. Drop chicken livers, one at a time, in hot oil. Fry until golden brown. Remove onions and livers and drain. Serve hot.

Serves: 4–6

Tommaso's Restaurant
Brooklyn, New York
Proprietor/Chef: Thomas W. Verdillo

MOZZARELLA IN CAROZZA (Carriage) WITH SAUCE NIÇOISE

4	slices mozzarella cheese (or substitute)
4	slices Italian ham (or substitute)
8	thin slices Italian or American bread
1/4	cup flour
1	egg and 2 tablespoons cream, whipped together
1/2	cup olive oil Sauce Niçoise (*see recipe below*) parsley, to garnish

Sandwich cheese and ham between bread. Flour sandwiches, then coat in egg-cream mixture. Heat oil to 340° and pan fry until golden brown. Remove to hot plate. Prepare sauce.

Cut sandwiches in half, diagonally. Return to hot pan and re-heat until cheese is melted again. To serve: spoon over with sauce and garnish with fresh parsley.

Sauce Niçoise

2	tablespoons butter
2	fillets of anchovies, diced
6	capers
3	tablespoons minced green and black olives
1/2	clove garlic
1/8	cup dry white wine

To prepare sauce: heat butter in pan, add anchovies, capers, olives, and garlic. Sauté until golden. Add white wine and reduce to half.

Serves: 4

The Versailles
New Orleans, Louisiana
Proprietor/Chef: Gunter Preuss

ESCARGOTS BOURGUIGNON EN CROÛTE (Snails in a Crust)

3 tablespoons butter or margarine
12 snails
1 teaspoon chopped green onion
2 shallots, chopped
2 small garlic cloves, minced
6 tablespoons Burgundy wine
1 cup brown sauce (*see recipe below*)
1 bay leaf
2 small sourdough loaves
   green onion tops
   lemon wedges

Melt 3 tablespoons butter in skillet. Add snails, green onion and shallots and saute about 1 minute. Add garlic, wine, brown sauce, and bay leaf. Cook, stirring often, 8–10 minutes. Discard bay leaf.

Cut tops from loaves and remove soft bread from center of bottoms, leaving at least 1″ of crust around sides and about 2″ in bottom. Cut slit in center of tops and insert 1 or 2 green onion tops as garnish. Spoon half of snails and sauce into each bread shell. Cover with tops.

Serve each in a folded napkin with lemon wedges.

Quick Brown Sauce

1 1/4 cups beef bouillon
2 teaspoons cornstarch
   seasoning, as needed

In a small saucepan, stir 2 tablespoons bouillon into cornstarch to make a smooth paste. Add remaining bouillon and seasoning to taste. Bring to a boil. Cook and stir over medium heat until slightly thickened, about 5 minutes. Makes about 1 cup.

Serves: 2

WINE: *Red Burgundy*

Soups

Repulse Bay Hotel
Hong Kong
Chef: Rolf Schneider

GAZPACHO

2 tablespoons chopped canned
   pimientos
2 tablespoons chopped fresh green
   pepper
3 tablespoons chopped, peeled
   cucumber
2 tablespoons minced carrots
1/4 cup tomatoes, peeled, seeded, and
   chopped
2 tablespoons chopped parsley
2 tablespoons tomato paste
2 tablespoons salad oil
5-8 drops tabasco sauce
1/2 teaspoon Worcestershire sauce
1 teaspoon lemon juice
4 cups chicken stock (*see index*)
   salt and pepper, to taste
   croutons

Mix together all the vegetables. Add tomato paste, salad oil, tabasco, Worcestershire, and lemon juice and mix well. Add the chicken stock and season to taste. Chill for several hours before serving with croutons.

Serves: 6–8

*Ramada Inn Restaurant
Portland, Oregon*

CHEDDAR CHOWDER

1/4 pound butter
1 cup flour
5 cups warm milk
1 medium-sized green pepper
3-4 green onions
4 large stalks celery
1/4 cup red pepper
1/2 cup frozen green peas
4-6 ounces cheddar cheese
4-6 ounces Swiss cheese
1/4 pound butter
1/8 teaspoon cayenne pepper
1 teaspoon garlic powder
1/4 cup sherry wine
   salt and pepper, to taste

To prepare cream sauce: in a double boiler, melt butter and slowly stir in flour to form a roux. Allow to cook enough to change the color from yellow to a cream color. Be sure to stir while cooking or it will scorch. Add warm milk and cook, allowing to thicken.

Dice vegetables and cheeses finely. Add cheese to cream sauce and allow the cheese to melt. Meanwhile, sauté vegetables in butter until tender. Add to soup and season with spices. Allow to simmer for about 5 minutes. Add sherry and adjust salt and pepper to taste.

Serves: 4–6

Soups   21

Stonehenge
Ridgefield, Connecticut
Proprietors: David Davis & Douglas Seville

SEAFOOD SOUP

	bones from 3 sole
3	mushrooms
2	sprigs parsley
1	onion
1	gallon water
1	carrot
1	celery stalk
1	leek (white part only)
3	medium-sized tomatoes
1	tablespoon olive oil
1	pound any white fish (cheapest available)
1/8	teaspoon thyme
1	bay leaf
1	clove garlic
1	ounce turmeric
1/8	teaspoon dill weed
1/2	cup cognac or Pernod
1	cup white wine
1/8	teaspoon salt
1	dash pepper
1	cup vermicelli
1/2	cup grated Parmesan cheese

To prepare fish stock: Combine fish bones, mushrooms, parsley, and onion with water and bring to a boil. Boil gently for 3 minutes. Strain and skim any sediment or fat.

Cut carrot, celery, leek, and tomatoes into 1″-pieces. Heat olive oil over a moderate heat. Add vegetables and fish. Allow to cook for 2 minutes, stirring constantly. Add thyme, bay leaf, garlic clove (uncrushed), turmeric, and dill. Stir well. Add cognac or Pernod, flame.

Add white wine and simmer for 2 minutes. Add fish stock, salt, and pepper and cook for 15 minutes.

Cook vermicelli separately, according to directions on packet. Add to the soup just before serving. Serve with Parmesan cheese on the side to be sprinkled over the soup.

Serves: 4–6

Villa Nova Restaurant
Newport Beach, California
Proprietor: Charlotte F. Dale
Chef: Walter Gentile

PASTA E FAGIOLI

4	ounces chopped salt pork or prosciutto fat
2	tablespoons chopped garlic
1	large grated or finely chopped onion
2	stalks chopped celery
1	small can chopped or diced tomatoes
2	diced potatoes
4	quarts beef or chicken broth
3	small cans white kidney beans
1	small can red kidney beans
1	teaspoon salt
1/2	teaspoon pepper
3-4	bay leaves
2	cups macaroni

Sauté salt pork or prosciutto fat to a golden brown. Add garlic and sauté about 1 minute with pork. Add onions, celery and tomatoes and add diced potatoes gently. Combine with beef or chicken broth and let boil until onion and celery are tender.

Add white kidney beans, red kidney beans, and salt and pepper to taste. Add bay leaves and cook for about 30 minutes.

Cook macaroni separately for about 8 minutes. Cool in cold running water and mix into boiling mixture.

Serves: 4–6

WINE: *Bolla Amarone*

Commander's Palace
New Orleans, Louisiana
Chef: Paul E. Prudhomme

GUMBO YA YA

1   large (5-pound) hen, cut into 10
    pieces
    salt
    cayenne pepper
    powdered garlic
2 1/2 cups flour
1   cup vegetable oil
2   cups chopped onions
1 1/2 cups chopped celery
2   cups chopped green pepper
6   cups chicken stock (*see index*)
1 1/2 teaspoons minced fresh garlic
1   pound diced andouille sausage (or
    any spicy smoked sausage, such as
    Kielbasa)
3   cups steamed white rice

Season chicken in advance with salt, cayenne pepper and powdered garlic and let stand for 30 minutes at room temperature. Place 2 1/2 cups flour in a large paper bag. Add chicken pieces and shake until chicken is well coated. Reserve flour.

In a large skillet, brown chicken in 1 cup very hot oil. Remove chicken when browned and set aside. Stir with a wire whisk to loosen the browned particles from the bottom of the pan. With the whisk, stir in 1 cup of the reserved flour and stir constantly until the roux is a very dark brown. Remove from heat and add onions, celery, green pepper, stirring continually so vegetables do not burn. Return to skillet to low heat and cook until vegetables are soft. Transfer all of the roux with vegetables to a large saucepan.

Add stock to roux vegetable mixture and return to heat. Bring to a boil. Lower heat to a quick simmer and add garlic and sausage. Continue cooking for 45 minutes.

Bone chicken and cut into 1/4'' chunks. Add chicken. Adjust seasonings with salt and pepper.

To serve: mound 1/2 cup steamed white rice in center of soup bowl and ladle 1 1/2 – 2 cups gumbo around it.

Serves: 5–6

WINE: *Chardonnay or Chablis*

Romeo Salta
New York, New York
Proprietors: Rosita and Salvatore Salta
Chef: Giacomo Spada

ZUPPA ZINGARELLA

1   tablespoon finely chopped shallots
3   tablespoons butter
1   cup dry white wine
3   tablespoons flour
1 1/2 cups clam broth
8   chopped clams
1 1/2 cups light cream
1 1/4 cups cooked puréed spinach
    salt and pepper, to taste
4   teaspoons grated Parmesan cheese

Sauté shallots in butter until golden brown. Add white wine and cook until reduced by 1/2. Gradually stir in flour, clam broth, and clams, and continue to stir until smooth. When the mixture begins to thicken, stir in light cream, spinach, and seasoning. Heat and stir but *do not boil*.

Just before serving, pour mixture into ovenproof bowls and top each with 1 teaspoon Parmesan cheese. Place bowls under broiler for 2 minutes or until cheese browns lightly.

Serves: 4

WINE: *Frascati Fontana Candida*

The Ponchartrain Hotel
Caribbean Room
New Orleans, Louisiana
Proprietor: Albert Aschaffenburg
Chef: Louis Evans

OYSTER BROTH

1	white onion
2	pieces celery (not whole stalk)
1/2	pound butter
2	ounces flour
1/2	gallon water
2	bay leaves
1/2	gallon oysters
	salt and pepper, to taste
	parsley, to garnish

Chop onion and celery. Sauté together in pan with butter, but do not brown. Add flour, water, bay leaves, and oysters. Bring to a boil. Simmer 10 minutes. Salt and pepper to taste. Strain and serve with parsley.

Serves: 10

Maxim's de Paris
Chicago, Illinois
Proprietor: Nancy Goldberg

BILLI BI (Cream of Mussels Soup)

1	pound mussels
2	ounces sliced onion
2/3	cup water
1	bouquet garni (thyme, bay leaf, celery)
	salt and pepper, to taste
1/3	cup white wine
1	pint whipping cream
1	teaspoon arrowroot

Place mussels, onion, water, bouquet garni, salt, pepper, and wine in a saucepan and cover. Cook for 10 minutes.

Strain the mussels, reduce the liquid to 2/3 of the original volume, add whipping cream and bring to a boil. Reduce heat and simmer for 10 minutes. Moisten the arrowroot with a little water and add to the mixture. May be served hot or cold.

Serves: 4

The Abbey
Atlanta, Georgia
Proprietor: William S. Swearingen
Chef: Hans Bertram

LOBSTER BISQUE

1	diced carrot
1	diced celery stalk
1/2	onion, diced
1/4	bunch fresh green onions, diced
1/2	cup diced mushroom stems
	butter, as needed
1	large boiled Maine lobster with shell
1/4	cup tomato paste
1/4	cup flour (approximately)
2	cups fish stock (*see index*)
	salt and pepper, to taste
2	bay leaves
	touch of garlic, thyme, and basil
1	tablespoon pickling spice
1	dash saffron
2	shots cognac
1/2	cup cream

Sauté all vegetables in butter. Remove meat from lobster body and dice. Reserve claws. Add diced lobster meat and shells to the sautéed vegetables. Braise this mixture for about 10–15 minutes. Add tomato paste and cook for about 5 minutes longer, stirring so as not to allow the mixture to stick to the pot.

Add flour, mix well, and fill the pot with fish stock. Then, add salt, pepper, bay leaves, thyme, basil, garlic, and pickling spice. Stir well and cook about 45 minutes. Be sure soup is of creamy consistency.

Remove from heat and strain soup through a fine strainer or cheesecloth. Return liquid to heat and bring to a boil. Add saffron, cognac and cream. While stirring, add bits of butter, a few at a time. Take cooked meat out of the claws and add to the soup.

Serves: 6

---

*Visko's Restaurant
Gretna, Louisiana
Proprietor: Joseph S. Vuskovich
Chef: Laura Ryan*

VISKO'S OYSTER SOUP

24	oysters
1/4	pound butter
1/2	cup chopped green onions bottoms
1/2	cup chopped green onions tops
1 1/2	cups milk
1/4	cup chopped parsley (fresh or dried)

Wash oysters in their own liquid; strain and reserve liquid.

In a saucepan, melt butter and add green onion bottoms. Cook until transparent. Add onion tops and sauté only until soft. Add oyster liquid and bring to a low boil.

Add oysters and cook for about 3 minutes only, or until edges begin to curl.

In a separate saucepan or double boiler, heat milk until just before boiling.

Serve in soup bowls or cups. Into each bowl add 3 parts soup liquid to 1 part heated milk and 6 oysters. Sprinkle soup with chopped parsley.

Serves: 4

WINE: *Vouvray white wine*

---

*Sheraton Inn-Portland Airport
Northwoods Dining Room
Portland, Oregon
Chef: Gunard Meier*

SHRIMP SOUP À LA CHEF MEIER

	butter, as needed
2	pounds diced mushrooms
4	large diced onions
2	cloves garlic, crushed
4	large diced green peppers
1	diced celery stalk
4	gallons fish stock (*see index*)
3	pounds fresh, peeled, diced tomatoes
4	pounds peeled Oregon shrimp
2	bay leaves
1	tablespoon MSG
2	tablespoons salt
1	teaspoon pepper
1	teaspoon tarragon
1/2	teaspoon dill weed
1	teaspoon chervil
1	teaspoon oregano
1	teaspoon sweet basil
1/2	cup parsley
4	cups sauterne

Sauté in butter the mushrooms, onions, garlic, green pepper, and celery. Add fish stock, diced tomatoes, and peeled shrimp. Add all seasonings and simmer for 1 1/2 hours. Add sauterne and serve with hot French bread.

Serves: 16–20

Le Chalet
Erawan Hotel
Bangkok, Thailand
Chef: Roland Laurenceau

LOBSTER SOUP "LE CHALET"

3	tablespoons olive oil
1	cup butter
1	cup chopped carrots
1	cup chopped turnips
1	chopped leeks
4	cups fish stock (*see index*)
1	pinch saffron
1	pinch nutmeg
2	cloves garlic
1/2	teaspoon thyme
1	teaspoon oregano
	salt and pepper, to taste
4	river lobster tails
4	tablespoons Pernod
1	medium onion, chopped
2	egg yolks
1/4	cup cream

Heat olive oil and 1/2 the butter in a flameproof casserole. Add the finely chopped vegetables and sauté gently for 5 minutes. Add fish stock, saffron, nutmeg, garlic, thyme, and oregano. Bring to a boil and cook until vegetables are tender. Season with salt and pepper.

Halve the lobster tails lengthwise and remove the long intestinal vein. Sauté gently in the remaining butter and flame with Pernod.

Sauté onion in a little butter. Pour in the previously prepared vegetable-stock mixture and boil for a few minutes.

Remove lobster-sauce mixture from heat. Beat the egg yolks. Stir several spoonsful of the hot sauce into the egg yolks, then pour the egg mixture back into the casserole. Add cream gradually, stirring constantly. Heat gently but do not allow to boil after egg yolks and cream are added.

Serve hot over toast or in pastry shells.

Serves: 4

Ocean's Bounty
Ft. Lauderdale, Florida
Proprietor: Daniel S. Janis
Chef: John Proteu

LOBSTER BISQUE

2	1-pound Maine lobsters
3	ounces Spanish paprika
1	ounce salt
1	teaspoon white pepper
2	medium-sized onions
2	cloves garlic
3/4	stick margarine or butter
3	tablespoons flour
1	quart half and half
4	ounces cooking sherry

Boil lobsters. Save tails, claws, and 1 pint of the water. Dice lobster meat from the bodies and simmer with paprika, salt, pepper, onions, and garlic. Reduce to 1/3 its original volume and strain.

Make a roux with butter and flour. Add half and half to roux. When bisque comes to a boil, add roux and whip with a whip. Add sherry.

Dice the meat from the lobster claws and tails and add to the bisque.

Serves: 8

WINE: *Sherry*

Chez Michel
Honolulu, Hawaii
Proprietor: Michel Martin

FRENCH ONION SOUP GRATINÉE

    4   medium onions
    3   tablespoons butter
        salt and pepper, to taste
    6   cups beef stock or bouillon
  1/4   cup sherry
1 1/2   cups white wine
        fresh grated Parmesan and Romano
          cheese
        day-old French bread

Slice onions and cook gently in butter until light brown. Add salt and pepper to taste. Add beef stock and bring to boiling point. Reduce heat, add sherry and wine and simmer for 10 minutes. Set aside. When ready to serve, heat to piping hot, sprinkle cheese on, and arrange in individual casseroles. Top with bread slices and more grated cheese. Set in oven long enough to brown cheese. (Make soup the day before and it will taste even better.)

Serves: 4

WINE: *Red Beaujolais*

The Hippogriff
St. Louis Park, Minnesota
Proprietor: B. Grossman
Chef: Darrel Rufer

FRENCH ONION SOUP (LES HALLES)

    2   small onions, halved then cut in
          julienne strips crosswise
    3   tablespoons butter
  1/4   cup sherry wine
        paprika, to color
        salt and white pepper, to taste
2 1/2   cups chicken stock (or bouillon
          cubes)
2 1/2   cups beef stock (or bouillon cubes)
  4-6   slices French bread
  4-6   slices, 3″ × 3″ × 1/4″ thick, fresh
          Parmesan cheese

Sauté cut onions in butter. Add wine, paprika (to lightly color onions), salt, and pepper. Add stock. Bring to simmer and adjust seasoning.

Ladle soup in ovenproof cups or stoneware. Add slices of French bread and top with fresh Parmesan Cheese. Place in oven until cheese melts and lightly browns.

Serves: 4–6

Rheinlander Haus
La Jolla, California
Chef: Erich Roesch

OXTAIL SOUP

1	pound oxtail, disjointed
3	tablespoons fat or oil
1/2	cup chopped onions
1/2	cup chopped celery
8	tablespoons flour
2	quarts water
	salt and pepper, to taste
1	teaspoon paprika
1/4	cup parsley

Brown the oxtail in fat or oil and remove oxtail. Fry onions and celery in same oil, dust with flour, and add water. Bring to a boil.

Add oxtail and boil until meat is soft. Remove meat from bones and add to the soup. Season with salt, pepper and paprika. Garnish with parsley.

Optional: add 1/2 cup red wine or dry sherry.

Serves: 6

The Fig Tree
Louisville, Kentucky
Chef: Chet Holden

CHEDDAR SOUP

2	tablespoons butter
2	tablespoons flour
3	cups hot milk
1	garlic clove
1	cup white wine
1	cup grated cheddar cheese
	salt, pepper, and nutmeg, to taste
2	egg yolks
2	tablespoons heavy cream
	grated cheddar cheese, to garnish

Melt butter and flour in a double boiler. Add hot milk and garlic clove. Cook over boiling water for 20 minutes. Discard garlic. Add wine, cheese, salt, pepper and nutmeg and cook gently, stirring until cheese melts.

Blend yolks and heavy cream in a separate bowl, then add slowly to hot mixture. Cook 3 minutes. *Do not boil.* Garnish with grated cheese.

Serves: 4–6

The Pantry
Portland, Oregon
Proprietor: Lee Hamblin
Chef: Ron Kern

CHICKEN BISQUE SOUP

1	3-pound stewing hen
3	tablespoons salt
4	celery stalks
4	carrots
2	onions
1	gallon water
1/2	pound butter
1	cup flour
1/2	cup chopped pimientos
1/2	cup chopped chicken
1/	cup blanched chopped peppers
1/2	teaspoon pepper
	yellow food coloring, as needed

Boil chicken with salt, celery, carrots, and onions in water until meat can be pulled from bone. Strain off 8 cups of chicken stock.

Make a butter roux by melting butter and adding flour. Bring the 8 cups of chicken stock to a very low boil, then slowly add the butter roux. Simmer 15 minutes or less until soup takes on a glaze. Add the chopped pimientos, chopped chicken, chopped peppers and pepper. Stir constantly. Add a few drops of yellow food coloring and serve.

Serves: 8–10

First Street Alley
St. Louis, Missouri
Proprietor: Dave Switzer
Chef: Ernestine D. Dunlap

HAM À LA ERNIE SOUP

1 1/2 gallons water
1/2 pound ground yellow onions
1/2 pound ground celery
3/4 jar Milani ham base (10 1/2-ounce jar)
1 1/4 ounces granulated garlic
3/4 ounce white pepper
3/4 pound Topic package
3/4 pound ground ham
3/4 pound melted butter
1 1/2 cups flour

Pour water into a large cooking pot. Let water get very hot, but not necessarily boiling. Add yellow onions, celery, ham base, garlic, pepper, and Topic. Cook for 1 1/3 hours. Then add ground ham and simmer. Make a roux by mixing melted butter and flour and add to mixture. Cook on low heat for 15 minutes.

Serves: 24

Marquette Hotel
Orion Room
Minneapolis, Minnesota
Chef: Peter Dexter

WILD RICE SOUP

1/4 cup butter
1/4 cup raw wild rice (or 2 cups cooked rice)
2 tablespoons blanched sliced almonds
1/2 cup finely diced onion
1/4 cup finely diced celery
1/2 cup finely diced carrots
soup stock (*see recipe below*)
2 teaspoons arrowroot, or as needed
1 pint whipping cream

Melt butter in a heavy casserole and sauté rice, almonds, onion, celery, and carrots. Add soup stock and simmer for about 1 1/4 hours. (If necessary, thicken with arrowroot dissolved in a small amount of the whipping cream.) Stir in cream just before serving.

Soup Stock

2 duck or chicken carcasses
1 smoked ham bone
1 medium onion, sliced
1 bay leaf
3 teaspoons Maggi seasoning or Knorr-Swiss Aromat seasoning
1/4 celery stalk, chopped
1 1/4 quarts water
2 carrots, chopped
salt and white pepper, to taste

To prepare stock: combine together all of the above ingredients and bring to a boil. Simmer approximately 1 1/2 hours. Strain and use in soup recipe.

Serves: 6

Yamato Restaurant
Los Angeles, California
Proprietor: Ken Ishizaki

CHAWAN MUSHI (Steamed Egg Custard Soup)

6 ounces boneless chicken, cut in
    small chunks
  water, as needed
6 slices fresh mushrooms
1 small bunch spinach, coarsely
    chopped
6 eggs, beaten
4 cups basic chicken stock (*see index*)

Parboil chicken chunks in small amount of water for 5 minutes. Parboil mushrooms and spinach and drain. Place all ingredients into chawan mushi bowls, dividing equally. (If a traditional chawan mushi bowl is not available, use a tall tea cup or bowl covered with foil.)

Pour egg and chicken stock not quite to top of bowl. Place bowl in steamer and cook approximately 15–20 minutes. Stick toothpick into custard to test

Serves: 6

Le Cellier Restaurant
Santa Monica, California
Proprietor: Jacques Don Salat
Chef: Jean Bellordre

CREAM OF SORREL SOUP

6-8 cups chicken broth
3 medium-sized potatoes, peeled and
    diced
1 1/2 pounds sorrel, well washed
  salt and pepper, to taste
1 cup cream
2 tablespoons chopped chives, to
    garnish

Bring chicken broth to a boil. Add potatoes and cook for 15 minutes. Add sorrel and continue simmering for 10 minutes more.

Purée the soup in a blender until smooth. Return to pot and reheat. Check seasoning and add salt and pepper if necessary.

Combine cream and chives and add to the soup. Serve hot.

Serves: 6–8

WINE: *Chablis or St. Emilion*

Restaurant La Terrasse
Philadelphia, Pennsylvania
Chef: Kamol Phutlek

COLD CREAM OF CUCUMBER SOUP

1/4 cup chopped onion
1/4 cup chopped shallots
3 tablespoons butter
1 1/2 pounds cucumbers, peeled and sliced
    into chunks
6 cups chicken stock (*see index*)
1 1/2 teaspoons wine vinegar
2 tablespoons chopped fresh dill
4 tablespoons rice
  heavy cream, as needed to thin soup
  salt and pepper, to taste
1 1/4 cups sour cream
  shredded cucumber, to garnish
1 tablespoon minced fresh dill, to
    garnish

In a saucepan, cook onions and shallots slowly in butter until tender but not browned. Add the cucumber chunks, chicken broth, vinegar and dill. Bring to a boil, then stir in the rice. Simmer, partially covered, for 20-25 minutes. Purée, and thin with heavy cream, if needed. Season with salt and pepper. Stir in 3/4 cup sour cream and refrigerate.

To serve: add 1 tablespoon sour cream to each cup. Top with shredded cucumber and dill. Serve chilled.

Serves: 6

La Zaragozana
San Juan, Puerto Rico

CUBAN BLACK BEAN SOUP

- 1 pound black beans
- 2 quarts water
- 2 tablespoons salt
- 5 garlic cloves, peeled
- 1/2 tablespoon cumin
- 1/2 tablespoon oregano
- 1 ounce white vinegar
- 5 ounces Spanish oil
- 1/2 pound onions, chopped
- 1/2 pound green peppers, chopped
- 1 cup cooked rice
  finely chopped raw onions, as needed
  Spanish oil and vinegar, as needed

Soak beans in water overnight. Add salt and boil beans until soft. Crush in a mortar the garlic, cumin, oregano and vinegar. Heat the oil in a pan, adding the onions and peppers, and fry until the onions are brown. Add the crushed ingredients, frying slowly. Drain some of the water off the beans before adding them to the pan and cook slowly until ready to serve.

Marinate cooked rice and very finely chopped raw onions in Spanish oil and vinegar. Add 1 soupspoon of this to each serving of the soup.

Serves: 6

The Stockman Restaurant
San Antonio, Texas
Proprietor: Billy R. Regan

THE STOCKMAN RESTAURANT CHEESE SOUP

- 1 cup grated carrots
- 1 cup minced celery
- 1/2 cup minced onion
- 1 1/2 quarts chicken stock (*see index*)
- 2 cups cream
- 1 cup butter
- 1 cup all-purpose flour
- 3/4 pound shredded sharp cheddar cheese
- 1 teaspoon salt
- 1/2 teaspoon white pepper
- 3 tablespoons Worcestershire sauce

Boil carrots, celery and onion in chicken stock until tender. Add cream and set aside.

Melt butter in a large skillet or saucepan and add flour. Cook until well blended. Add stock mixture and cook to make a smooth sauce. Add shredded cheese, salt, pepper, and Worcestershire sauce. Stir until cheese is melted. Serve hot.

Yields: 1 gallon

The Wine Cellar
North Redington Beach, Florida

TEDS SWISS CHEESE SOUP

1	tablespoon butter
2	ounces flour
21	ounces milk
10	ounces chicken stock (*see index*)
8	ounces Kraft's Cheese Whiz
8	ounces Swiss cheese, shredded
	salt
	white pepper
10	ounces sauterne wine
	kirschwasser

Melt butter in sauce pan and slowly add flour to make a roux. Add milk and chicken stock, stirring constantly. Bring to a boil and let simmer 15 minutes. Stir in Cheese Whiz and Swiss cheese. Stirring constantly, simmer for an additional 5 minutes. Salt and pepper to taste.

Just before serving, add sauterne and let simmer for an additional minute. After dishing out in soup cups, put a small dash of kirschwasser on top of each serving.

Serves: 10

Cordon Bleu
Kansas City, Missouri
Chef: Ari Camburako

POTAGE WINDSOR

2	pounds chicken
1/2	gallon water
	salt and white pepper, to taste
1	bay leaf
1/2	pound coarse tapioca
1/4	cup 12% cream
3	ounces sherry
3	egg yolks, beaten
1	pinch parsley

Boil chicken in water with salt, pepper, and bay leaf. Cook for 1 hour. Remove chicken. Add tapioca and cook until velouté. Just before serving, add cream, sherry, and beaten egg yolks to the potage. Garnish with parsley.

Serves: 6–8

Salads

Windows on the World
New York, New York
Director: Alan Lewis
Chef: Henry Boubee

ORANGE AND ONION SALAD WITH CUMIN DRESSING

6	oranges, sectioned and membranes removed
1	medium red onion, sliced thinly
1/3	cup pitted Niçoise olives
	Cumin Dressing (see recipe below)
1	bunch watercress, stems removed

Combine orange sections, onion, and olives in a bowl, then prepare dressing.

Cumin Dressing

1/2	cup olive oil
1/2	teaspoon ground cumin
1/4	cup orange juice
2	pinches salt
1/2	teaspoon garlic, chopped
2	tablespoons white vinegar

Combine all dressing ingredients. Add to salad ingredients and mix well. Make a nest of watercress in a serving dish. Place salad mixed with dressing in center of the watercress.

Serves: 8

Renaissance Restaurant
Hotel Syracuse
Syracuse, New York
Proprietor: John J. Farrell

SALAD NIÇOISE

1	head Boston or romaine lettuce
1	pound white tuna fish
1/2	cup finely chopped celery
1/2	cup mayonnaise
2	cups prepared French potato salad
2	cups green beans, blanched and marinated in oil, vinegar, salt, and pepper
3	medium tomatoes, quartered
3	hard-boiled eggs, sliced
1/2	cup pitted black olives
1/4	cup capers
12	anchovy fillets
1	cup vinaigrette dressing (*see index*)

Make a bed of lettuce on 6 dinner plates.

Mix tuna with celery and mayonnaise. Arrange about 4 ounces tuna mix, 1 scoop potato salad, and 1 spoonful green beans in center of each plate. Decorate with tomato wedges, eggs, olives, and capers. Crisscross 2 anchovies over potato salad, add 1 tablespoon vinaigrette dressing over tomatoes and potato salad.

Serves: 6

WINE: *Macon Blanc, Louis Jadot*

ANANAS AUX CREVETTES

3 baby pineapples
3 ounces diced celery
8 ounces peeled shrimp
1/4 pint mayonnaise
2 teaspoons double cream
2 teaspoons curry powder

Cut pineapples in half lengthwise. Remove the flesh and place in a bowl with diced celery and shrimp. Mix mayonnaise, cream, and curry powder together, add to pineapple mixture and stir. Place in pineapple halves and serve.

Serves: 6

La Petite Ferme
New York, New York
Proprietor: Charles Chevillot
Chef: Rainer Langbein

MOULES VINAIGRETTE (Mussels Vinaigrette)

6 quarts (6 pounds) mussels, well scrubbed
2 cups coarsely chopped red onion
1/2 teaspoon freshly ground pepper
Sauce Vinaigrette (*see recipe below*)
1/2 cup finely chopped parsley

In a very large, heavy, metal casserole, put in the mussels and scatter half the onions over all. Sprinkle with pepper. Do not add salt or liquid. Cover the casserole and cook over high heat about 6–10 minutes, or until the moment the steam starts to escape from the casserole. Shake the casserole so that the mussels are redistributed. Remove from heat as soon as the mussels are open. Do not overcook or the mussels will fall out of the shells. Pour off the cooking liquid immediately. Let stand, uncovered, until ready to serve.

Put the mussels in a large salad bowl and scatter the remaining onion over all. Spoon the Sauce Vinaigrette over the mussels and toss with finely chopped parsley.

Serves: 4

La Petite Ferme's Sauce Vinaigrette

2 tablespoons imported mustard
6 tablespoons red wine vinegar
6 tablespoons peanut oil
6 tablespoons olive oil
salt and freshly ground pepper, to taste

Spoon the mustard into a mixing bowl and add the vinegar. Start beating with a wire whisk and gradually beat in the oils. Add salt and pepper to taste.
Yields: about 1 1/4 cups

Gold Coast
Hollywood Beach, Florida
Proprietor: Joe Sonken
Chef: Adolph Fassa

DELIZIE DI MARE HOT SALAD

1 tablespoon chopped garlic
6 tablespoons olive oil
1 #2 can whole tomatoes, crushed
8 cherrystone clams
4 lobster tails, split
1 pound shrimps, peeled and deveined
1 pound linguine or spaghettini

Sauté garlic in olive oil, add crushed tomatoes, and cook over slow heat for 5 minutes. Add remaining ingredients, cover tightly, and bring to a boil. Let simmer for 10 minutes and serve.

Serves: 4

WINE: *White*

Hydens Restaurant & Oyster Bar
Spring, Texas
Proprietor/Chef: James Pinero

SHRIMP SALAD

3	cups cooked small shrimp
1 1/2	cups chopped celery
1	cup mayonnaise
1	teaspoon celery salt
1/2	teaspoon white pepper
2	hard-boiled eggs, chopped
1	cup chopped green onions with tops
2	tablespoons sweet red peppers

Combine shrimp and celery. Moisten with mayonnaise, season with salt and pepper, fold in diced eggs, green onions, and red peppers.

Serving suggestion: arrange in lettuce cup with shredded lettuce and garnish with tomato and lemon wedges.

Serves: 4–6

WINE: *Green Label Deinhard*

Café des Artistes
New York, New York
Proprietor: George Lang
Chef: Andre Guillou

AVOCADO WITH CURRIED MUSSELS

120	mussels
2	tablespoons curry powder
1	quart mayonnaise
2	capfuls of white vinegar
12	avocados
	lettuce leaves, as needed
	chopped parsley, as needed
	sliced cucumber and sliced green peppers, to garnish
	lemon wedges, to garnish

Steam mussels open in saucepan with cover. Shell and allow to cool.

In a mixing bowl, combine curry powder with mayonnaise, whisking well. Beat in vinegar, mix in shelled mussels and keep chilled.

Halve the avocados as needed. Shave a strip off the bottom of each half so they sit evenly and straight. Shape a few tablespoons of the mixture domelike over the avocado halves and set on a serving dish lined with lettuce leaves. Sprinkle the mixture with chopped parsley. Garnish with cucumber, green pepper, and lemon wedges.

Serves: 12

WINE: *Chablis*

The Tower Hotel
London, England
Chef: P. Ricks

STUFFED AVOCADO

1	ripe avocado
2	ounces baby prawns
1/2	ounce chopped stem ginger (preserved)
1/2	ounce diced fresh or canned pineapple
2	ounces Thousand Island Dressing (prepared)
	pinch cayenne pepper

Cut the avocado in half lengthwise and remove the stone. Spoon out the flesh in one piece, if possible, and cut into 1/4″ dices. Place into a small mixing bowl.

Add the rest of the ingredients and bind together with the dressing. Refill the avocado skins with the mixture. Place on a lettuce leaf in a china avocado dish and garnish with slices of lemon, roundels of cucumber, sprigs of parsley, etc.

Serves: 2

Stonehenge
Ridgefield, Connecticut
Proprietors: David Davis & Douglas Seville

FRESH MUSHROOMS AND COUNTRY SAUSAGE

1/2 pound raw mushrooms, rinsed and
     sliced finely
     juice of 1 lemon
1/4 cup onion, finely chopped
1/4 cup celery, finely chopped
1 teaspoon salt
1/4 teaspoon pepper
1/4 cup corn oil
1 5-ounce well-seasoned smoked
     sausage (Kielbasa or cervelat)
4-6 lettuce leaves

Moisten mushrooms with lemon juice in a salad bowl. Add onion, celery, salt, pepper, and oil. Skin the sausage and slice very thin into the mushroom salad. Mix and serve well chilled on a lettuce leaf.

Serves: 4–6

Modesto Lanzone
San Francisco, California
Proprietor: Modesto Lanzone
Chef: Gino Laghi

CALAMARI SALAD

2 cloves
1 onion cut in half
1 small bay leaf
8 peppercorns
1 gallon water
2 pounds calamari
3/4 pounds shrimp
2 lemons
1 lime
     olive oil, vinegar, salt and pepper,
      to taste
     chopped parsley

Place one clove in each half of the onion. Boil the onion halves, bay leaf, and peppercorns in a gallon of water for 15 minutes. Clean and skin the calamari and boil in the seasoned water for 5 minutes. Drain and cut in thin slices (lengthwise). Mix with shrimps and marinate with the juice of the lemons and lime, olive oil, vinegar, salt, pepper, and chopped parsley. Serve chilled.

Serves: 6

Da Vinci Restaurant
Philadelphia, Pennsylvania
Proprietor: Steve Wernovsky
Chef: Alfio Gaglianese

ALFIO SALAD

1 medium-sized garlic clove
1/2 teaspoon salt
     peppercorns, as needed
     juice of 1/2 lemon
1 teaspoon red wine vineger
4 ounces olive oil
3 teaspoons chopped oregano leaves
12 leaves romaine lettuce, broken into
     small pieces
12 wedges of tomatoes
12 black olives
1 cup chickpeas

Peel garlic clove and put into wooden salad bowl. Sprinkle salt and grind a small amount of peppercorns into the bowl. With a fork and tablespoon, mash the garlic and rub well into the bowl. Add lemon juice, vinegar, olive oil, and oregano leaves. With fork and tablespoon, mix well. Add romaine, tomato wedges, olives and chickpeas. Mix well and serve.

Serves: 4

Theatrical Restaurant
Cleveland, Ohio
Proprietor: I.B. Spitz

CAESAR'S SALAD

1	head romaine lettuce
6	anchovies
	juice of 1 lemon
	juice of 1 clove garlic
6	tablespoons oil
1 1/2	tablespoons wine vinegar
1	dash Worcestershire sauce
1	teaspoon dry English mustard
	croutons
1	coddled egg
	grated Parmesan cheese

Tear lettuce by hand.

Cut and mash anchovies in lemon juice until almost completely dissolved. Blend the garlic juice, oil, wine vinegar, Worcestershire sauce, and mustard with a fork.

Add lettuce, croutons, coddled egg and blend gently and well together. Add Parmesan cheese to taste.

Serves: 4

The Hilton Inn at Inverrary
Lauderhill, Florida
Proprietor: Gregg Pate
Chef: Dan Ristau

CLASSIC DRESSING

3	egg yolks
3	teaspoons minced shallots
6	teaspoons Dijon mustard
2	teaspoons coarse black pepper
2	cups salad oil
1/4	cup dry red wine
1/2	cup red wine vinegar
	salt, to taste

Place egg yolks, shallots, mustard and pepper in bowl. Slowly add oil and whip to make a mayonnaise consistency. When oil is finished, add red wine and vinegar. Let dressing set 1/2 hour, then adjust seasoning with salt and possibly more vinegar.

Suggestions: use dressing on Bibb lettuce. To make a unique Caesar Salad, add anchovies, garlic, and Parmesan cheese.

Yields: 1 quart

Casimir's Restaurant
Denver, Colorado

CHICKEN MADRAS

3	cups extra heavy mayonnaise
1	cup freshly squeezed orange juice
1/2	cup freshly squeezed lemon juice
3	tablespoons sour cream
3	tablespoons Madras curry powder
1/2	teaspoon white pepper
1/2	teaspoon seasoning salt
3	pounds boiled chicken meat, chopped
1	pound seedless white grapes
4	Mandarin oranges
2	large Golden Delicious apples, peeled and diced
1	cup chopped celery

Combine mayonnaise, orange juice, lemon juice, sour cream, curry powder, pepper, and salt in one large bowl. Add large chopped pieces of chicken meat; add grapes. Peel mandarin oranges and separate segments. Add to mixture. Add apples and celery and mix together. Serve on chilled Bibb lettuce.

Serves: 4

WINE: *Frascati Superior*

Valentino's Restaurant
Charlotte, North Carolina
Proprietor: William P. Georges
Chef: Peter Amfaldern

SALAD WITH DILL DRESSING

2 heads iceberg lettuce
1 cup mayonnaise
1 tablespoon dill weed
2 cups catsup
1 tablespoon Worcestershire sauce
2 dashes tabasco sauce

Cut lettuce into four wedges each. To prepare dressing: blend all other ingredients. Serve dressing over lettuce wedges.

Serves: 8

Cellar Restaurant
Fullerton, California
Proprietor: Louis Schnelli

LA SALADE NOUVELLE

1 tablespoon dark sesame oil
3 ounces freshly chopped shallots
12 ounces aged, seasoned Japanese rice vinegar
2 ounces best champagne wine vinegar
2 teaspoons imported French mustard
1 tablespoon freshly chopped basil
1 tablespoon freshly chopped tarragon
1 tablespoon freshly chopped chives
1 pinch freshly chopped thyme
1 1/4 cups light sesame oil
4 handfuls fresh spinach
4 handfuls butter lettuce hearts, cut in 2"-squares
1 cup large white mushrooms, sliced
1 handful whole leaves of fresh basil

Sauté lightly in dark sesame oil the chopped shallots; do not brown. Add next eight ingredients and bring to a boil.

Place spinach, butter lettuce hearts, sliced mushrooms, and whole basil leaves in a large mixing bowl. Pour hot dressing over all. Toss lightly and serve immediately to avoid wilting the greens.

Serving suggestion: heat 1 crab leg, split lengthwise, in the dressing and serve on top of salad for garnish.

Optional: season with sea salt and freshly ground black pepper.

Serves: 4

Anthony's
Indianapolis, Indiana
Proprietor: Ray Mastellon

ANTIPASTO SALAD

1 head iceberg lettuce
1 head romaine lettuce
1/4 cup chopped Spanish olives
1 small can artichoke quarters
5 medium pepperoncini, chopped
2 medium tomatoes, cut in wedges
6-8 red onion rings
6 large sliced mushrooms
1 garlic clove
1/2 cup light oil
2 anchovy fillets, finely chopped
2 lemons
1/3 cup grated Parmesan cheese

Coarsely chop lettuce into large wooden bowl. Add next 6 ingredients. Using a garlic press, squeeze garlic into oil, then add anchovies. Pour over salad and mix well. Squeeze lemon juice over salad and mix well. Sprinkle with cheese.

Serves: 4-6

WINE: *Orvieto Secco*

Canlis' Restaurant
Honolulu, Hawaii
Chef: Peter Canlis

CANLIS' SPECIAL SALAD

2	tablespoons olive oil
	salt
1	large clove garlic
2	peeled tomatoes, cut in eighths
2	heads romaine lettuce, cut in 1"-strips
1/4	cup chopped green onion
1/2	cup freshly grated Romano cheese
1	pound rendered finely chopped bacon
1/4	cup lemon juice
1/2	teaspoon fresh ground pepper
1/4	teaspoon chopped fresh mint
1/4	teaspoon oregano
1	coddled egg
1	cup olive oil
1	cup croutons

In a large wooden bowl, pour in 2 tablespoons olive oil, sprinkle with salt, and rub firmly with the large clove of garlic. Remove garlic and place the tomatoes in bottom of bowl. Add the romaine. (Optional: add other vegetables, but put heavy vegetables in first with romaine on top.) Add green onion, cheese, and bacon.

To prepare dressing: pour the lemon and seasonings in a separate bowl. Add coddled egg and whip vigorously. Then add olive oil, whipping constantly.

When ready to serve, pour dressing over salad, add croutons last, and toss.

Serves: 4–6

Jamil's
Dallas, Texas
Proprietor/Chef: Mike Elias

TABOLI SALAD

3	whole tomatoes, diced
1	large bell pepper, diced
1	cucumber, diced
1	bunch parsley, chopped
2	bunches green onions, chopped
1	pound crushed wheat
3	whole lemons
1	cup salad oil
1	cup tomato juice (optional)
	salt, to taste

In a large bowl, combine tomatoes, pepper, cucumber, parsley, onion, and crushed wheat. In a separate bowl, squeeze lemon juice into oil, then add tomato juice, if desired, and mix with other mixture. Salt to taste. Set and chill 45–60 minutes. May be served on leaf of romaine.

Serves: 6

Valentino's Restaurant
Charlotte, North Carolina
Proprietor: William P. Georges
Chef: Peter Amfaldern

SALAD WITH SWEET AND SOUR DRESSING

4	heads Boston lettuce
3	egg yolks
	juice of 1 lemon
2	tablespoons sugar

Cut lettuce heads in half. To prepare dressing: blend together all other ingredients and serve over lettuce halves.

Serves: 8

Vinchenzo's
Pasadena, California
Chef: Keith W. Garton

ANN'S SALAD

2 cups medium diced turkey
1/3 cup shredded coconut (fresh if possible)
1/3 cup finely diced celery
1/2 cup medium diced water chestnuts
1 tablespoon grated onion
1/4 cup toasted sliced almonds
1 cup homemade mayonnaise (or prepared)
1 cup bean sprouts (mung)
salt and pepper, to taste
soy sauce (optional)

In a 2-quart bowl, mix the first 7 ingredients. Refrigerate for 1/2 hour. Just before serving, toss the turkey mixture with the bean sprouts, salt, and pepper.

Serves: 6 as a side dish,
4 as a main dish

WINE: *Semi-dry white*

Stonehenge
Ridgefield, Connecticut
Proprietors: David Davis & Douglas Seville

FRESH PEACH STUFFED WITH CURRIED HAM OR CHICKEN

1/3 pound cooked ham or cooked chicken
1/2 teaspoon curry powder
3 tablespoons softened butter
1 teaspoon chutney syrup from jar
1/2 ounce dry sherry
1 pinch salt
1 pinch pepper
4 large fresh peaches
lettuce leaves, as needed

Put the ham or chicken through the fine blade of a grinder. Blend with the curry powder, butter, chutney syrup, sherry, salt and pepper to make a smooth paste. Chill while preparing the peaches.

Dip the peaches into boiling water for a few seconds, remove skin. Cut the top off of each peach and, with a sharp-pointed spoon, remove the pit. Slice 1/8″ off bottoms of peaches so they will stand firmly. Fill each peach with the mousse, piling it high above the top. Serve the peaches well chilled on a bed of lettuce leaves.

Serves: 8

The Mansion
Atlanta, Georgia
Proprietor: William S. Swearingen
Chef: Hans Bertram

BELGIAN ENDIVE LEAVES AND TOMATOES WITH NEUCHATEL SAUCE

1/2 pound cream cheese
2 ounces mayonnaise
3 tablespoons sour cream
2 teaspoons paprika
2 teaspoons curry powder
salt and white pepper, to taste
1 touch finely chopped parsley
1 touch finely chopped dill
4 green onions, finely chopped
cream, as needed
1 head romaine lettuce
6 large Belgian endives
2 tomatoes, sliced
parsley, to garnish
sliced hard-boiled eggs, to garnish

To prepare Neuchatel sauce: Put cream cheese in a mixer. Add mayonnaise, sour cream, and all of the seasonings. Mix well. Add parsley, dill, and green onions and mix until sauce is smooth. If too thick, add a little fresh cream.

Place romaine leaves on a plate and lay endive leaves around them to form a star design. Place slices of tomato in the center and top with the Neuchatel sauce. Garnish with parsley and boiled eggs.

Serves: 6

Bastille
Chicago, Illinois
Proprietor: George Badonsky

SALADE NIÇOISE AU POULET FROID

2	heads Boston lettuce
4	small potatoes, cooked, peeled and sliced
2	tomatoes, quartered
1/2	pound green beans, parboiled and chilled
16-20	black olives
1	small tin anchovy fillets
3-4	chicken breasts, poached and diced
4	hard-boiled eggs, quartered
2	egg yolks
1	tablespoon Dijon mustard
	salt and pepper, to taste
1	teaspoon tarragon leaves
16	ounces oil (approximately)
2-3	ounces white vinegar

Divide first 8 ingredients into four serving portions and assemble on dinner plates or in shallow bowls in order indicated. Serve with dressing.

To prepare Classic French Dressing: mix egg yolks, mustard, salt, pepper and tarragon. Pour oil slowly while whisking briskly (or use a blender) until mixture thickens. Thin to proper consistency with vinegar.

Serves: 4

WINE: *Pouilly Fumé*

Peachtree Plaza
Atlanta, Georgia
Chef: Waldo Brun

SALAD DENNONE

1	head lettuce
12	ounces shrimp (San Francisco Bay)
8	cherry tomatoes cut in half
24	mandarin orange sections
	Curry Fruit Dressing (*see recipe below*)

Cut lettuce in 1-inch squares. Top lettuce with shrimp. Surround with tomatoes and orange sections. Serve curry dressing on the side.

Serves: 4

Curry Fruit Dressing

1/2	fresh Golden apple, diced
1/6	fresh pineapple, diced
1	ounce marachino cherries, diced
1	ounce apricots, diced
1	teaspoon lemon juice
1/2	quart mayonnaise
8	ounces apricot juice
	salt and pepper, to taste
2	tablespoons curry powder

Pulverize all the fruit, then add other ingredients, mix well. Shelf life is 3 to 4 days.

SECTION TWO

Meat Entrées   *Poultry Entrées*

Seafood Entrées

Vegetable Specialties

Meat Entrées

Doro's
San Francisco, California
Proprietor: Don Dianda
Chef: Paolo Bermani

VEAL SCALLOPINE À LA DORO'S

12	thin slices veal loin, pounded flat
	salt
	pepper
	flour, to dust
1	cup butter
1	tablespoon shallots, chopped
1/4	cup dry sauterne wine
1/2	cup brown sauce
1	pound sliced mushrooms
	olive oil
12	slices eggplant
2	tablespoons butter

Season veal with salt and pepper. Dip in flour to lightly cover both sides. Melt the cup of butter in a large skillet, then add the veal slices to it when it bubbles.

When veal is browned on both sides, pour off excess butter. Add the shallots, pour in wine, and simmer for 3 minutes. Add brown sauce.

In a separate pan, sauté sliced mushrooms in olive oil. In a separate pan, sauté sliced eggplant in olive oil.

Alternating veal and eggplant, arrange on a bed of sautéed sliced mushrooms.

To the rest of sauce in skillet, add 2 tablespoons of solid butter. Shake skillet to swirl and melt butter, then pour sauce over the veal and eggplant slices.
Serve immediately with rice.

Serves: 4

WINE: *Soave*

Russell's Restaurant
Philadelphia, Pennsylvania
Proprietor: Ron Wesner
Chef: Barbara McCloskey

VEAL AMARETTO WITH PEACHES

	flour, as needed
6	6-ounce veal tenders, flattened
6	tablespoons clarified butter
1	cup heavy cream
3	sliced peaches
6	tablespoons amaretto liqueur
6	tablespoons toasted sliced almonds
	salt, to taste

Flour the veal and cut into 2 pieces each. Sauté in clarified butter until lightly browned. Remove veal and pour off excess butter. Add cream to pan and reduce until thick. Add peaches and amaretto and cook until soft. Pour cream and peaches over veal and sprinkle with almond. Salt to taste.

Serves: 6

WINE: *Riesling or Gewürztraminer*

Barbuto's Restaurant
Syracuse, New York
Proprietor/Chef: Anthony Barbuto

VEAL CHABLIS

6	tablespoons clarified butter
1/4	cup flour
24	thinly sliced pieces of veal, 3" × 3"
1/4	teaspoon garlic salt
1/8	teaspoon white pepper
1/4	cup room temperature Chablis wine
	juice of 1/2 lemon
4	lemon wedges

Heat butter in skillet until hot. Flour individual pieces of veal and sauté in hot butter until lightly browned on either side. Season with garlic salt and pepper. Deglaze skillet and veal with Chablis and lemon juice. Reduce wine and lemon until light gravy forms. Serve on hot plates with lemon wedges.

Serves: 4

Club El Morocco
New York, New York
Chef: Pierre Laverne

ESCALOPES OF VEAL CHASSEUR

3	escalopes of veal (6-7 ounces) or veal chops (8-10 ounces)
	salt and pepper
	flour, to dust
4-5	ounces clarified sweet butter
1	teaspoon chopped shallots
6-8	mushrooms, sliced
3/4	cup white wine
1 1/4	cups prepared brown sauce, thickened slightly with cornstarch
2	tablespoons peeled and chopped tomatoes
1	teaspoon chopped tarragon
1	teaspoon chopped chervil
1	tablespoon butter

Flatten the escalopes. Season with salt and pepper and dust with flour. Cook in clarified butter to a golden brown, then remove from pan and keep warm.

In the frying pan, add chopped shallots and sliced mushrooms. Brown for a few seconds. Moisten with white wine. Reduce. Add brown sauce and chopped tomatoes. Boil for a few seconds. Add chopped tarragon and chervil and a tablespoon of butter.

Arrange the veal on a dish and pour the sauce over.

Serves: 3

WINE: *Beaujolais*

La Pace
Hackensack, New Jersey
Proprietor: James D'Agostinos
Chef: Paul R. Bernal

VEAL SCALLOPINE SORRENTINO

	flour, to dust
12	veal scallopine, 1 1/2 ounces each
	olive oil, to sauté
12	tablespoons tomato sauce
6	tablespoons brown gravy
3	ounces butter
8	slices prosciutto ham
4	sliced fresh eggplants
8	slices mozzarella cheese

Flour the veal and sauté in olive oil. Remove from pan and set in casserole. Add tomato sauce, brown gravy and butter to casserole. Place ham, eggplant slices, and cheese on top. Bake for 5 minutes in hot oven. Serve immediately.

Serves: 4

WINE: *Corvo white*

The Mill Falls Restaurant
Newton, Massachusetts
Proprietor: Lawrence A. Wolozin
Chef: Robert G. Meyer

ESCALOPE DE VEAU WITH CHAMPAGNE CHANTERELLE SAUCE

8	ounces chanterelles (fresh or canned) or use 1 1/2 ounces dried chanterelles
2	minced shallots
8	ounces brut champagne
10	ounces white veal stock (or chicken stock)
2-3	ounces roux (1/2 butter, 1/2 flour)
6	ounces light cream
2	ounces flour
	salt and white pepper, to taste
1 1/2	pounds veal in 2-ounce slices pounded thinly
4-6	ounces clarified butter
1	ounce butter

Soak the chanterelles in water for 1 1/2 hours. Poach chanterelles and shallots in 1/2 the champagne and veal stock for 8–10 minutes over low heat. Remove chanterelles and shallots and reserve.

Thicken the liquid (using wire whip) with roux. Bring to a boil and add warm cream and remaining champagne. Sauce should be thick enough to coat a spoon.

Lightly flour and season the veal and sauté in butter over medium heat. Do not let butter burn. Sauté until veal is lightly brown on both sides. Remove veal from pan and place on paper towel to absorb excess butter. Arrange on warm silver tray or china serving platter.

Remove remaining butter from pan and deglaze pan with the sauce. Strain sauce; swirl in raw butter (to make sauce shine). Add chanterelles and shallots and pour sauce over the veal and serve.

Serving suggestion: serve with rice pilaf and a green vegetable.

Serves: 6

WINE: *Champagne, Vouvray, Gewürztraminer*

Mauro's Restaurant
Glendale, California
Chef: Giuseppe Pupillo

VEAL ZINGARA GYPSY STYLE

4	ounces sweet red peppers, julienne
4	ounces fresh mushrooms
4	ounces green peas
	butter and oil, as needed
	flour, to dust
1	pound eastern veal provino, sliced thinly and gently pounded
	salt, to taste
8	ounces butter
6	ounces dry white wine

Sauté peppers, mushrooms, and peas in butter or oil and set aside.

Flour both sides of veal and salt lightly. Sauté in butter under low heat for 4 minutes. Turn once. Add white wine. After wine evaporates, add sautéed vegetable mixture. Cook for 4 more minutes and then add 1 teaspoon butter. Serve immediately.

Serves: 4

WINE: *Vernaccia(white), or Santa Chiara (red)*

Cappuccino Restaurant & Club
Dallas, Texas
Chef: L. J. Jones

VEAL MARSALA

5 pounds veal, sliced thinly
  flour, as needed
1/3 pound butter
1/2 cup thinly sliced shallots
1 cup dry Marsala wine
3 cups beef au-jus
1 cup sliced mushrooms
  salt and pepper, to taste
  peach halves, to garnish
  parsley, to garnish

Dust veal lightly with flour. Place in sauté pan with butter, shallots, Marsala wine, beef au-jus, and mushrooms. Salt and pepper to taste. Sauté over medium-high heat for about 1 minute. Garnish with peach halves and parsley.

Serves: 6

WINE: *Valpolicella*

Bagatelle Restaurant
Dallas, Texas
Proprietor: Leodegar Meier
Chef: Hubert Treiber

VEAL FRANCAISE BAGATELLE

5-6 ounces white veal, sliced into 3
  escalopes and pounded lightly
  flour, to dust
2 tablespoons vegetable oil
1 tablespoon butter
1 ounce demi-glaze sauce (light brown
  sauce)
1 ounce white wine
1 tablespoon grated lemon peels

Coat veal lightly with flour. Brown on both sides in skillet in oil and butter at medium-high heat. Sauté quickly to avoid toughening meat.

Place veal on plate or platter.

Pour demi-glaze and wine into skillet and bring to a boil for 2 minutes. Pour over veal.

Sprinkle grated lemon peel on top of veal and serve immediately.

Serves: 1

WINE: *Montrachet–Château de la Maltroge*

Ernie's Restaurant
San Francisco, California
Proprietors: Victor and Roland Gotti
Chef: Jacky Robert

MIGNONETTES DE VEAU NORMANDE

8 2-ounce slices of veal loin, pounded
  to 1/4" thick
  salt and pepper, to taste
3 ounces butter
1 ounce chopped shallots
4 ounces sliced mushrooms
4 teaspoons Calvados
2 pints heavy cream
2 Pippin apples, peeled and quartered

Season veal. Sauté veal in 1 ounce butter. Cook to medium doneness, remove from pan and put on serving tray.

Clean sauté pan, then lightly sauté shallots in 1 ounce butter. Add mushrooms, sauté together, and deglaze with Calvados. Add cream and reduce to smooth thickness. Add more seasoning if necessary and pour over veal.

In another pan, sauté the apples in the remaining 1 ounce of butter until crisp and garnish the veal with them.

Serves: 4

VEAL SLICES PYRÉNÉENNE

1/2	pound sweet onions, sliced
4	tablespoons melted butter or cooking oil
1	cup Béchamel Sauce *(see recipe below)*
2	egg yolks
1/4	cup light cream or milk salt and white pepper, to taste
8	thin round slices of veal flour, as needed
1	tin imported pâté de foie gras (goose liver pâté)
16	mushroom caps
2	sliced truffles
2	tablespoons chopped chives

Sauté the onion slices in melted butter or oil. Add the Béchamel Sauce and heat over low heat, blending the onion with the sauce. Remove from heat and beat in the egg yolks that have been mixed with the cream. Salt and pepper to taste.

Heat the remaining 2 tablespoons of butter or oil in a heavy skillet. Dust the veal slices with flour and brown quickly on both sides.

Sandwich the pâté in the centers. Arrange the veal in an ovenproof serving dish surrounded with mushrooms sautéed in skillet with butter or oil. Pour the onion sauce over the veal and top with slices of truffle. Sprinkle with chives. Place under broiler and glaze quickly to a golden brown.

Serves: 4

WINE: *Chardonnay*

Béchamel Sauce

2	cups milk (or equal parts milk and fish, chicken or vegetable stock, depending on type of dish sauce is to be served with)
4	tablespoons butter
1/4	cup minced onion
4	tablespoons flour
2	egg yolks
1/4	cup heavy cream salt and white pepper, to taste

Bring the milk to a boil and remove from heat. Heat the butter and onion in a heavy saucepan, but do not allow onion to brown. Add flour and stir to make a roux. Cook and stir the roux over low heat, being sure not to brown the flour. Add the hot milk gradually, and whip until sauce is smooth and thick. Remove from heat and whip in the egg yolks and heavy cream to make a thicker and richer sauce. Season with salt and pepper. Strain onions out if desired. Béchamel is a basic sauce. By adding either cheese or mustard or anchovy paste, the character can be changed to suit any use.

Yields: approximately 3 cups

Doro's
Chicago, Illinois
Proprietor/Chef: Michael Scoby

COSTOLETTA VOLTOSTANA
(Stuffed Veal Chop)

2	veal rib chops (frenched and butterflied)
2	slices Muenster or mozzarella cheese
2	thin slices prosciutto
2	tablespoons grated Parmesan cheese
	flour, as needed
1-2	well beaten eggs
2	tablespoons oil
2	tablespoons butter
1-2	ounces white wine
1	teaspoon chopped parsley
3	tablespoons butter
2	ounces chicken stock *(see index)*
2	ounces brown gravy (or beef stock)
2	pinches salt

Preheat oven to 400°.

Open veal chops on work board, cover with waxed paper and pound them with a flat mallet. Remove paper, lay slice of cheese, prosciutto, and sprinkle of grated Parmesan cheese on 1/2 of each chop. Then, fold other halves of chops over and pat down. Flour and dip chops thoroughly in egg.

Melt oil and butter in 8–10″ ovenproof pan over medium-high heat. When oil and butter are hot, slip chops in pan. Cook until chops are brown (about 2 minutes) and turn over. Cook an additional minute then place in oven for approximately 20 minutes.

Remove pan from oven and pour off liquid. Place pan back on medium burner. Add white wine, parsley, butter, chicken stock, brown gravy, and salt. Let simmer in sauce for a few minutes to enhance flavor.

Serving suggestion: serve hot with potato and/or vegetable.

Serves: 2

WINE: *White or light red*

Golden Table
Washington, D.C.
Chef: Jimmy Chue

ESCALOPE OF VEAL MONSEIGNEUR

3	thinly sliced pieces of veal from the leg (approximately 6 ounces each)
3	thinly sliced pieces of ham, each 1 1/2 ounces
3	thinly sliced pieces of Swiss cheese, each 3 ounces
	salt and pepper, to taste
	flour, as needed
2	beaten eggs
1	1/2 cups mushroom sauce *(see recipe below)*
3	tablespoons fresh butter
1	tablespoon Madeira wine
1 1/2	cups cooked white rice

On each slice of veal place 1 slice ham and 1 slice Swiss cheese. Roll veal. Sprinkle with salt and pepper and flour and dip in the beaten eggs.

Place on greased pan (which has been preheated in hot, 550° oven) and cook for 5 minutes. Do not overcook or cheese will melt and burn. Take out of oven and immediately remove grease from pan.

Pour mushroom sauce, pieces of butter, and Madeira wine into pan. Pick up veal and set upon bed of rice. At the same time, shake the pan and when butter melts completely, pour the sauce over veal and rice and serve immediately.

Serves: 3

WINE: *Soave*

Mushroom Sauce

1/2   pound fresh mushrooms, sliced
2   tablespoons finely chopped onion
1   tablespoon finely chopped peeled tomato
3   tablespoons butter
1   teaspoon full meat glaze
1   tablespoon flour
1 1/2   cups veal stock *(see recipe below)*
1-2   tablespoons chooking sherry
   salt and pepper, to taste

Sauté mushrooms, chopped onion, and chopped tomato in 2 tablespoons butter until light brown. Add another tablespoon butter. Blend in, away from heat, the meat glaze and flour. Pour in stock, sherry, and stir over heat until mixture comes to boil. Season with salt and pepper to taste.

Veal Stock

2-3   pounds crushed veal bones
1   carrot
1   whole onion, cut into lumps
1   stalk celery
2   bay leaves
1/2   cup tomato purée
4   cups water

Bake veal bones in hot (550°) oven for 45 minutes. Add remaining ingredients and cook 2 hours. Strain and save juice.

Jamar Restaurant
La Mesa, California
Proprietor: Dean Hansen
Chef: Paul Hoffman

VEAL ALASKA

8   5-ounce veal cutlets pounded and lightly breaded
8   3-ounce portions Alaskan King Crab meat
8   slices Swiss Cheese
   paprika, as needed
   wine sauce *(see recipe below)*
   parsley sprigs, to garnish

Grill veal cutlets one minute on each side. Place on greased cookie sheet, cover with crabmeat, and put in 550° oven for 5 minutes. Remove and cover with Swiss cheese and sprinkle with paprika. Return to oven and leave until cheese melts. Remove to individual plates. Ladle 4 ounces of wine sauce on top of each cutlet. Garnish with parsley sprigs and serve.

Serves: 8

Wine Sauce

1   bell pepper, julienne
1   medium onion, julienne
1   cup fresh mushrooms, chopped
2   ounces butter
1/3   cup Burgundy wine
1   cup canned diced tomatoes
   dash of whole Greek oregano
1   quart beef gravy

Sauté pepper, onion and mushrooms in butter until onions are limp. Add Burgundy wine, diced tomatoes, and oregano. Bring to a boil and remove from heat.

In a 2-quart container, put beef gravy and add the mixture. Stir together, bring to a boil, and simmer 45 minutes.

Hampshire House
Boston, Massachusetts
Proprietor: Thomas A. Kershaw
Chef: Nicholas Francisco

VEAL OSCAR

3 ounces veal scallopine
3 ounces Parmesan cheese
1/2 cup melted butter
1/2 cup cooking sherry
4 ounces Mornay Sauce *(see index)*
2 ounces crabmeat
2 ounces crab leg
2 white asparagus spears
2 ounces Mousseline Sauce

Roll the veal on Parmesan cheese and sauté in hot butter. Pour in wine and add Mornay sauce and crabmeat. Arrange the scallopine on a platter and pour the mixture over. Garnish with crab legs and asparagus spears and top with Mousseline sauce. Brown in broiler and serve immediately.

Serves: 1

Clive's
Bond Court Hotel
Cleveland, Ohio
Chef: Erwin Buttiker

VEAL CHOPS À LA CLIVES

4 5-ounce veal chops, bone in
   salt and pepper
   flour
2 ounces butter
1/2 clove garlic, chopped finely
1/2 cup freshly sliced mushrooms
1/2 cup diced onions
1/2 cup diced tomatoes
1/4 cup Chablis wine
1/2 teaspoon oregano

Season veal chops with salt and pepper and dust with flour. Heat butter in a 10″-skillet. When butter is hot, add veal chops and sauté until golden brown. Add garlic, mushrooms, onions, and tomatoes and cook about 10 minutes. Add wine and oregano and simmer 5 minutes more. Arrange veal chops on serving platter or plates and pour sauce over it.

Serving suggestion: serve with rice or spaghetti

Serves: 2

Lido di Venezia
Arlington, Virginia
Chef: Jeffrey Bleaken

OSTRICHE DI VITELLO

6 eggs
14 ounces firm ricotta cheese
   salt and pepper, to taste
4 5-ounce veal cutlets
4 slices boiled ham
4 slices mozzarella cheese
   oil, for frying
   flour, for dusting
   Sauce Marsala al Panna *(see recipe below)*

Mix 1 egg with ricotta cheese and season with salt and pepper. Refrigerate for 20 minutes.

Pound cutlets with mallet until very thin, carefully making no holes. Season with salt and pepper.

Place 1 slice ham and 1 slice mozzarella cheese on each cutlet. Place an ice cream scoop of ricotta mixture in the center of each cutlet. Bring edges of cutlets to top of ricotta and pull together, leaving no openings. Place on a plate, seam side down, and refrigerate 60 minutes.

Place 1/2″ oil in heavy, ovenproof large frying pan and heat to 375°. Dust all 4

Ostriche with flour and place in bowl with remaining eggs, well beaten. Coat well the entire surface, lift out, and place into hot oil, seam side up. When golden brown, turn with tongs and place entire pan into preheated 425° oven for 5 minutes.

Remove to serving plates and top with Sauce Marsala al Panna.

Serves: 4

WINE: *Fontana Candida Frascati*

Sauce Marsala al Panna

1	finely chopped shallot
4	tablespoons butter
3/4	cup sweet Marsala wine
1/2	pint heavy cream
	seasoning, to taste

Sauté shallot in butter until melted but not brown. Add Marsala. Reduce to half, then add heavy cream. Simmer and reduce until thick enough to coat a wooden spoon. Season to taste.

La Belle Rive
Houston, Texas
Proprietor: Merle W. Lommer
Chef: Carlos Contreras

CÔTES DE VEAU "EXCELSIOR"

6	6-ounce veal cutlets
	butter, as needed
1	small chopped shallot
4	ounces sliced fresh mushrooms
4	ounces sliced artichoke bottoms
6	medium cherry tomatoes, halved
	juice of 1 lemon
	white wine, as needed

Sauté the cutlets on both sides in butter, then place them on a plate and keep warm.

Heat the chopped shallot in the same skillet and sauté the mushrooms, artichoke bottoms, and, at the very last moment, the tomatoes, lemon juice, and wine. Pour mixture over the veal and serve.

Serves: 4–6

WINE: *Piesporter*

Chez Vendôme
David William Hotel
Coral Gables, Florida

VEAL CHOP VALLÉE D'AUGE

	flour, as needed
4	veal chops (10-12 ounces)
3	ounces butter
2	teaspoons oil
	salt and pepper, to taste
1/2	cup applejack
2	whole shallots, chopped
30	pieces medium mushrooms, sliced
1/2	pint heavy cream

Flour the veal chops and sauté for 6 minutes on each side in butter and oil. Add salt and pepper to taste.

Flambé chops with warm applejack. Add chopped shallots and sliced mushrooms and stir for 3 minutes. While stirring, add heavy cream.

Remove veal chops after 3 minutes, set on plate, and continue to cook sauce. Correct seasoning. Garnish veal, covered with sauce, with chopped parsley.

Serves: 4

WINE: *Rosé d'Anjou*

The Caribbean Café
Bel-Air Sands Hotel
Los Angeles, California
Proprietor: Ralph Woodworth
Chef: Stephen White

MEDAILLONES DE VEAU DE SLANDRIES

3 bunches leeks
  butter, as needed
1 quart heavy cream
  salt and pepper, to taste
3 pears, peeled, seeded, and sliced
  lengthwise
1/2 pint heavy cream
2 veal loins, trimmed and cut into
  medallions
2 ounces pear liqueur
2 avocados, peeled and sliced
  lengthwise

To prepare leek coulis: wash and clean leeks. Chop into small pieces and sauté lightly in butter. Add 1 quart heavy cream and reduce slowly. Once cream has reduced to desired consistency, strain the liquid (coulis), pressing the leeks with a rubber spatula to extract as much taste as possible. Season to taste. Reserve the coulis and keep warm.

To prepare pears: in a separate pan, simmer pears in 1/2 pint heavy cream until tender and cream is thickened.

To prepare veal: sauté veal medallions and deglaze with pear liqueur. Put one nice ladle of coulis on each plate, dressing the veal on top. Put alternating slices of the avocados and pears on top of the veal, seeing to it that the pears are coated well with the reduced cream. Garnish with vegetables.

Serves: 6

Viking Restaurant
St. Louis, Missouri
Proprietor: Ed Kreutz
Chef: Bob Eaves

VEAL SMITANE

  flour, seasoned with salt and pepper
4 3-ounce portions of veal, cubed
4 tablespoons butter
4 chopped green onions, bottoms and
  tops
4 tablespoons sour cream
  Smitane Sauce *(see recipe below)*

Lightly flour each piece of veal in seasoned flour. Sauté veal in hot buttered skillet until golden brown on one side. Turn over and put green onions in the drippings and allow to half cook. Remove veal from pan and keep hot while making Smitane (white) sauce. Leave green onions in drippings.

Stir in sour cream to drippings and add 4 tablespoons Smitane Sauce. Stir all until hot and pour over veal portions. Serve.

Serves: 2

Smitane Sauce

1 ounce salted butter
1 ounce all-purpose flour
2 cups heavy cream

Melt butter in pot, stir in flour. Cook over low heat, stirring constantly for 8–10 minutes. Do not allow roux to brown.

Heat heavy cream to boiling in separate pot, stir in roux gradually, beating briskly until sauce is thickened and smooth.

Simmer for 5 minutes, stirring occasionally. Bring to a boil. Strain through china cap.

A. Bastion's Vendome
Clearwater, Florida
Proprietor/Chef: A. Bastion

VEAL À LA MARENGO

2	pounds veal
2	ounces butter
3	tablespoons olive oil
1	onion, cut in small pieces
2	ounces flour
1	garlic clove
1	glass dry white wine
1	tablespoon tomato purée
	bay leaf, rosemary, thyme, to taste
6	ounces mushrooms

Sauté the veal in a skillet with butter and oil. Brown well on all sides, making sure the oil is very hot. When veal is nicely brown, add onion, flour, and garlic. Let the onion brown a little, then add wine and tomato purée. Add a few drops of water. Put in seasoning, cover pot, and let it cook on low heat for about 1 hour. Five minutes before turning off the heat, add the mushrooms.

Serving suggestion: serve topped with chopped parsley and bread croutons.

Serves: 4

Valentino's Restaurant
Charlotte, North Carolina
Proprietor: William P. Georges
Chef: Peter Amfaldern

VEAL FLORENTINE

2	pounds veal loin
	pepper and salt, to taste
	flour, as needed
1/2	pound butter or margarine
2	pounds spinach
1	dash nutmeg

Slice veal thinly into 8 slices. Pound each slice until flat. Season with pepper and salt to taste. Dip each piece of veal in flour and sauté in pan in butter over medium-high heat until medium (not well done).

Boil spinach and drain. Sauté spinach in butter, add salt and pepper and dash of nutmeg.

Place spinach on a platter, top it with veal, and pour 1/4 cup brown melted butter over entire dish.

Serves: 4

WINE: *Bechtheimer Pilgerfad, Kabinett*

The Stanhope Hotel
The Rembrandt Room
New York, New York
Proprietor: Rawdon A. Conyers

WIENER SCHNITZEL HOLSTEIN

4	4-ounce veal cutlets, pounded thinly
1/4	cup flour
2	eggs, beaten
1	cup bread crumbs
2	ounces butter
4	whole eggs (to be fried)
	lemon slices, anchovies, and capers (optional)

Dip each cutlet in flour, then in beaten egg, and finally in bread crumbs. Sauté in melted butter until golden brown.

When the cutlets are nearly done, fry eggs in separate pan. Serve each cutlet topped with an egg. Garnish with sliced lemon, anchovies, and capers, if desired.

Serves: 4

WINE: *Rosé*

The Tower Hotel
London, England
Chef: P. Ricks

ESCALOPE OF VEAL "WESTERN ISLES"

2 ounces peeled prawns
2 ounces Scotch whiskey
  cooking oil
  salt and pepper, as needed
2 5-ounce escalopes cut from veal
    topside, flattened
  flour, as needed
1 ounce butter
1 ounce finely chopped shallots
3 ounces sliced button mushrooms
4 ounces double cream
1 teaspoon chopped chives

Marinate the prawns in whiskey for at least 2 hours.

Heat some cooking oil in a thick-bottomed, shallow frying pan. Season the veal and dredge with flour. Shake off the excess. Just before oil begins to smoke, quickly brown the veal on both sides. Remove and keep warm.

Discard the oil in the pan and return pan to heat. Melt the butter and add shallots. Soften until translucent. Place mushrooms in the pan and stir briskly. Blend in the prawns and whiskey. Flame. Pour in cream and allow to boil for about 2 minutes.

Place the veal in a serving dish. Check the sauce for seasoning. With a perforated spoon, collect most of the prawns and mushrooms and place in the center of the meat. Pour the remainder of the sauce over. Sprinkle with chopped chives and serve.

Serves: 2

L'Escoffier
Beverly Hills, California
Chef: Raymond Dreyfus

FILLET OF VEAL GENTILHOMME

6 8-ounce milk-fed veal fillets
  salt, pepper, flour, and butter, as
    needed
2 egg whites, beaten
6 small tomatoes
3 ripe avocados
3 cups Mornay Sauce *(see recipe below)*
3 cups Madeira Sauce *(see recipe below)*

Split the fillets and flatten rather thinly. Dip in flour and egg. Pan fry rapidly in butter. Dice and reduce tomatoes, season. Place veal on silver platter with reduced tomato in center and top with sliced avocado. Cover fillets with Mornay sauce and glaze under broiler. Serve with a thin line of sauce surrounding the finished preparation of Madeira sauce.

Serves: 6

WINE: *White Burgundy*

Mornay Sauce

2 cups Béchamel (basic white sauce, prepared) *(or see index)*
4 ounces heavy cream
4 ounces grated cheese (Swiss, cheddar, Parmesan)
2 tablespoons butter (optional)

Prepare basic white sauce in a non-aluminum pan, add cream, and bring to a boil. Stir in cheese, remove from burner. Add butter, beating with a wooden spoon until butter is melted.

Madeira Sauce

4 cups Espagnole (basic brown sauce, prepared)
8 ounces Madeira wine
   seasoning, as needed

Simmer brown sauce to a rolling boil and reduce to half its volume. Adjust seasoning, strain through cheesecloth, add Madeira wine. Cover and keep warm without allowing to boil.

La Scala Restaurant
Ft. Lauderdale, Florida
Proprietor: Ciro Gentile

SALTIMBOCCA À LA SCALA

1   pound spinach
4   tablespoons sweet butter
12   small veal scallopine
12   leaves sage
12   slices prosciutto
4   slices mozzarella cheese
3   teaspoons sweet butter
6   drops lemon juice
3   pinches rosemary
1/2 cup dry white wine

Drown spinach in butter for 5–10 minutes and then set aside. Prepare veal by pounding it tender, sprinkling with sage, and topping with 1 slice prosciutto on each.

Sauté in a skillet with sweet butter, but *don't* turn the veal. Place the veal on top of the spinach, top each with mozzarella cheese, and keep in hot broiler or oven.

Using the same skillet in which veal was sautéed, add 3 teaspoons sweet butter, lemon juice, rosemary, and dry white wine. When the sauce thickens slightly,

pour it over the veal and serve immediately.

Serves: 3

WINE: *Dry white wine*

Ferdinand's Restaurant
Cambridge, Massachusetts
Proprietor/Chef: Isaac Dray

VEAL DRAY

4   artichoke hearts
1/2 pound mushrooms
1   medium onion
1   tablespoon butter
     puff pastry *(see index)*
4   4-ounce veal cutlets
4   slices Swiss cheese
1   egg
     Béarnaise Sauce *(see index)*

To prepare stuffing: coarsely chop artichoke hearts, mushrooms, and onion. Sauté onion in butter until wilted, add mushrooms and artichokes. Cook gently over low heat until vegetables are tender. Allow mixture to cool.

On a 4″ × 6″ section of puff pastry (1/8″ thick), place two tablespoons of Veal Dray stuffing. On each cutlet, place one slice Swiss cheese and roll tightly, tucking in the ends. Set the veal roll on top of stuffing. Beat one egg and paint a border round the edges of the pastry. Fold the pastry over the veal dressing gently to seal. With the tines of a fork, seal the two ends, paint the outside of the pastry with egg, and bake at 400° for 15–20 minutes until golden brown.

Serve with Béarnaise sauce.

Serves: 4

WINE: *Alsace Riesling Renée Schmidt*

Sign of the Dove
New York, New York
Chef: Guy Gauthier

VEAL CORDON BLEU, SIGN OF THE DOVE

2   veal cutlets (2 1/2-3 ounces each, ask butcher to flatten extremely well)
2   teaspoons Dijon mustard
1   slice prosciutto ham (1 ounce)
1   slice imported Swiss cheese (1 1/2 ounces)
    flour
1   raw egg
    bread crumbs
2   ounces cooking oil
1   ounce butter
1/2 cup veal stock or beef broth (optional)

Coat both veal cutlets with mustard, one side only. On one of the cutlets, place the slice of prosciutto ham, then put the Swiss cheese over the mustard spread. Place the other cutlet over it, mustard side down. Join them by applying pressure around the sides of the cutlet so they will not separate.

Then, flour the cutlets, dip in egg, then dip into bread crumbs. Again, squeeze the sides of the cutlets with your forefingers to insure a good bond.

Sauté in oil and butter until both sides are a golden brown. Place in 375° oven for 10 minutes. (Optional: boil the veal stock or beef broth with the remaining mustard, reduce to half the original quantity and serve with the cutlet.)

Suggestions: this recipe can be made with pork chops and with cooked ham substituted for the prosciutto.

Serves: 1

WINE: *Brouilly Château de la Chaize*

At Marty's
Los Angeles, California
Proprietor: Martin Tunick

LAMBUCCO

1/2   pound softened butter
1/2   bunch chopped fresh mint
6-12 cloves fresh garlic, chopped
1/4   pound chopped bacon
1/2   bunch freshly chopped parsley
1/4   cup red wine vinegar
1   medium can whole tomatoes, crushed with juice
1   medium can tomato juice
1   teaspoon tomato paste
6   crushed bay leaves
1   teaspoon dill
1   teaspoon rosemary
1   teaspoon whole thyme
1/2   teaspoon ground pepper
1   tablespoon Worcestershire sauce
2   10-ounce cans chicken broth
1   10-ounce can beef broth
4-6   fresh lamb shanks, trimmed of gristle and membrane
3   onions, sliced in circles
6   carrots, sliced in wedges
1   pound pitted prunes

Preheat oven to 375°.

To prepare butter-mint paste: combine butter, mint, garlic, bacon, parsley, and vinegar and mix well. Set aside.

To prepare tomato-based sauce: combine crushed tomatoes, tomato juice, tomato paste, bay leaves, dill, rosemary, thyme, pepper, Worcestershire sauce, chicken broth, beef broth, and 1/4 of the butter-mint paste in a saucepan. Simmer 30 minutes.

While sauce is simmering, braise lamb shanks in ovenproof pan on top of stove at high heat in 1/4 of the butter-mint paste, turning constantly until dark brown.

Drain pan and arrange shanks in the

pan and cover them with onion circles and carrot wedges. Ladle 1/2 of the tomato-based sauce over lamb, carrots, and onions. Cover with foil and place in oven.

Cook 1 hour. Remove pan from oven, remove foil, dot with more butter-mint paste and return pan to oven uncovered and cook 1 hour more. (Baste at 30 minutes.)

Remove from oven, rotate the shanks to the top, and carrots and onions to the bottom of pan. Add pitted prunes and return to oven for additional 30 minutes or until meat is sufficiently tender.

Serves: 4–6

WINE: *Zinfandel*

Clos Normand
New York, New York

CÔTE DE VEAU NORMANDE (Veal Chops with Mushrooms and Cream)

4   veal chops, 3/4" thick (about 2
      pounds)
1   tablespoon cooking oil
      salt
      pepper
2   tablespoons butter
2   tablespoons minced shallots
1/2   cup dry white wine
1/2   cup chicken broth
1   cup sliced fresh mushrooms
2   tablespoons butter
1/4   cup apple brandy
1/2   cup whipping cream
1/4   teaspoon salt
1/8   teaspoon pepper

In ovenproof skillet, brown chops in hot oil 5 minutes per side. Season with salt and pepper. Remove and set aside. Pour off fat. To skillet, add 2 tablespoons butter and shallots. Cook until tender but not brown. Add white wine and chicken

broth. Boil, scraping pan, until reduced to 1/2 cup. Return chops to skillet and spoon juices over them. Cover and bake in 400° oven for 15 minutes.

In a small saucepan, cook mushrooms in 2 tablespoons butter. Remove chops to platter and keep warm. To the skillet, add brandy; flame. Add cream to skillet, cook and stir until mixture thickens. Add 1/4 teaspoon salt, 1/8 teaspoon pepper, and mushrooms. Spoon over chops and serve.

Serves: 4

WINE: *Rosé*

The Red Timbers
Novi, Michigan
Proprietors: Bill Stavropoulos
and Charles Miller
Chef: Charles Miller

RACK OF LAMB PARISELLE

3   pound rack of lamb
      salt, rosemary, garlic, to taste
3   cups water

Remove blade bone from lamb rack. Score back with sharp point of knife, trimming the bottom so the bones protrude. Remove all meat from bone tips.

Rub back of rack with season salt, crushed rosemary, and garlic. Cover bone tips with aluminum foil to prevent burning.

Place lamb on rack with fat side up. Pour water in bottom of roaster. Place in preheated 400° oven. Roast for 30–45 minutes, depending on desired degree of doneness.

Skim and strain natural juices. Serve the reserved juice over lamb slices. Serve with wild rice and fresh vegetables.

Serves: 2–4

WINE: *Red wine*

India House
San Francisco, California
Proprietor: Sarwan S. Gill
Chef: Raminder Sekhon

LAMB CURRY KHORMA

4	pounds lamb shoulder, fat removed, cut in 1″ cubes
1 1/2	tablespoons turmeric
3	cups oil
6	medium onions, chopped
3	cloves garlic
6	whole cardamom seeds
6	bay leaves
6	whole cloves
1	stick cinnamon
	water, as needed
1/4	teaspoon mace
1/4	teaspoon ginger
2	tablespoons cumin
1	teaspoon ground coriander
1/4	teaspoon cayenne pepper
1/4	teaspoon nutmeg
1 1/2	teaspoons dill
	salt, to taste

Roll the lamb cubes in the turmeric. Heat the oil and add the onions and garlic; brown well.

In a separate pan, boil the cardamom seeds, bay leaves, cloves and cinnamon stick in a little water for 10 minutes.

In a separate bowl, combine the mace, ginger, cumin, coriander, pepper, nutmeg and dill and mix well.

When onions and garlic are browned, add the mixed spices and cook for 10 minutes. Add the meat and salt to taste. Strain the spices which have been boiled and add the liquid to the meat. Cook until the meat is tender.

Serves: 8

WINE: *Paul Masson Gewürztraminer*

The Selfridge Hotel
London, England
Chef: Erich Himowicz

CARRE D'AGNEAU À LA BOUQUETIÈRE

2	best ends of lamb (ask butcher for trimmings)
1	diced onion
1	diced carrot
1	diced stick celery
2	bay leaves
2	pints beef stock
	salt and pepper, to taste
18	*each* barrel-shaped and cooked vegetables: turnips, carrots, and asparagus tips

Roast lamb to desired degree of doneness with the diced onion, carrot, celery and bay leaves. Remove the lamb and keep warm. Place roasting pan on stove, add stock, season, and bring to a boil. Simmer about 20 minutes. Strain sauce and serve separately.

Place meat in center of oval dish and surround with cooked vegetables. Place cutlet frills on end bones of lamb and serve.

Serves: 6

HUNAM LAMB

3/4	pound leg of lamb (trimmed weight), thinly sliced
1/2	tablespoon cornstarch blended with 1/2 tablespoon water
1	egg white
5	pieces black mushrooms, soaked in water for 5 minutes before using
6	pieces bamboo shoots
1 1/2	tablespoons dark soy sauce
1/2	teaspoon sugar
1/2	teaspoon vinegar
2	tablespoons dry sherry
1/2	teaspoon sesame seeds
1/2	teaspoon MSG (optional)
1 1/2	teaspoons chili paste with garlic
2	cups vegetable or corn oil
1	cup leeks cut 2 1/2" long

In bowl #1: place lamb, add cornstarch and egg white. Blend well and set aside.

In bowl #2: place black mushrooms and bamboo shoots. Set aside.

In bowl #3: mix soy sauce, sugar, vinegar, sherry, sesame seeds, (MSG), and chili paste. Set aside.

Heat 2 cups of oil in a wok or skillet. Add contents of bowl #1 when oil is hot. Stirring, cook about 30 seconds. Add contents of bowl #2, cook about 10 seconds. Remove all the meat and vegetables. Drain in a sieve-lined bowl to catch the drippings. Pour all but about 1 tablespoon oil from the wok.

Put leeks into the wok. Cook about 30 seconds. Add lamb and vegetables back into wok. Add contents of bowl #3. Cook about 10 seconds and serve.

Serves: 2–4

WINE: *Wan Fu*

PETROS' ROAST LAMB (Arni Psito)

3	pounds leg or shoulder of lamb
4	cloves garlic
	rosemary
2	tablespoons lemon juice
1/2	cup olive oil
	salt and pepper
1	teaspoon oregano
1	cup water
6	potatoes, peeled and quartered

After cleaning the meat, make incisions to insert the garlic cloves and a little rosemary in it. Rub the meat with the lemon juice, olive oil, and salt and pepper. Place the meat in a roasting tin and pour over it the rest of the olive oil and lemon juice. Sprinkle generously with oregano, salt and pepper, and add a cup of water. Surround the meat with the potatoes. Bake in a hot (400°) oven until tender. Add more water if necessary. The potatoes must absorb all the water and be nicely browned.

(For variety, use chestnuts instead of potatoes. In this case, boil the chestnuts before peeling and omit the garlic and oregano.)

Serves: 4–6

WINE: *Roditys*

La Caravelle
New York, New York
Proprietors: Fred Decre and Robert Meyzen
Chef: Roger Fessaguet

SADDLE OF LAMB AUX PETITS LÉGUMES

- 1 saddle of lamb (ready to cook, 4–5 pounds)
- 2 medium-sized carrots, cut in strips
- 2 medium-sized cucumbers, cut in strips
- 2 medium-sized zucchinis, cut in strips
- 4 medium-sized white turnips, cut in strips
- 3 medium-sized potatoes, cut in strips butter, as needed
- 1 bunch of watercress

Roast lamb uncovered in 450° oven 40–45 minutes (10 minutes per pound) for medium rare. Let rest 1/2 hour.

Cook all vegetables "al dente" and sauté them in butter. Parboil potatoes and cook in butter.

Dress saddle on a serving dish. Garnish with bouquets of vegetables by arranging colors. Decorate with watercress.

Pour a little bit of lamb drippings around the saddle and pour the rest in a sauce bowl.

Serving suggestion: finish with noisette butter on saddle and vegetables.

Serves: 4–5

Chárdás Restaurant
Arlington, Virginia
Proprietor: Ivan Galitzin
Chef: Marta Galitzin

PRINCE ESTERHÁZY BEEF ROSTELYOS SERVED WITH POTATO PANCAKES

- 10 4-ounce rib eye steak slices, lightly pounded to make them even salt and pepper, as needed flour, as needed vegetable oil
- 2 large onions, chopped
- 2 green peppers, chopped
- 3 tomatoes, chopped
- 1 parsnip
- 1 large carrot, quartered lengthwise Burgundy wine, as needed water, as needed potato pancakes (see recipe below)

To prepare Beef Rostelyos: season beef with salt and pepper. Dredge in flour and shake off excess. In a large saucepan, heat enough oil to cover bottom of pan 1/2". Brown beef, 3 or 4 medalions at a time, over medium heat. Remove all browned meat to a plate and hold.

Loosen all flour stuck to the bottom of saucepan with a wooden spoon. Add about 4 ounces of oil, heat, and lightly sauté chopped onions. Do not burn or brown, just yellow. Add green peppers, tomatoes, parsnip and carrot, and sauté for about 3 minutes more.

Return all meat to saucepan, cover, and simmer over medium heat until tender. Take care to have meat always covered with liquid. Prepare a mixture of 2/3 Burgundy and 1/3 water (about 16–20 ounces total) and keep adding to saucepan slowly, in small amounts, until meat is tender.

When meat is tender, remove to a plate and set aside. Separate gravy from vegetables, using a colander, and liquefy vegetables in a strainer, blender, or similar equipment. Pour liquefied vegetables back into the gravy in the saucepan and season to taste, adding more Burgundy, salt, pepper, or water as the taste requires. (1/3 to 1/2 of smallest size can tomato purée may be added, but tomato taste must not dominate the sauce.) Gravy consistency should be medium.

Return meat to saucepan and heat in gravy.

Potato Pancakes

3 eggs
4 ounces flour ("Wondra" or similar)
4 ounces finely chopped onions
  salt and ground black pepper
4 large potatoes
  vegetable oil

To prepare potato pancakes: in a bowl, mix together eggs, flour, onions, salt, and pepper. Peel potatoes (keeping them in cold water after peeling so they won't blacken). Dry potatoes, one by one, and grate into a separate bowl. Squeeze out all liquid from the grated potatoes and mix into flour mixture.

Heat oil 2" deep in a saucepan. Use a slotted spoon as a measure for each pancake. Flatten pancake in hot oil so that pancake will be of even thickness, but *not too thin.* Fry and serve immediately.

Preferably in an oval platter, serve 2 beef medallions and 1 potato pancake per person. Place gravy on meat only.

Serves: 4–6

WINE: *Hungarian: Szekszardi Vörös or Bull's Blood from Eger*

Don Pepe
Kansas City, Missouri
Chef: Jose Fernandez

SPANISH PALLARDA

4 8–10-ounce beef fillets
1 medium onion, chopped
1/2 stick butter
6 ounces crabmeat, chopped
6 ounces shrimp, chopped
2 ounces bread crumbs
1 bay leaf
1 clove garlic, chopped
1 pinch parsley
2 ounces white wine
1 ounce dry sherry
1 cup chicken broth
1 cup cream
1 bay leaf
1 teaspoon white pepper
4 ounces white wine
1/2 ounce 151-proof rum

Pound fillets thinly to form 6× 8 cm strips.

To prepare stuffing: sauté onion in butter. Add crabmeat, shrimp, and bread crumbs to onion, then add bay leaf, garlic, and parsley. Cook 8–10 minutes, adding wine and sherry just before done.

Place mixture on beef strips and roll up. Bake in 375° oven for 20–30 minutes.

To prepare sauce: mix together chicken broth, cream, bay leaf, white pepper, and wine in a saucepan. Cook for 15–20 minutes, but do not boil.

Put fillet rolls on serving platter. Pour sauce on beef. When ready to serve, add rum and flame.

Serves: 4

WINE: *Federico Paternina Banda Azul*

The Selfridge Hotel
London, England
Chef: Erich Himowicz

FILET DE BOEUF ELIZABETH

4	pounds fillet
	salt and pepper
1/4	pint oil
	diced carrots, celery stick, and onion
2	bay leaves
1	pound beef bones chopped in small pieces
1	tablespoon tomato purée
2	tablespoons flour
2	pints stock
1/2	gill sherry
1/2	gill brandy
1	ounce truffle, chopped
1/4	pound butter

Trim the fillet and season with salt and pepper. (Keep the trimmings for sauce.) Place a shallow roasting tray on stove, add oil, and heat. Put fillet in pan and brown all over. Place in a moderate oven for 20 minutes. Add diced vegetables, bay leaves, bones, and trimmings, and place back in oven for another 10 minutes. Remove fillet and keep warm.

To prepare sauce: place the same roasting tray on top of stove and add tomato purée and flour. Mix together with wooden spoon and return to the oven for 5 minutes. Remove from oven, add stock, and bring to a boil. Simmer for 20 minutes. Strain into a saucepan and bring back to a boil. Add sherry, brandy, and diced truffle to mixture and stir in butter just before serving.

Serving suggestion: place fillet in center of oval dish. Garnish with endive, stuffed tomatoes, stuffed artichoke bottoms, and Parisienne potatoes placed around the beef. Slice 6 ounces of pâté de foie gras into six slices and place on top of fillet. Sauce is served separately to be ladled over beef.

Serves: 6

The Buccaneer Inn
Longboat Key, Florida
Proprietor: Herbert Field
Chef: William Hallisey

PRIME RIBS OF BEEF OVER CHARCOAL

7	pound standing rib roast
1 1/2	cups salad oil, to marinate
1	teaspoon garlic powder
1	teaspoon onion powder
1/4	cup lemon juice
	onion rings and parsley, to garnish

Preheat oven and cook roast at 325° for 1 1/2 hours or until meat is rare. Remove from oven and allow meat to rest.

Slice into 1" thick slices. (Usually there will be a rib bone in every other slice.) Marinate slices in oil, garlic powder, onion powder and lemon juice for as long as possible.

Drain meat and grill over charcoal, searing both sides first. Cook to order. Serve with a garnish of onion rings and parsley.

Serves: 6

The Villa Nova
Winter Park, Florida
Proprietor: Jeanne Rodriguez
Chef: Ann Pantilione

KING JACQUES

1/8	pound butter
2	5-ounce center cut tournedos
1	ounce cognac
1	cup brown sauce
2	tablespoons chives
2	tablespoons green peppercorns
1/2	cup clarified butter
8	ounces Alaskan King Crab meat
1/2	cup sliced almonds
1	ounce crème de noyaux
	bouquetierre of sautéed vegetables, to garnish

Heat two separate pans.

To prepare tournedos: melt butter and sauté tournedos. Add cognac, flambé, and remove tournedos. Add brown sauce and chives and mix. Return tournedos to pan and spread peppercorns over. Cook to desired degree of doneness.

To prepare crabmeat: pour in clarified butter to second heated pan. Add crabmeat and almonds and simmer until heated through. Add noyaux and flambé. Serve on plate with tournedos. Garnish with bouquetierre.

Serves: 2

WINE: *Cabernet Sauvignon*

Bavarian Village
Ft. Lauderdale, Florida
Proprietor: E. Heintze

SAUERBRATEN

2	cups vinegar
2	teaspoons salt
10	peppercorns
3	cloves
2	bay leaves
2	chopped onions
2	sliced carrots
4-6	pounds beef
3	tablespoons butter
1 1/2	cups boiling water
1/2	pint sour cream

Combine in a saucepan vinegar, salt, peppercorns, cloves, bay leaves, onions, and carrots. Bring to a boil. Remove from heat and cool for 30 minutes. Place beef in a bowl and pour mixture over it. Marinate for 3–5 days in the refrigerator. Turn the meat several times and baste occasionally.

Drain the meat, reserving the marinade, and dry with paper towel. Melt butter in a heavy cast-iron pot or Dutch oven. Brown on all sides. Add the marinade and boiling water and cook over low heat for 3 hours or until meat is tender. Add sour cream, stirring constantly, and simmer for 15 minutes. Slice and serve with the gravy.

Serves: 6–8

WINE: *Burgundy*

The Library
Hilton Hotel
Ft. Lauderdale, Florida
Chef: Richard Saywell

TOURNEDOS SOUTHERN CROSS

4   strips bacon, cut up
8   fresh oysters on half shell
    salt, pepper, and lemon juice, as
      needed
    Worcestershire and tabasco sauces,
      as needed
8   4-ounce tournedos of beef
8   croutons
4   ounces Bordelaise Sauce

Place cut bacon on oysters and sprinkle with salt, pepper, lemon juice, Worcestershire sauce, and tabasco sauce. Cook on a bed of rock salt.

Broil tournedos to desired degree of doneness. Place on croutons. Pour Bordelaise sauce over and serve with oysters.

Serves: 4

WINE: *Zinfandel*

La Paloma
San Antonio, Texas
Proprietor: Amin George, Jr.
Chef: Janie Villanueva

LA PALOMA RESTAURANT CHILI

10   pounds ground round beef
1/3   cup salt
1/3   cup cumin
1/2   cup granulated garlic
1   cup chili powder
3   gallons water
3   cups shortening
1/2   cup chili powder
      flour, as needed

Place first five ingredients in a 5-gallon pot with 3 gallons of water. Boil for about 1 1/4 hours or until meat is tender.

In a smaller pan, make chili pastry as follows: heat shortening and 1/2 cup chili powder over medium heat. Gradually add flour until a thick paste base is attained.

When meat is ready, add small amounts of pastry until a rich creamy gravy is attained. Do not add too much pastry too early. The longer the cooking time, the thicker the pastry.

Serves: 20

WINE: *Sangria (see index)*

Peppertree Restaurant
Holiday Inn-Airport
Portland, Oregon
Proprietor: B. Sullivan
Chef: Reinhold Antoni

STEAK DAVID

2   4-ounce peeled tenderloin steaks
4   Dungeness crab legs
    butter, to sauté
    white wine, as needed
4   fresh asparagus spears
    chicken broth, as needed
4   ounces Béarnaise Sauce *(see index)*

Cook tenderloin to desired degree of doneness. Lightly sauté crab legs in butter and white wine. Cook asparagus in chicken broth. Place tenderloin steaks on serving platter, top with asparagus spears, add Béarnaise sauce, and place crab legs on top of all.

Serves: 1–2

John Charles Restaurant
San Antonio, Texas
Proprietor/Chef: John W. Casey III

TENDERLOIN BITS & CRUNCHY VEGETABLES

3   ounces peanut oil
4   cups coarsely cut vegetables: Italian
      onions, yellow zucchini, goose-
      neck squash, bell pepper, broccoli
      stalk slices, Jerusalem artichoke
      slices
1   teaspoon dry tarragon
1   tablespoon chives
1   clove garlic, pressed
1   teaspoon cracked pepper
12 ounces tenderloin bits, 3/4 inch-
      1 1/2 inch cubes
1 1/2 teaspoons salt
8   cherry tomatoes
2   ounces brandy

Heat skillet with oil and add the 4 cups of vegetables. Season with tarragon, chives, garlic, cracked pepper, and salt. Stir fry vegetables for 5 minutes over high heat. Add tenderloin pieces and stir for 2 minutes. Add cherry tomatoes and stir 1 minute. Add brandy and flame, stirring and dipping liquid during flaming. Stir 2 minutes. Total cooking time about 12 minutes. Place mixture on white plate and serve "neat" or over rice.

Serves: 2

The Wildwood Restaurant
South Lake Tahoe, California
Proprietor: Jim Simpson
Chef: Ron Brown

STEAK OSCAR

8   egg yolks
1/2 ounce lemon juice
1/3 teaspoon cayenne pepper
1   pound butter at room temperature
1   tablespoon tarragon leaves
8   3-ounce fillets of beef
8   ounces crabmeat
16 asparagus spears
4   slices toasted, buttered sourdough
      bread

To prepare sauce: beat together egg yolks, lemon juice, and cayenne pepper. Cook on double boiler until it starts to thicken. Remove from heat. Add butter and whip into egg mixture very slowly. Add tarragon leaves to mixture and let set.

Broil fillets to desired doneness.

Divide crabmeat into 4 2-ounce portions on baking sheet. Lay asparagus spears across crabmeat. Heat at 300° for 4–5 minutes.

Lay 2 fillets over each piece of bread and lay crabmeat and asparagus on top. Top with 2 ounces of sauce, garnish, and serve.

Serves: 4

King Arthur's Pub
Chicago, Illinois
Proprietors: Arthur, Michael,
and Robert Lieberman
Chef: Fritz Allgaier

STEAK & KIDNEY PIE CASSEROLE

8 ounces tenderloin tips, cubed
1 tablespoon vegetable shortening
6 ounces veal kidneys, cubed
  salted water, as needed
1/4 medium onion, minced
4 tablespoons beef stock
2 teaspoons flour
1 pinch marjoram
  salt and pepper, to taste
  cooked chopped celery, mushrooms,
    and diced carrots (optional)
  puff pastry pie crust (*see index*)
1 egg yolk, beaten

Place tenderloin cubes in skillet with shortening and brown. In a separate pan, place cubed kidneys in salted boiling water, blanch, strain, and rinse. Place kidneys in with tips, add onions, and brown. Add beef stock and flour and stir until smooth. Add seasonings (and optional items) and simmer until meat is tender.

Place steak and kidney stew in two small casseroles. Flatten pie dough and shape to just overlap casserole. Rub egg yolk around edge of casserole. Place dough on top and press overlapping dough around casserole. Brush top of dough with egg yolk. Bake at 350° for 10–15 minutes.

Serves: 2

WINE: *Côtes du Rhône Rouge wine*

L'Affair
Mission Hills, California
Chefs: Michel and John Casarubbia

ENTRECÔTE MARCHAND DE VIN

1 chopped shallot
1 glass red wine
1/2 teaspoon beef broth
1 1/2 ounces unsalted butter
1 teaspoon chopped parsley
1 N.Y. or Delmonico steak, enough to
  serve 1
1 dash lemon juice

In a saucepan combine shallot, wine, beef broth, butter, and parsley. Bring to boil, simmer to reduce to sauce consistency.

Grill steak to desired doneness. Just before serving, add a dash of lemon juice to sauce, stir well, and pour sauce over steak.

Serves: 1

WINE: *Red Burgundy*

The Little Cafe
Detroit, Michigan
Proprietor: Ted Colo
Chef: Mike Colo

BEEF ROULADEN

2 pounds top round steak, cut 1/2"
  thick
8 teaspoons spicy brown mustard
1/2 pound bacon, cooked and diced
2 medium onions, diced
  flour
  salt and pepper, to taste
  water, as needed
1 tablespoon Maggi seasoning
1 tablespoon liquid gravy browner
2 tablespoons spicy brown mustard
1/2 cup flour
1/2 cup water

To prepare beef: cut round steak diagonally to make 8 thin strips. Pound to flatten and spread one side of each strip with 1 teaspoon mustard. Place equal amounts of bacon and onions at one end of each piece of steak. Roll up and secure with food picks.

Place beef rolls in Dutch oven or casserole. Sprinkle lightly with flour, season with salt and pepper. Add water to come halfway up sides of beef. Bake, covered, in 325° oven for about 2 hours, or until tender. With slotted spoon, remove beef rolls from pan to serving platter.

To prepare gravy: to liquid in pan, add Maggi, liquid gravy browner, and mustard. Bring to a boil. In a separate bowl, stir together flour and water until smooth. Whisk into boiling liquid. Cook several minutes or until thick. Strain. Add water, if necessary, to thin gravy to desired consistency. Serve over Rouladen.

Serves: 4

L'Hotel de France
Minneapolis, Minnesota
General Manager: John F. Lehodey
Chef: Daniel Hubert

FILET MIGNON POÊLE MAÎTRE DES CAVES

1/2   liter white wine
1   ounce chopped shallots
2   bay leaves
    salt and pepper, as needed
1/2   liter veal stock (*see index*)
1   teaspoon horseradish
2   teaspoons Dijon mustard
    brandy, as needed
    cornstarch, as needed
3   ounces bleu cheese, well-crumbled
3   ounces butter
4   filets mignons

In a saucepan, reduce the white wine with the shallots, bay leaves, salt and pepper to half. In another saucepan, reduce the veal stock to half.

Add the veal stock and horseradish to the wine mixture and reduce for another 10 minutes. Add the mustard and brandy and then the cornstarch to make a thin sauce.

Strain the sauce through a fine sieve, add the cheese, and as soon as it begins to boil, thicken the sauce with butter. Serve over the filets, sautéed to the desired doneness.

Serving suggestion: serve with broccoli, Belgian endive, sautéed potatoes.

Serves: 4

WINE: *Côtes de Bergerac or Cahors*

Coal Hole
Clayton, Missouri
Proprietor: Shel Waldman

TOURNEDOS PROVENCAL

2   4-ounce medallions of beef tenderloin
    butter or oil, to sauté
1/2   clove fresh minced garlic
1/2   cup fresh mushrooms, sliced
2   tablespoons diced onion
2   tablespoons diced green peppers
1 1/2   cups brown sauce (*see index*)
1 1/2   ounces Madeira wine
1/2   cup diced tomatoes

Braise tenderloin lightly and remove from heat. In a separate skillet, sauté garlic, mushrooms, onions, and green peppers. Add brown sauce and let simmer for 3 minutes. Add Madeira wine, diced tomatoes, and tenderloin medallions. Let simmer until beef reaches desired degree of doneness.

Serves: 1

That Steak Joynt
Chicago, Illinois
Proprietor: Billy Siegel
Chef: Riley Simmons

STEAK MARINER WITH BÉARNAISE SAUCE

1/2	cup olive oil
4	ounces Burgundy wine
4	teaspoons chopped parsley
4	tablespoons finely chopped shallots
2	finely chopped garlic cloves
2	teaspoons crushed black peppercorns
1	pinch salt
4	8-ounce butterflied fillets from a prime tenderloin
12	ounces Alaskan crabmeat
4	tablespoons butter
4	teaspoons chopped chives
4	sliced mushrooms
4	tablespoons sherry wine
12	jumbo asparagus spears
1	cup rich chicken broth
	Béarnaise Sauce (*see recipe below*)

Combine first 7 ingredients to make a marinade. Place steak in a glass casserole and pour marinade over steak. Turn steak to saturate. Cover dish and refrigerate for 6 hours.

Sauté crabmeat in butter. Add chives and mushrooms. Cook for about 3–4 minutes. Add wine and set aside.

Poach asparagus spears in chicken broth until tender. Remove and dry on a napkin.

Sear steak quickly in hot skillet on both sides, then cook steak to desired degree of doneness in broiler.

Top asparagus spears with a little brown butter. Top steak with Béarnaise sauce and place on platter accompanied with crabmeat and asparagus.

Serves: 4

WINE: *Cabernet Sauvignon*

Béarnaise Sauce

1/4	cup terragon vinegar
1/4	cup lemon juice
1/4	cup white wine
2	finely chopped shallots
1	teaspoon crushed peppercorns
1	teaspoon chervil
5	egg yolks
10	ounces butter
1	pinch salt
1	teaspoon chopped tarragon

Mix together vinegar, lemon juice, wine, shallots, peppercorns, and chervil in a saucepan. Cook until reduced 2/3. Remove from heat and let the pan cool a little. Add the egg yolks to the reduction. Place in a double boiler and stir constantly with a wire whip until very creamy. Remove from heat. Add butter very slowly. Stirring constantly, add salt. Strain through a fine sieve. Add chopped tarragon.

The Torch Restaurant
Dallas, Texas
Proprietor: Chris Victor Semos

DOLMADES AVGOLEMONO

1	medium head cabbage
2	cups water
1 1/2	pounds ground beef
1	medium onion, grated
1/2	cup parsley
1	egg
1	cup rice
	salt and pepper, to taste

Discard coarse leaves of cabbage and cut out tough stalk. Separate leaves and parboil in 1 cup of water.

In a medium-sized bowl, combine

ground beef and all other ingredients except water, mixing thoroughly to make a meat filling. On each cabbage leaf, place one tablespoon of meat filling. Roll and fold the sides over.

In a deep saucepan, arrange Dolmades in layers and cover with a plate to keep them in order. Add the remaining 1 cup of water, cover pan, and cook slowly until rice is tender, about 1 hour. After cooking, drain off approximately 1 cup of liquid. Save to use in sauce.

Avgolemono Sauce

3 eggs
1/2 teaspoon flour
   juice of 2 lemons
   broth from cooked Dolmades

Beat eggs well, slowly adding flour and then lemon juice. Stir in warm broth from Dolmades.

Pour sauce over Dolmades. Heat slowly so sauce won't curdle. Serve immediately.

Serves: 4

WINE: *Greek white wine, chilled*

A. Bastion's Vendome
Clearwater, Florida
Proprietor/Chef: A. Bastion

BOEUF À LA BOURGUIGNONNE

2 pounds beef, cut in cubes
2 tablespoons olive oil
3 ounces bacon
1 onion
3 ounces mushrooms
   salt, pepper, thyme, bay leaf,
      rosemary, as needed
3 glasses dry red wine
3 tablespoons tomato purée
1 tablespoon flour
   chopped parsley, to garnish

In a skillet, sauté meat in hot olive oil. Add bacon, onion, mushrooms, and seasoning and continue to sauté. After 10 minutes, add wine, tomato purée, and flour. Cover and let cook for about 2 hours (adding water, if necessary) on a very low heat. Garnish with parsley and serve.

Serves: 4

The Oaks Restaurant
Dallas, Texas
Proprietor: Tony Braxton
Chef: Leon Dial

BEEF STROGANOFF

1/2 teaspoon salt
1/4 cup flour
1 pound tenderloin steak cut into 3" strips
1/3 cup butter
1/4 teaspoon oregano
1 teaspoon Worcestershire sauce
1/2 cup onion, finely chopped
3/4 cup fresh mushrooms, thinly sliced
1 pinch nutmeg
1 teaspoon paprika
1 1/2 cups beef stock
   salt and pepper, to taste
1/2 cup sour cream
1/4 cup sherry wine

Blend salt in flour. Coat strips of tenderloin in mixture. Heat butter in a large skillet and, when hot, quickly brown the coated meat strips on all sides. Remove meat from skillet and reserve.

Add all other ingredients, except sour cream and wine, to hot pan. Reduce heat and simmer until onions are tender.

Return meat strips to pan, stir in sour cream, then wine, and serve immediately over noodles or toast.

Serves: 4–6

Shiro of Japan
Houston, Texas
Proprietor: Hideo Matsuoka
Chef: Tony Luk

SHOGUN STEAK

1/2   cup soy sauce
1/4   cup sake
1/4   cup mirin (sweet cooking wine)
  2   teaspoons freshly ground ginger
1/4   cup sugar
  2   tablespoons ground sesame seed
  1   dash kono-sansho (Japanese pepper)
  1   3-4-pound fillet of beef, 1″ thick

Combine first six ingredients and simmer over slow heat for 1 hour. Add dash of kono-sansho. Cool sauce.

Marinate fillet for 5 minutes in sauce. Cook on grill. After cooking, dip into sauce and serve.

Serves: 6–8

WINE: *Chablis*

Les Tournebroches
New York, New York
Proprietor: Charles Chevillot

BROCHETTE DE BOEUF (Cubed Beef on Skewers) WITH BÉARNAISE SAUCE

1 1/4   pounds sirloin steak in one piece
  16   1″-squares cored, seeded green peppers
   2   tablespoons peanut, vegetable, or corn oil
      salt and freshly ground pepper, to taste
      Béarnaise Sauce (*see recipe below*)

Cut steak into cubes of about 1″–1 1/2″. (There should be about 48 pieces.)

Arrange the pieces of beef on skewers, starting with one piece of green pepper. Add 4 pieces of beef, another green pepper piece, 4 of beef, another green pepper piece, 4 more pieces of beef, and finally, a pepper piece. Repeat with 3 more skewers.

Place the skewered foods in a flat dish and brush all over with oil.

Place the brochettes on a heated grill and cook about 3–4 minutes on one side. Sprinkle with salt and pepper and turn the brochettes to cook on the other side, about 3–4 minutes. Serve immediately with Béarnaise sauce.

Serves: 4

Béarnaise Sauce

1/2   pound butter
  2   tablespoons finely chopped shallots
  2   tablespoons tarragon vinegar
  1   teaspoon crushed peppercorns
  1   teaspoon dried tarragon
  2   egg yolks
  1   tablespoon cold water

Melt butter slowly in a small, heavy saucepan. Skim off film from top carefully.

Heat the shallots, vinegar, peppercorns and tarragon in another small, heavy saucepan and cook until all the liquid evaporates. Remove from heat and let the saucepan cool slightly.

Add the egg yolks and water.

Return the saucepan to the stove and, using very low heat, stir the yolk mixture vigorously. Do not overheat or the eggs will curdle. Remove the saucepan from the heat and place on a cold surface. Add the melted butter, ladle by ladle, stirring vigorously. Do not add too rapidly.

Yields: about 1 cup

THE TOWER HOTEL
London, England
Chef: P. Ricks
Loup de Mer

THE SELFRIDGE HOTEL
London, England
Chef: Erich Himowicz
Rouget à la Niçoise

△ LA PETITE FERME
New York, New York
Chef: Rainer Langbein
Poached Lobster

▽ GAGE & TOLLNER
Brooklyn, New York
Lobster Newburg

△ CAFÉ JOHNELL
Fort Wayne, Indiana
Chef: Nike Spillson
Sole Bonne Femme aux Epinards

▽ THE BARBADOS HILTON
Bridgetown, Barbados
Caribbean Flying Fish in Crust

ALEXIS
San Francisco, California
Chef: Theodore Gugolz
Koulebiaka of Salmon

△ VARGO'S
Houston, Texas
Scampi

▽ DOCK OF THE BAY
Berkeley, California
Chef: Leonard Riley
Jambalaya

THE TOWER HOTEL
London, England
Chef: P. Ricks
Escalope of Veal "Western Isles"

LA ROTISSERIE
New York, New York
Coq au Vinaigre

△ ALLGAUER'S FIRESIDE
Northbrook, Illinois
Chef: Jesse Cobb
Baked Dover Sole with Salmon
Mousse Florentine, en Croûte

▽ THE JAMAICA HILTON
Ocho Rios, Jamaica
Breast of Chicken "Conquistador"

THE SELFRIDGE HOTEL
London, England
Chef: Erich Himowicz
Filet de Boeuf Elizabeth

△ HUNGARIA RESTAURANT
  New York, New York
  Chef: Bank Szerenyi
  Chicken Strudel

▽ LAKESIDE RESTAURANT
  Newport Beach, California
  Chef: Edward Swindler
  Fillet of Beef Wellington

△ THE MAYAGUEZ HILTON
Mayaguez, Puerto Rico
Chef: Dieter Hannig
Tropical Fruit Strudel ''Mayaguezano''

▽ LES TOURNEBROCHES
New York, New York
Raspberry Tarte

HAROLD RESTAURANT
Santa Monica, California
Chef: Luis Carrido
Chocolate Mocha Ice Cream Pie

MICHEL'S AT THE COLONY SURF
Honolulu, Hawaii
Chef: Gordon W.K. Hopkins
Bouillabaisse

Ichabod Crane's Tarry Town Tavern
Torrance, California
Chef: Harry Prod

ROASTED PRIME RIBS OF BEEFE

1   16–18-pound prime rib roast
    pre-mixed pickling spice, as needed

Refrigerate roast overnight.

Pre-heat oven to 500°.

(Take roast directly from refrigerator to oven. Do not bring to room temperature.) Place fat side up in shallow roasting pan. Add pre-mixed, ordinary pickling spice to fat side of beef. Roast freely.

Insert meat thermometer, making sure tip does not touch bones. Roast for 20 minutes at 500°. Reduce oven heat to 325° for approximately 2 1/2 hours or until meat thermometer reaches 130° for rare, 160° for well done.

Remove from roasting pan to room temperature. Let stand idle for 15–20 minutes before carving.

Serves: 12–15

WINE: *Cabernet Sauvignon*

Hotel Dorset
New York, New York
Chef: William J. Spry

JULIENNE OF BEEF À LA DORSET

3   pounds shell of beef (sirloin)
    salt and pepper to taste
1/2 cup flour
9   ounces chopped shallots or onions
1/2 pound butter
    cooking oil
1   fifth bottle red Burgundy wine
1   teaspoon Lea & Perrins Sauce
    (Worcestershire sauce)
2   tablespoons fresh chopped parsley

Remove all fat from beef, then slice into 1/2" steaks. Cut steaks into julienne (or finger) strips, season with salt and pepper, dredge with flour. Sautée shallots (or onions) in a little butter and oil for about 3–4 minutes, but do not brown. Set aside.

In a very hot pan, sauté the julienne of beef to sear the edges, add the cooked shallots (or onions) and stir well. Cover the beef with the wine and simmer for about 10 minutes. Remove any scum or fat which may form on top. Add the Lea & Perrins Sauce before serving, garnish with parsley.

Serving suggestion: rice pilaf or buttered noodles.

Serves: 6

WINE: *Cabernet Sauvignon*

Danny's Restaurant
Baltimore, Maryland
Proprietor/Chef: Danny Dickman

STEAK DIANE FLAMBÉ

8   4-ounce tenderloin fillets
    salt and pepper
6   tablespoons clarified butter
8   ounces sliced mushrooms
1/4 cup chopped shallots
1   tablespoon snipped parsley
1   teaspoon snipped chives
1/4 cup cognac
1/4 cup condensed beef broth
2   tablespoons Madeira wine
2   tablespoons bottled Sauce Robert
1/2 teaspoon Worcestershire sauce

Season meat with salt and pepper and set aside. Melt butter in blazer pan of chafing dish or in skillet over medium heat. Add mushrooms; cook 2 minutes. Add shallots, parsley, and chives; cook for 2 minutes more. Remove vegetables, reserving butter in pan. Increase heat. Cook half of the beef at a time in butter in the same pan, 2–3 minutes per side for rare or medium rare.

Return vegetables and meat to pan. Add cognac; flame. When flame is extinguished, add beef broth, wine, Sauce Robert, and Worcestershire sauce. Cook 1 minute. Season to taste with salt and pepper. Serve over wild rice.

Serves: 4

WINE: *Nuits St. Georges*

Lakeside Restaurant
Newport Beach, California
Proprietor: Irwin Milman
Chef: Edward Swindler

FILLET OF BEEF WELLINGTON

1 1/2 pounds fillet of beef (from head of
      tenderloin)
  1/2 cup butter
      salt
      ground black pepper
  1/4 cup sliced celery
  1/4 cup sliced onions
  1/2 cup sliced carrots
    1 bay leaf
  1/4 teaspoon dried rosemary, crumbled
    6 ounces pâté de foie gras (prepared or
      see index)
      puff pastry (*see recipe below*)
    2 egg yolks
  1/2 cup veal stock (prepared or *see
      index*)
    1 truffle or 1/4 cup chopped
      mushrooms

Remove all fat and sinew from meat. Wrap in towel and flatten to approximately 2 1/2" thick. Tie meat with string to keep round shape. Spread meat generously with butter. Sprinkle with salt and pepper. Spread all the vegetables, bay leaf, and rosemary over the bottom of a shallow baking pan. Place roast on top. Cook at 450° after preheating oven. Cook for 20–25 minutes, depending on how well done you prefer the meat. Remove roast from oven and cool completely.

When roast is cold, remove string. Spread 4 ounces of pâté de foie gras over entire surface of roast. Roll pastry to 1/8" thick. Cut one piece 1/2" larger than roast. Place roast in center. Cut another piece of pastry dough large enough to cover meat completely. Cover meat with pastry dough and seal by pressing moistened edges together. Decorate with strips of pastry dough laid over top in any design desired. Place in baking pan, seam side down. Brush crust with beaten egg yolk. Prick crust in a few places to allow steam to escape. Bake in preheated oven at 450° for 15–20 minutes, or until baked to a golden brown. Place roast on platter.

Combine veal stock, 2 ounces of pâté de foie gras, and chopped truffles (or mushrooms) in roasting pan. Simmer 10–15 minutes or until mixture is of sauce consistency. Strain mixture and place in sauce boat to be served with roast.

Serves: 2

WINE: *Cabernet Sauvignon, Pinot Noir*

Puff Pastry

1 1/2	cups (3 sticks) butter
3	cups plus 2 tablespoons all purpose flour, sifted
3/4	teaspoon salt
2	teaspoons lemon juice
2/3	cup ice water

Cut each stick of butter lengthwise into 3 strips. Sprinkle waxed paper with additional 2 tablespoons flour. Arrange the 9 strips of butter on waxed paper. Wrap in waxed paper and refrigerate until ready to use. Mix flour and salt in bowl. Combine lemon juice and ice water and add to flour, using circular motion. This mixture should be firm, but not sticky. Knead dough 20 minutes until smooth and satin-like. Cover dough and let it rest 20 minutes.

Roll dough 1/4" thick onto a 12" x 8" rectangular well-floured board. Place chilled butter strips side by side on half of the dough, within 1/2" of edge. Fold remaining dough over butter strips. Press edges together firmly. Wrap in waxed paper or foil and refrigerate 30 minutes.

Using a rolling pin, tap dough lightly to flatten butter. Roll out dough on a well-floured board until dough is 12" x 8" and approximately 1/4" thick. Do not roll over the edges until it is 12", then roll very gently. Fold both ends of the dough into the center, making sure that edges and corners are even. Press edges together firmly. Fold dough in half. Wrap in waxed paper or foil and refrigerate 30 minutes.

Roll dough again into rectangular shape, fold as before, and chill 30 minutes. Repeat this procedure 3 more times. The last time, chill dough for 3 hours.

When baked, this dough should be flaky and layered.

Rheinland Haus
Charlotte, North Carolina

ROULADEN

12	1/8"-thick center cut rare roast beef slices
	yellow mustard
	salt and pepper
23	ounces chopped onions
1/2	pound bacon, diced
3	large kosher dill pickles, cut in 4 lengthwise strips
	cold water

Lay slices of beef flat. Spread evenly with mustard. Sprinkle with salt and pepper. Mix together onion and bacon. Sauté until onions are transparent. Spread onion mixture on roast beef (divide mixture between 12 slices). Top mixture with one strip of pickle. Starting at narrow end of beef, roll up and secure with skewer. Place the rolls in a baking dish and cover halfway with water. Bake at 350° for 35–40 minutes.

Serves: 6

WINE: *Medium-dry Chablis*

La Bibliothèque
New York, New York
Proprietors: William Gordon
and Steve Meisels
Chef: Witold Karcz

PRIME FILLET OF BEEF WELLINGTON "WILLIAM SHAKESPEARE"

1	5-ounce filet mignon
1/4	pound clarified butter
1/2	pound chopped fresh mushrooms
2	ounces chopped calves liver
2	ounces chopped fillet of veal
2	tablespoons bread crumbs
2	eggs
	salt and pepper
2	tablespoons sherry
1/2	pound puff pastry (*see index*)
	watercress

Brown filet mignon in clarified butter. Remove from heat and set aside. Sauté mushrooms in clarified butter. In a separate pan, sauté calves liver.

Combine mushrooms, liver, veal, bread crumbs, one egg, salt, pepper, and sherry in a mixing bowl.

Roll out puff pastry to 1/4" thickness. Cut a circle of dough slightly larger than the filet mignon. Place 1/2 of the stuffing on the circle cut of dough and place filet mignon on that.

Cut an additional circle of dough twice the size of the first. Cover the filet mignon with stuffing and wrap with the larger piece of puff pastry dough. Beat the remaining egg and brush over the Wellington.

Bake in a 350° oven for 15 minutes (rare) or 20 minutes (medium rare). Garnish with watercress and serve.

Serves: 1

Stonehenge
Ridgefield, Connecticut
Proprietors: David Davis & Douglas Seville

MEDALLIONS OF PORK WITH ROASTED CHESTNUTS

14	ounces loin of pork, boned and trimmed of fat
	salt, pepper and paprika, to taste
	flour, as needed
	butter, to fry
1 1/2	ounces shallots
1 1/2	cups dry white wine
1 1/2	pints brown stock
1	tablespoon chives, chopped
3	ounces bacon
1 1/2	ounces finely chopped onion
16-20	pieces canned whole chestnuts
	Béarnaise Sauce (optional)
	chopped parsley, to garnish

Slice the loin of pork thinly to yield 3 slices per portion. Flatten slightly. Sprinkle with salt, pepper and a little paprika. Dip in flour and shallow fry in melted butter for a few seconds on each side until golden brown. Remove from pan and keep warm.

To prepare brown sauce:

Add shallots to pan with white wine, brown stock, and chopped chives. Bring to a boil and allow to reduce by 1/4.

In another pan, sauté the bacon, chopped onions, and chestnuts. When the onion is golden brown, add the contents of the pan to the reducing liquid in the other pan.

Place the sliced pork on a plate and spoon over the brown sauce and chestnuts. Top with Béarnaise sauce, if desired, and sprinkle with chopped parsley.

Serves: 2

MOUSAKA (Eggplant Casserole)

    1 pound chopped meat
    2 medium onions, chopped
  1/2 cup olive oil
    1 cup water
  1/2 cup tomato paste
    2 tablespoons minced parsley
  1/4 pound butter
       salt and pepper, to taste
    2 medium eggplants
       flour, as needed
  1/2 cup bread crumbs
    2 eggs, well beaten
  1/2 cup grated cheese and bread crumbs
       mixed

Brown the meat and onions in olive oil. When well browned, add water, tomato paste, parsley, butter, salt and pepper. Let it simmer on low heat for 1 hour or more until paste is thickened.

Peel and cut eggplants lengthwise in 1/4″-thick slices. Sprinkle with flour and sauté in separate pan in oil or butter to a golden brown color.

Add 2 tablespoons bread crumbs to the already cooked chopped meat mixture and mix well.

Butter a baking dish well and sprinkle with bread crumbs. Place 1/2 the eggplant slices in the dish and spread 1/2 the chopped meat on them. Add the remaining eggplant slices and chopped meat paste alternately. Pour well beaten eggs on top and spread evenly. Sprinkle with grated cheese and bread crumb mixture and bake in medium oven for about 1/2 hour or until golden brown.

Serves: 4–6

WINE: *Red*

CASSOULET DU CHEF DE CAFE BERNARD

  1/4 cup onion, diced
  1/4 cup carrot, diced
  1/4 cup celery, diced
  1/8 cup fat (pork or fowl)
    4 cloves garlic
    1 pint tomatoes, diced
  1/2 cup Burgundy, reduced to half
  3/4 pound lamb, boned
  3/4 pound pork loin, boned
    4 ounces garlic sausage
    4 ounces Polish sausage
1 1/2 pounds white beans, soaked for 2
         hours
    3 pound duck, cut into eighths
    4 ounces salt pork
    3 quarts water
       salt and pepper, to taste
    2 tablespoons thyme
    2 bay leaves

In a large pot, sauté onion, celery, and carrot in fat until soft. Add all other ingredients, cook over medium heat until beans are soft (approximately 2 hours). Remove from heat and remove meat items. Slice sausages, lamb, pork, and salt pork. Layer in a large casserole as follows: 1/4 beans, sliced lamb, 1/4 beans, sliced sausages, 1/4 beans, sliced pork, 1/4 beans, sliced salt pork and duck on top. Cover and bake at 375° for about 2 hours.

Serves: 5–7

WINE: *St. Emilion Château Fombrauge*

Steckley's Olde House
Carmel, Indiana
Proprietor: James Steckley

BARBECUED PORK RIBS

5 1/2 pounds pork loin back ribs
       water, as needed
       salt, pepper, and rubbed thyme, to
         taste
       thick barbecue sauce (*see index*)

Remove membranes from back of ribs. Cut rib in four equal parts. Cover with water in roaster pan. Add to taste salt, pepper and thyme. Cover pan with foil and boil 2 hours or until tender and blunt end of spoon will drop through ribs.

Drain and chill for 1 day.

Coat with thick barbecue sauce. Bake in preheated 350° oven for 20 minutes and serve.

Serves: 4

Mario's
Dallas, Texas
Chef: Raffaele Scudieri

LASAGNA VERDI PAVAROTTI

       Green Pasta (*see recipe below*)
       Meat Sauce (*see recipe below*)
       Béchamel Sauce (*see recipe below*)
    4 ounces grated Parmesan cheese
         blended with
    4 ounces grated mozzarella cheese
       butter for coating and top browning

Green Pasta

   16 ounces all-purpose flour
    3 eggs
    1 cup cooked spinach, finely chopped
         and well-drained

To prepare noodles: sift flour onto pastry board and make a well in the center. Add eggs and spinach, working the dough energetically until it becomes smooth and pliable. Roll the dough paper thin. Sprinkle lightly with flour to prevent sticking. The dough can be cut immediately or left 30 minutes to dry. Cut into 3"-strips.

Meat Sauce

1 1/2 ounces butter
    3 tablespoons olive oil
    1 onion, finely chopped
    1 carrot, finely chopped
    1 stalk celery, finely chopped
    3 ounces bacon
    6 ounces minced pork
    6 ounces minced beef
    2 ounces sausage meat
    3 chicken livers
    1 cup dry white wine
       salt and pepper
    2 tablespoons tomato paste
       beef stock, as needed
    4 ounces mushrooms sautéed in
         butter, garlic, and parsley

To prepare meat sauce: heat the butter and all the oil. Add vegetables and bacon and fry gently until they begin to brown. Add pork, beef, sausage meat and liver. Moisten with wine until it evaporates. Season with salt and pepper. Dilute tomato paste with a little stock and add to mixture. Cover and cook slowly for 1 hour. After sauce is ready, add sautéed mushrooms.

Béchamel Sauce

    6 tablespoons butter
    6 tablespoons all-purpose flour
    1 teaspoon salt, or as needed
    6 cups hot milk

To prepare Béchamel sauce: melt butter in pan, stir in flour and salt and cook without letting it brown. Gradually add hot milk, stirring with wire whisk. Continue to cook until thick and smooth.

To prepare lasagna: butter a deep round baking dish. Cover the bottom with a layer of pasta. Cover the pasta with a layer of Béchamel. Cover the Béchamel with a layer of meat sauce, followed by a layer of grated cheese mixture. Then, continue the process, layering in the same order and ending with pasta.

Sprinkle some grated cheese mixture on top of pasta and dot top of casserole with butter. Bake in 375° oven for 1 hour or until top turns to a golden crust. Serve directly from oven.

Serves: 8

WINE: *Barolo, 1969*

Cantina d'Italia Ristorante
Washington, D.C.
Proprietor/Chef: Joseph Muran de Assereto

CONIGLIO AL LIMONE (Rabbit in Lemon-Raisin Sauce)

24	pieces rabbit
	cold water, as needed
1	quart lemon juice
1/2	cup olive oil
1	cup sweet butter
1	cup grated lemon rind
5	cloves garlic, minced
1/2	cup freshly chopped parsley
1/2	cup crumbled bay leaves
1	cup dried sage leaves
	salt
2	quarts heavy cream
5	cups Chablis wine
1	tablespoon wine vinegar
1	cup potato flour
3	cups Sultana raisins
	cracked black pepper

Marinate the rabbit pieces in enough cold water to cover, flavored with 3 cups lemon juice, for 24 hours.

Drain and dry each piece of rabbit. In 1 or 2 large frying pans, put olive oil and 1/2 cup of butter. Sprinkle with lemon rind and garlic. Heat the mixture. When it is hot, add parsley and rabbit. Add bay leaves and sage and sprinkle with salt.

Reduce the heat and sauté the rabbit until golden brown on each side. Heat the cream and remaining butter in a large pan, add the browned rabbit pieces and simmer for 15 minutes.

Remove the sage and bay leaves with a slotted spoon. Add the Chablis and vinegar to the drippings in the frying pan and simmer 5 minutes.

Return rabbit to the frying pan with pincers. Add potato flour to cream. Stir briskly until blended. Pour the mixture over the rabbit and sprinkle with raisins and cracked black pepper. Stir well and bake in 300° oven for 30 minutes.

Remove, transfer to heated platter and serve with fried potatoes.

Serves: 6

WINE: *Pinot Bianco, Fontana, Tredda*

Poultry Entrées

La Caravelle
New York, New York
Proprietors: Fred Decre and Robert Meyzen
Chef: Roger Fessaguet

VOLAILLE EN CHAUD-FROID

2 chickens, 2 1/2 - 3 pounds each
chicken broth, as needed (*see index*)
1 quart of aspic
1 quart Sauce Supreme
1 sliced truffle
2 green leaves of leek
1 hard-boiled egg, sliced
1 red pepper (canned pimientos)
parsley, to garnish

Dress chickens and blanch them. Cook them in chicken broth for 25 minutes. Remove and let cool in refrigerator. Remove skin and place chickens on decorating grill.

Add 10 sheets of gelatin to Sauce Supreme. Dip both chickens a couple of times in mixture. Refrigerate chickens a few minutes between each dipping. Then, refrigerate 1 hour.

Remove chickens from refrigerator and decorate them with truffles, leek, hard-boiled egg, and red pepper by dipping each in melted aspic before placing them on the chickens. Refrigerate entire dish for 1/2 hour.

Cut out excess sauce and aspic around each chicken and dress on serving platter which has been previously coated with a thin coat of aspic. Decorate with chopped aspic and branches of parsley. Keep refrigerated until serving.

Serves: 4

King Cole
Dayton, Ohio
Proprietor: Bruce Comisar

COQ AU CHAMBERTIN

1 frying chicken, 1 1/2 pounds
salt and pepper
flour, to dust
butter, to sauté
1 large chopped onion
2 celery stalks, chopped
2 large carrots, chopped
1 small can chicken broth
fifth Chambertin or other red Burgundy wine
oregano, bay leaf, thyme, to taste
8 ounces halved or quartered mushrooms, sautéed
16 cooked pearl onions
4 ounces slab bacon, cut in small cubes and browned in oven

Cut chicken into 4 pieces, season with salt and pepper, dust with flour, and sauté in butter until golden brown. Remove chicken and put aside.

To prepare sauce: add chopped onion, celery, and carrots to the pan juices and sauté for a few minutes. Add chicken broth and wine, season with oregano, bay leaf, thyme, black pepper and salt. Let cook 2–3 hours. Strain sauce through a fine strainer.

Add the sautéed chicken pieces to the sauce and finish cooking until tender. Before serving, add pearl onions, sautéed mushrooms, and bacon.

Serves: 4

Siple's Garden Seat
Clearwater, Florida
Proprietor: Richard B. Siple
Chef: Louis Mantzanas

CHICKEN BREAST GORGONZOLA

butter or oil, to sauté
2 ounces minced onions
2 ounces sliced fresh mushrooms
4 boneless 8-ounce chicken breasts, skinned, flattened, and seasoned with salt and fresh ground pepper
3-4 ounces crumbled bleu or Gorgonzola cheese
3 ounces dry white wine
2 ounces chicken stock (*see index*)
roux

Heat oil in sauté pan and, when hot, sauté onions and mushrooms briefly. Cook the seasoned, flattened chicken breasts on both sides. Add cheese, wine, and stock. Simmer for a few moments. Thicken the sauce with roux only slightly.

Serving suggestion: serve over rice baked in stock with chopped onion, celery, and pimiento.

Serves: 4

Normandy French Restaurant
Denver, Colorado
Proprietor: Heinz E. Gerstle

COQ AU VIN ROUGE

2 frying chickens, 2 1/2 pounds each, cut in pieces
1 teaspoon salt
1/2 teaspoon white pepper
2 chopped shallots
1 clove garlic, chopped
  flour, as needed
1 cup vegetable oil
1 quart chicken broth
2 tablespoons Kitchen Bouquet
1 #3 can tomatoes
  bouquet garni (herb bunch)
2 cups red Burgundy wine
1 can tiny whole onions
1 pound cooked mushrooms
1/2 cup diced fried bacon

Rub the chicken pieces with salt, pepper, shallots, and garlic and dip into flour, coating chicken thoroughly. Preheat oil to smoking point in a heavy skillet. Add chicken and fry until golden brown on all sides. Remove from skillet.

Pour drippings from skillet into a pot; add chicken broth, Kitchen Bouquet, tomatoes, and Bouquet Garni. Bring to a boil. Thicken with flour (or cornstarch) to the consistency of a sauce or gravy.

Add chicken pieces and cook them in this sauce for 20 minutes. Add the wine and continue to cook 15 more minutes. Add onions, mushrooms, and bacon and cook until chicken is done, approximately 10 more minutes. (Total cooking time: about 45 minutes.) Serve hot.

Serves: 6

Wine: *Gevrey Chambertin*

India House
San Francisco, California
Proprietor: Sarwan S. Gill
Chef: Raminder Sekhon

MURGHI MASALA (Chicken Curry)

2/3 cup peanut, vegetable, or corn oil
1 large onion, coarsely grated (about
     1 1/2 cups)
1 4"-piece cinnamon stick
2 whole cardamom seeds or 1/2
     teaspoon ground cardamom
1 tablespoon finely minced garlic
2 cups water
1 cup yogurt
1/3 cup fresh ginger cut in thin strips
     (or 1 tablespoon grated ginger)
1 teaspoon turmeric
2 teaspoons sweet paprika
1 teaspoon ground ginger
1/2 teaspoon ground cumin
1 teaspoon ground coriander
1 3-pound chicken, skinned and cut in
     several pieces
     salt, to taste
1/2 cup heavy cream

Heat oil in a large, heavy kettle and add onion. Cook over medium heat, stirring, about 5 minutes until onion is dry but not brown. Add the cinnamon and cardamom seeds and continue cooking, stirring, until onion is golden brown. Add garlic and 1/4 cup water.

Add yogurt and cook briskly, stirring, about 5 minutes. Add chopped ginger, turmeric, paprika, powdered ginger, cumin, coriander, and 1 cup of water.

Cook, stirring about 5 minutes, then add chicken pieces. Add salt to taste. Cook about 20 minutes, stirring frequently.

Add the remaining water, if necessary, and cook about 10 minutes, stirring often. Add cream and bring to a boil. Cook about 2 minutes.

Serving suggestion: serve hot with an Indian rice.

Serves: 4–6

Yee's Restaurant
Dallas, Texas
Proprietor: Kenny Yee

HUN SU GAI KEW WITH CHICKEN

2 eggs, beaten
1/2 cup all-purpose flour
1/4 cup cornstarch
1/2 teaspoon baking powder
1/4 teaspoon salt
3/4 cup water
2 quarts vegetable oil
3 tablespoons toasted sesame seeds
1 cup uncooked boneless chicken
     breast, diced
2 tablespoons vegetable oil
1 small garlic clove, crushed
2 cups bok choy, cut in 1" diagonal
     slices
1/4 cup canned sliced mushrooms,
     drained
1/2 cup canned water chestnuts, drained
1/4 cup canned bamboo shoots, drained
1 1/2 cups chicken broth
1 cup snow peas, fresh if possible
1 tablespoon cooking sherry
1/2 tablespoon MSG
1 tablespoon cornstarch well mixed
     with 2 tablespoons water

To prepare batter: in a bowl, mix eggs, flour, cornstarch, baking powder, salt, and water. Stir until batter is smooth.

Heat vegetable oil in a large skillet until very hot. Sprinkle sesame seeds on chicken pieces, then dip each chicken piece into the batter, coating completely. Place into hot oil and deep fry for 4 minutes. Drain on paper towel and set aside.

Preheat wok and swirl around 2 tablespoons vegetable oil. Add crushed garlic, bok choy, mushrooms, water chestnuts, and bamboo shoots. Toss gently. Add chicken broth and cover for 2 minutes. Add snow peas, cooking sherry, MSG, and cornstarch-water mixture. Stir thoroughly. Add chicken.

Remove to platter and serve.

Serves: 4

WINE: *White*

Foulard's Restaurant
Houston, Texas
Proprietor: Chef Foulard
Chef: George Finch

POTTED CHICKEN, FOULARD'S

  1 chicken 2 1/2-2 3/4 pounds
     salt and white pepper, to taste
  2 tablespoons very finely chopped
        shallots
     clarified butter, as needed
  1 cup dry white wine
10-12 medium oysters, coarsely chopped
  1 cup macaroni, small cuts, pre-cooked
        in salted chicken stock
1/2 cup whipping cream
  1 dash nutmeg
  2 tablespoons grated Swiss or Gruyère
        cheese
     butter, as needed
  1 tablespoon brandy
1/2 cup brown sauce flavored with 2
        tablespoons blanched celery stalk,
        strained or blended
     flour and water paste
  1 beaten egg

Completely bone the chicken without breaking the skin. Season with salt and white pepper.

To prepare stuffing: sauté shallots in clarified butter. Discard the butter and add wine. Reduce until almost dry, then add oysters and cover for a few seconds. Add macaroni and moisten with whipping cream. Season with salt, white pepper, and a touch of nutmeg. Boil briefly and finish with grated cheese.

Stuff and close the chicken. Wrap around it a band of oiled paper to hold it in shape and place in a buttered pan. Brush the top with fresh butter and bake it at 450° until golden. Lower the temperature to 350° and leave it bake for 25–30 minutes more, depending on size of chicken.

Unwrap chicken and place it in a terrine or cocotte with brandy and flavored brown sauce. Close and seal the lid with an unsweated paste made of flour and water. Brush paste with beaten egg and bake dish again.

When paste is hard, chicken is ready to serve. To open lid, break up paste. Slice chicken in 2 and serve with the sauce.

Serves: 2

WINE: *Montrachet*

L'Auberge Bretonne French Restaurant
Chesterfield, Missouri
Proprietor: Jean Claude Guillossou
Chef: Marcel Keraval

BREAST OF CHICKEN IN MADEIRA SAUCE

3   ounces flour
12 breasts of chicken, boneless and
    skinless
3   ounces oil
6   ounces butter
1   medium onion, chopped
2   tablespoons tomato paste
1   pint beef broth
1   pinch thyme
1   small piece bay leaf
    salt and pepper, to taste
4   ounces sliced cooked mushrooms
5   ounces Madeira wine

Flour the breasts of chicken very lightly. Heat oil and butter in a large, heavy pan. When hot, sauté the chicken breasts on both sides to a nice brown. Then, add and sauté the onion. Add the remaining flour, stir, then add tomato paste, beef broth, thyme, and bay leaf and salt and pepper to taste. Cook for 20 minutes, then remove chicken from pan. Cook the sauce a little longer. Strain. Add sliced cooked mushrooms and Madeira and pour over chicken. Serve.

Serves: 6

The Old Place
Grosse Pointe Park, Michigan
Proprietor: Diamond Phillips

DIAMOND'S SPECIAL CHICKEN

1   double chicken breast
    salt and pepper, to taste
    flour, as needed
2   tablespoons butter
2   ounces crabmeat
1   slice Swiss or mozzarella cheese
4   tablespoons Madeira wine
1   teaspoon chopped parsley

Lightly flatten chicken breast. Season with salt and freshly ground pepper and drench in flour. Sauté breast in skillet with butter. When brown, turn over. Lay crabmeat on top, cover with cheese, and cover skillet. When cooked and cheese has melted, add wine and re-cover. Wine will steam and flavor chicken. Serve on hot dish sprinkled with parsley.

Serves: 1

Wine: *Sweet White*

Camelot
Bloomington, Minnesota
Proprietor/Chef: Hans Skalle

FRICASSEE OF CHICKEN (or Veal)

1   pound chicken (or veal) cut into 1"
    pieces
    water, as needed
3   stalks celery
4-5 white leeks
1   pound peeled carrots
3   tablespoons margarine
4   tablespoons flour
2   cups chicken (or veal) stock (*see*
    recipe below)

To prepare chicken (or veal) and vegetables: cover chicken (or veal) with water. Bring to a boil and simmer until desired doneness (do not overcook). Remove fat. Drain off water (and save to add to stock). Cut celery into 1"-pieces and boil to desired doneness. Cut leeks into 1/2"-pieces; boil to desired doneness. Cut carrots into 1" pieces, round edges for add attractiveness; boil to desired doneness. Drain all vegetables and set aside.

To prepare sauce: melt margarine in large skillet or saucepan. Add flour; stir to remove all lumps. Gradually add 2 cups strained stock while stirring constantly. Simmer until volume is reduced 2/3. Season to taste. Add vegetables and meat to sauce.

Serving suggestion: pour fricasse into a casserole dish and garnish with small boiled potatoes and parsley.

Serves: 4

WINE: *Pinot Chardonnay, Pouilly Fuisse, Chablis*

Chicken (or Veal) Stock

4 quarts water
1/2 pound large carrots
2 pound chicken carcass (or veal knuckle bone)
1 heart of celery and celery trimmings
4-5 leek tops
1 quartered onion

To prepare stock: Place all ingredients into water and bring to a boil. Simmer until stock is reduced 1/3. Skim off fat and strain. If time allows, refrigerate overnight and remove additional fat layer. Stock can be refrigerated until needed.

The Charles Restaurant
Boston, Massachusetts
Proprietor: Nate Grifkin
Chef: Edmund Sportini

CHICKEN À LA STROZZI

1/2 pound butter
6 skinless chicken breasts
1 pound cooked button mushrooms
4 ounces brandy
4 ounces chicken stock (*see index*)
6 slices Danish Fontina cheese

Melt butter in a large frying pan. Add chicken and cook to a golden brown color. Add mushrooms, brandy, and wait until it reduces. Then, add chicken stock and let simmer about 6 minutes.

Remove chicken and cover each breast with a slice of cheese, put under broiler until cheese melts, then serve with sauce.

Serves: 6

WINE: *Pinot Grigio Friuli (white)*

Valentino's Restaurant
Charlotte, North Carolina
Proprietor: William P. Georges
Chef: Peter Amfaldern

CHICKEN CORDON BLEU WITH MILANAISE SAUCE

8	boneless breasts of chicken (5-6 ounces each)
	salt and pepper, to taste
1/4	pound sliced ham
1/4	pound sharp Swiss cheese, sliced
2	cups flour
2	eggs, beaten
	butter or oil, to sauté
2	pounds spaghetti
2	cups sliced fresh mushrooms
1	cup diced onions
1	cup diced ham
2	cups catsup
1	cup tomato purée
1/4	cup butter

Place the 8 chicken breasts skin-side down on board. Season with salt and pepper to taste. Place 1 slice ham and 1 slice cheese in middle of each breast. Fold in half. Dip in flour, then in beaten egg. Sauté over medium heat until golden brown (about 15 minutes). Remove from pan and drain on paper towel.

Cook the spaghetti.

To prepare Milanaise Sauce: sauté mushrooms, onions, and ham. Simmer for 5 minutes. Add catsup, tomato purée, and salt and pepper to taste. Simmer 5 minutes more.

Drain the spaghetti and mix the sauce with it. Place chicken on top of spaghetti-sauce mixture. Pour 1/4 cup melted brown butter over entire dish and serve.

Serves: 8

WINE: *Soave Bolla*

La Zaragozana
San Juan, Puerto Rico

BONELESS CHICKEN SAUTÉ ANDALUZA

2	tablespoons raisins
2	ounces Spanish manzanilla (dry sherry wine)
1	2 1/2-pound chicken
1	peeled garlic clove
1/8	ounce chopped parsley
1	ounce orange juice
2	ounces flour
4	ounces Spanish oil
1/4	pound butter
2	tablespoons sliced almonds
3	ounces small Spanish olives
	salt, to taste

Marinate raisins in manzanilla for at least 2 hours before adding each to recipe when indicated.

Cut the chicken in half, remove bones.

Crush garlic, parsley, and orange juice together in a mortar, then macerate (soak) the chicken in this mixture. Bathe the chicken in flour and then fry in Spanish oil until nice and brown. Remove chicken and pour off oil from pan.

Add butter and Spanish manzanilla in pan and heat until glazed. Add raisins, almonds, olives and chicken. Fry everything on low heat for 15 minutes. Salt to taste.

Serving suggestion: serve with Spanish fried potatoes.

Serves: 2

Dock of the Bay
Berkeley, California
Chef: Leonard Riley

JAMBALAYA

1	tablespoon olive oil
2	tablespoons butter
3	ounces diced onions
1 1/2	ounces diced celery
1 1/2	ounces diced bell pepper
1/2	ounce diced salt pork
3	ounces diced raw shrimp
3	ounces diced chicken breast
1	teaspoon minced garlic
4	ounces chicken stock (*see index*)
12	whole large shrimp, peeled and deveined
3	coarsely chopped tomatoes
2 1/2	cups cooked long grain rice
	bouquet garni (parsley stems, bay leaf, and whole thyme, tied in muslin)
2	teaspoons saffron powder blended with 2 ounces chicken stock
	salt and pepper, to taste

Sauté together the first 8 ingredients until translucent (half cooked). Add remaining ingredients. Bring to a boil, cover, and place in 375° oven for 12 minutes.

Serves: 6

WINE: *Chardonnay*

The Russell
Dublin, Ireland
Chef: Jackie Needham

CHICKEN CHAUD-FROID

2	3 1/2-pound (1.75-kilogram) chickens
2	carrots, sliced
2	onions
2	whole cloves
1/2	tablespoon salt
2	cups heavy cream
1	cup butter
1	cup flour
	salt and freshly ground pepper, to taste
2	tablespoons unflavored gelatin
2	cups chicken consommé
2	tomatoes, sliced
1/2	cup pitted black olives, sliced
1/2	cup chopped leeks (green portion)

Truss chickens and cook for 35 minutes in water to cover with carrots, onions (with a clove inserted in each) and salt. When chickens are cooked, remove from water and allow to cool. Cover chickens with a damp cloth.

Reduce chicken stock by half. Strain stock and add cream. Reduce still further and thicken with a roux of butter and flour. Remove from heat and add salt and pepper to taste. Soften the gelatin in 1/4 cup cold water. Add half of it to the sauce. Chill.

Bring consommé to a boil. Add other half of softened gelatin. Chill until aspic is the consistency of unbeaten egg whites.

Quarter each chicken and remove skin. When cold, cover with sauce and allow to set. Decorate chicken portions with tomato slices, olive slices and leeks. Finally, coat chicken with aspic jelly. Arrange on silver dish and decorate with chopped aspic jelly.

Serves: 4–6

La Rotisserie
New York, New York

COQ AU VINAIGRE (Chicken in White Wine Vinegar)

4	tablespoons butter
2	tablespoons olive oil
1/2	pound fat bacon in 1 piece
10	small white onions
10	small mushrooms
1	2 1/2-pound broiling chicken, cut in 6 pieces
1/2	cup flour
1/2	teaspoon salt
1/8	teaspoon ground white pepper
	salt and white pepper, to taste
2	cloves garlic, finely chopped
2	sprigs thyme
2	bay leaves
2	sprigs parsley
1	cup white wine vinegar
2	tablespoons butter
2	tablespoons flour
2	tablespoons finely chopped parsley

Heat 4 tablespoons butter and olive oil together with the fat bacon cut in small cubes in an ovenproof deep casserole or Dutch oven. Stir. When the bacon begins to turn golden, add the onions. Cook for 2 minutes and then add mushrooms. Sauté this mixture until the onions begin to turn transparent and the mushrooms brown. Remove everything from casserole with a slotted spoon to another dish and keep warm.

Sprinkle the chicken pieces with flour seasoned with salt and pepper. Sauté the chicken in the fat for 5 minutes. Using pincers, turn the chicken pieces over to brown the other side. When they are well browned, add the sautéed vegetables and bacon to the chicken, sprinkle with salt and pepper. Add garlic, thyme, bay leaves, and parsley. Cover the casserole and cook at 375° for 30 minutes.

Remove contents of casserole to another dish and keep warm. Skim off excess fat from the juices in the casserole. Place casserole over high heat and add the white wine vinegar. Reduce to half its original quantity. Thicken by dropping a mixture of 2 tablespoons each of butter and flour mixed together into the juices and stir well until blended. Strain the sauce into a deep ovenproof serving dish. Place the chicken pieces, bacon, and vegetables in the dish. Cover and simmer in 300° oven for 20 minutes, or until ready to serve. Sprinkle with chopped parsley.

Serves: 4

WINE: *Bordeaux*

The Farmer's Daughter
Orland Park, Illinois
Proprietor: Kandy Norton-Henely

CHICKEN GOURMET

1/2	cup margarine
1	clove garlic, minced
1	teaspoon salt
1/4	teaspoon chili powder
1/8	teaspoon pepper
1/8	teaspoon dry mustard
4	chicken breasts, each cut in half
2	tablespoons flour
1/2	cup coffee cream
1/2	cup milk
1	teaspoon fresh parsley, minced
2	tablespoons toasted and slivered almonds

Melt margarine in frying pan. Blend in garlic, salt, chili powder, pepper, and dry mustard. Brown chicken breasts on both sides. Cover pan. Bake in preheated 350° oven for 40 minutes or until tender. Place chicken on heated platter.

Add flour to pan juice and stir until thick. Slowly pour in cream and milk until it thickens. Add salt and pepper to taste.

Spoon sauce over chicken breasts. Sprinkle with parsley and almonds.

Serves: 4

Marrakesh
Newport Beach, California
Proprietor/Chef: Ali Rabbani

CHICKEN WITH LEMON AND OLIVES

- 1 chicken, 3-4 pounds, cut up
- 5 tablespoons olive oil
- 1 sliced onion
- 1 clove garlic, chopped
- 1 teaspoon chopped parsley
- 1 pinch saffron
- 1/2 teaspoon black pepper
- 1 quart water
- 1 teaspoon salt
- 1 can green olives
- 3 lemons, quartered and pickled (by soaking in salted water for 30 minutes)

Brown chicken in a pot with olive oil, onion, garlic, parsley, saffron, and pepper. Add water and salt. Cover and bring to a boil. Cook for 40 minutes. Remove chicken. Reduce the heat; add olives and lemon to the sauce and cook on medium heat for 15 minutes.

Place chicken in a serving dish, pour sauce over, and serve.

Serves: 4

WINE: *Moghrabi Rosé*

Johnson's Del Prado Restaurant
Sacramento, California
Chef: Roger Flores

CHICKEN SAUTÉ SEC

- 1 whole chicken, cut in 10 pieces
- 1/2 cup flour
  butter or oil, to sauté
- 1/2 cup white wine
- 1/2 cup finely diced onions
- 1/2 cup sliced fresh mushrooms
- 1/2 cup finely diced chives
- 1 clove fresh garlic, chopped
- 1/2 cup tomato sauce
  salt and pepper, to taste
- 1/2 teaspoon Worcestershire sauce
- 1/4 cup grated Parmesan cheese

Powder chicken with flour. Sauté in frying pan, browning all around. Drain oil from pan. Pour wine over chicken and add onions, mushrooms, chives, and garlic. Sauté for 2 minutes, then add tomato sauce. Cover pan and simmer 35-45 minutes on low heat. Add salt and pepper to taste. Add Worcestershire sauce, garnish with Parmesan cheese, and serve.

Serves: 4

WINE: *Chablis*

Fran O'Brien's Steak and Seafood
Restaurant
Annapolis, Maryland

CHICKEN AND CRAB

1   6-ounce boneless breast of chicken
1   tablespoon white wine
4   tablespoons mayonnaise
1   tablespoon Dijon mustard
1   dash white pepper
1   teaspoon lemon juice
    chopped pimiento
3   ounces backfin crabmeat
    sliced pimiento

Boil chicken breast (about 5 minutes), remove skin, and place on cooking dish. Sprinkle white wine on top of chicken. Combine mayonnaise, mustard, white pepper, and lemon juice to make Imperial sauce. Fold 3/4 of the sauce into crabmeat and add chopped pimiento. Place crabmeat mixture on top of breast and spread crabmeat to cover breast. Spread remaining Imperial sauce on top of crabmeat and garnish with sliced pimiento. Bake in preheated 450° oven for 20–25 minutes until light brown.

Serves: 1

WINE: *White or dry Chablis*

Casa Mauricio
San Antonio, Texas
Proprietor: Maurice Huey
Chef: Armando Chavez

ENCHILADAS BLANCA

1   large chicken
2   cups water
1   large onion, chopped
1/2   teaspoon comino
2   teaspoons salt
1   teaspoon garlic
1/2   teaspoon black pepper
1   teaspoon shortening
1   dozen soft corn tortillas
      oil, as needed
2   pounds Monterey Jack cheese,
      grated

To prepare chicken filling: add chicken, onion, seasonings, and shortening to water and simmer 1 1/2 hours. Remove cooked chicken from bones and chop into small pieces. Return to broth and keep hot.

Heat corn tortillas, one at a time, in hot oil. Fill with chicken filling and roll. Top with generous amount of cheese and put under broiler until melted.

Serves: 6

Casa Mauricio
San Antonio, Texas
Proprietor: Maurice Huey
Chef: Armando Chavez

ENCHILADAS VERDE

1 large chicken

1 large onion, chopped

2 cups water

1/2 teaspoon comino

2 teaspoons salt

1/2 teaspoon black pepper

1 teaspoon garlic

1 teaspoon shortening

1 dozen soft corn tortillas
  oil, as needed
  Verde Sauce (*see recipe below*)

1 pint sour cream

To prepare chicken filling: stew chicken and onion in water with seasonings and shortening for 1 1/2 hours. Remove bones and chop chicken into small pieces. Return to broth and keep hot.

Heat corn tortillas, one at a time, in hot oil. Fill with chicken filling and roll. Top with a generous serving of hot Verde sauce and a large dollop of sour cream.

Serves: 6

Verde Sauce

4 pounds Fresadia tomatoes (special
  Mexican tomatoes)

3 pounds green tomatoes

1 cup chopped onion

3 stalks celery

2 bell peppers

2 hot peppers

1 teaspoon comino

1 teaspoon garlic

2 teaspoons salt

1/4 teaspoon black pepper

1 drop green food coloring

To prepare sauce: chop all vegetables finely. Put into a large pot with seasonings and simmer for 1 1/2 hours. Add food coloring and stir well. Serve hot.

Chez Jean Restaurant Francais
Indianapolis, Indiana
Proprietor/Chef: Jean Marc Milesi

LE COQ AU VIN JEUNE FLANGUE DE MORILLES (Chicken in Yellow Wine with Morels)

1 chicken, 3 1/4 pounds
  salt, freshly ground pepper, and
    flour, as needed

8 ounces sweet butter

2 cups dry yellow wine

6 ounces fresh morels (mushrooms)

2 cups heavy cream

Quarter chicken, season with salt and pepper, dredge lightly in flour, set aside.

Heat butter in heavy casserole, add chicken to casserole, sauté very lightly for 10 minutes.

Remove casserole from stove, cover, and put in 300° preheated oven for 30 minutes. Remove from oven, uncover, and put on medium heat on stove. Add wine, heat 1–2 minutes, reduce heat to low. Add morels and cream and cook 10–15 minutes.

Serving suggestion: serve with rice.

Serves: 4

Chateau Madrid
New York, New York
Proprietors: Joseph Portela, Serafin Portela,
and Joseph Pineiro

PAELLA VALENCIANA CHATEAU MADRID

1	2 1/2-pound chicken cut into 12 pieces
1	cup diced pork
2	ounces Spanish sherry wine
1	green pepper, chopped finely
1/2	large Spanish onion, chopped finely
3	cloves of garlic, chopped finely
2	ounces olive oil
1	pound uncooked shelled shrimp
1	pound scallops
	mussels (3 per person)
	clams (1 per person)
	lobster (optional)
1	chorizo (Spanish sausage) cut into thin slices
12	ounces uncooked rice
	pinch of saffron
	pinch of cumin powder
	pinch of white pepper
2	teaspoons salt
1	bay leaf
30	ounces chicken broth
1	teaspoon monosodium glutamate
	cooked green peas
	Spanish pimiento

Brown the chicken and pork in a separate pan, adding some sherry. Sauté the pepper, onion, and garlic in olive oil over low heat until brown.

Place the mixture in a casserole. Add the sautéed chicken and pork. Add the seafood and sausage. Mix in the rice and saffron. Mix all together over heat for a short time. Pour a little sherry wine over the mixture. Add the other seasonings.

Pour the chicken broth over the entire mixture and boil on top of the stove for 5 minutes. Reduce heat and simmer for 15 minutes, covered (or, in 300° oven). Garnish with cooked green peas and Spanish pimiento. Sprinkle with sherry just before serving.

Serves: 4–6

The Jamaica Hilton
Ocho Rios, Jamaica

BREAST OF CHICKEN "CONQUISTADOR"

4	ounces skinless, boneless chicken breast
	salt and pepper, to taste
2	tablespoons brandy
1	ounce truffled goose liver pâté
1	slice green bacon (tossino) (salted pork fat back)
1	ounce sweet butter
1	teaspoon chopped shallots
2	ounces spinach leaves
1	ounce very thin sliced smoked ham
3	ounces puff pastry (*see index*)
1	egg, beaten

Place the chicken breast between waxed paper and pound thin. Sprinkle with salt and pepper and brandy; marinate for 4 hours. Wrap the goose liver pâté with the slices of green bacon. Melt butter, sauté shallots, and add spinach leaves. Season with salt and pepper, cool well before using.

Roll goose liver pâté and chicken breast together. Cover the chicken breast, next, with the spinach leaves. Wrap all in the thinly sliced ham. Roll the puff pastry dough thinly and wrap around the chicken breast in a nice round shape. Brush with egg glaze and bake at 350° for 20 minutes.

Serving suggestion: peel the skin of a

medium-sized tomato. Cut the top half off and scoop out the seeds. Heat slowly in oven and stuff with sautéed baby corn and okra.

Serves: 1

Champeaux's
The Ilikai Hotel
Honolulu, Hawaii
Chef: Vlastimil Lebeda

CHICKEN BREAST HANA

6   chickens (2 1/3–3 pounds each)
    salt
4   tablespoons flour
1   cup pineapple, fresh or canned
2   eggs
1/4   cup whipping cream
    sage
    pepper
8   tablespoons bread crumbs
6   tablespoons butter
    sauce (*see recipe below*)

Remove skin from chicken and separate breast from the legs. Bone out the breasts, leaving only the drumstick bone. Flatten breasts to 1/4″ with a meat hammer and sprinkle with salt and flour.

To prepare stuffing: bone out drumsticks and thighs and grind the meat in a meat grinder. Dice pineapple in small pieces and mix together with meat, eggs, cream, sage, salt, pepper, and bread crumbs.

Stuff chicken breasts with stuffing, roll in flour, and fit chickens tightly together in a preheated casserole with butter. Bake at 325° for approximately 30 minutes. Pour sauce over chicken and bake for approximately 5 minutes more. Serve.

Sauce

1   medium onion, chopped
1   apple, diced
1   banana, sliced
10   tablespoons butter
2   tablespoons curry powder
3   cups chicken stock or water
    roux (melted butter and flour)
15   mushrooms, sliced
1/2   cup whipping cream
4   tablespoons mango chutney
    salt and pepper

To prepare sauce: sauté chopped onions, diced apple, sliced banana, and 1/2 amount of butter for approximately 5 minutes. Dust with curry powder, mix well, and add chicken stock. Bring to a boil. Thicken sauce with roux and cook for about 20 minutes. Strain through a fine sieve. Add sliced mushrooms, sautéed in remaining butter. Finish sauce with cream, finely chopped mango chutney, and salt and pepper.

Serves: 12

WINE: *Beaujolais Blanc, Louis Jadot*

The Elms Inn
Ridgefield, Connecticut
Proprietor: Robert Scala

CHICKEN SCALA

1   2 1/2-pound broiler chicken or 4
    boneless chicken breasts
1   ounce clarified butter
    salt, pepper, and flour, as needed
2/3   cup chicken stock (*see index*)
1/2   cup sour cream
2   tablespoons grated Parmesan cheese
4   slices truffles (optional)

Either bone the chicken or purchase boneless chicken breasts.

Clarify butter as follows: melt in top of a double boiler. Pour off butter, leaving impurities in bottom of pan.

In a 12″-sauté pan, place the clarified butter and put on stove at a moderately high heat. Season and dredge in flour each piece of chicken. Place gently into the hot sauté pan. Sauté the chicken in hot butter for 2–3 minutes, or until the first side down is light golden brown. Turn the pieces over and reduce to a moderate heat.

Add the chicken stock to the chicken. Add sour cream and blend with the stock and chicken breasts. Reduce heat to a low simmer and continue cooking for 15 minutes, stirring occasionally. (As the chicken cooks, the stock and sour cream will reduce to produce a sauce used in the presentation of the dish.)

Remove the chicken from the pan to an ovenproof serving dish. Spoon the sour cream sauce over each piece, then sprinkle generously with the Parmesan cheese. Brown lightly and top with truffle slice.

Serves: 2–4

Rene Verdon Le Trianon
San Francisco, California
Proprietors: Rene and Yvette Verdon

SUPREME DE VOLAILLE "TRIANON"

4   chicken breasts, boned and halved
    salt and white pepper, to taste
1   tablespoon Dijon mustard
2   ounces Roquefort cheese
2 1/2   ounces imported fresh grated Swiss
    cheese
1/2   ounce unsalted butter
1/2   pound butter, clarified
1   egg, slightly beaten
1   tablespoon salad oil
1   cup flour
    soft bread crumbs

To prepare each breast half, carefully remove all skin. Using a smooth-surfaced meat hammer or rolling pin, flatten each breast and "fillet", cut side up, to about 1/4″ thick. Be careful not to tear meat. Lightly salt, pepper, and spread a thin layer of mustard on chicken.

To prepare cheese filling: place Roquefort cheese, grated Swiss cheese and 1/2 ounce butter in a food processor or blender and blend together just enough to form into a roll. Divide into 8 rolls.

Place cheese filling roll lengthwise on each breast half. Roll and fold each breast so that the cheese is completely enclosed. Wrap in waxed paper or aluminum foil and chill in the refrigerator.

Clarify butter by melting in top of double boiler. Pour off butter, leaving impurities in the bottom of the pan.

Mix egg and oil. Spread flour in shallow pan. Remove chicken breasts from refrigerator. Roll each breast in the flour to coat evenly. Dip each breast into the egg-oil mixture. Roll chicken generously in bread crumbs rendered fine in blender. Chicken breast must be well-sealed to retain cheese.

Using about 1/4 cup clarified butter in heavy frying pan, cook 1 or 2 chicken rolls at a time, turning until evenly golden brown. Place browned chicken on oven pan. Repeat with remaining chicken. Oven should be preheated to 325°. Bake for 10–15 minutes or until chicken is tender. Serve with a light Madeira Sauce (*see index*).

Serves: 4

WINE: *Nuits St. Georges
(red Burgundy from France)*

---

*Hungaria Restaurant
New York, New York
Proprietor: George Lang
Chef: Bank Szerenyi*

CHICKEN STRUDEL

2	tablespoons vegetable oil
1/2	pound Spanish onion, chopped
1	medium-sized clove garlic, chopped finely
1	tablespoon salt
2	tablespoons sweet Hungarian paprika
1/2	teaspoon ground white pepper
1	medium-sized tomato, diced
1	green bell pepper, diced
1/2	cup warm water
3	2-pound chicken fryers, quartered
2	cups sour cream
1 1/4	pounds puff pastry (frozen and thawed or *see index*)
1	egg

Heat the oil in a 2-quart Dutch oven. Sauté the onion gently until translucent, 5–8 minutes. Stir in the garlic, salt, paprika, pepper, tomato, green pepper, and 1/2 cup water. Add the chicken pieces. Stir carefully to coat each piece with some of the vegetable mixture. Cover the pot and simmer 25–30 minutes until the chicken is tender.

Take pan from heat; remove chicken and reserve. Slowly stir the sour cream into the sauce. Return pan to low heat; cook gently 5 minutes. Strain the sauce through a sieve; reserve.

Keeping the white and dark meat separate, remove the skin and bone the chicken pieces. Cut each breast lengthwise in half; reserve. Cut the dark meat into 1/4"-pieces. In a small bowl, mix the dark meat diced chicken with half the sauce; reserve.

Roll out the puff pastry to 1/8"-thick and cut into 6 even squares. Proceed as follows, filling and forming each strudel individually: on one side of a dough square, place 1 heaping tablespoon of the chicken/sauce mixture. Spread it out to form a 1 1/2"-strip, 3/4" from the sides and one edge of the square. In the center of the square, place one piece of the white chicken meat. Fold the sides of the square toward the center. Then carefully roll the dough and the chicken mixture around the chicken breast into the strudel shape.

When all strudels are formed and placed on a lightly greased baking sheet, beat the egg and brush it across the tops of the strudels. Refrigerate for 20 minutes, while preheating the oven to 400°.

When ready to bake, puncture the tops of the rolls with a fork several times. Reset the oven to 350°. Cover the strudels with aluminum foil, place in the oven, and bake for 15 minutes. Remove the foil and continue baking 15 minutes more.

When done, serve with the reserved warm sauce. Do not pour the sauce over the strudel, but serve it on the side.

Serves: 6

WINE: *Gewürztraminer*

René Chez Vous
Torrance, California
Proprietor/Chef: René Bouter

SUPREME DE POULET

24 ounces boneless, skinless chicken
    breast
2 heavy tablespoons butter
    flour, as needed
3 pinches salt
2 pinches ground white pepper
1 tablespoon fresh lemon juice (or
    more to taste)
1/2 cup cream
    chopped parsley

Pound chicken breast to 1/4"-thick. Melt butter over medium heat; do not brown. Lightly flour chicken and sauté on both sides until lightly golden. Sprinkle with salt and pepper and pour lemon juice over it. Let chicken cook one more minute. Pull pan away from heat, cover chicken with cream, and swivel vigorously until lemon mixes with cream. Sprinkle with chopped parsley and serve immediately.

Serving suggestion: serve with rice pilaf.

Serves: 4

WINE: *Red Beaujolais or White Chablis*

Flamingo Motel & Restaurant
Portland, Oregon
Proprietor: Joel Soderlund
Chef: John Brough

CHICKEN BREAST MARIE ANTOINETTE

6 7-ounce boneless and skinless
    chicken breasts, flattened
6 slices sugar-cured ham
6 slices Monterey Jack cheese
6 pats butter
    beaten egg, as needed
    oil, as needed
1 pinch thyme
1 teaspoon dry mustard
    salt and cayenne pepper, to taste
    sauterne wine, to taste
1/4 cup chopped celery, sautéed
1/4 cup chopped mushrooms, sautéed
1/4 cup chopped onions, sautéed
2 cups prepared white sauce

Lay out chicken breasts on a flat surface. Place 1 slice ham on each; place 1 slice cheese on the ham; place 1 pat butter on cheese. Fold up sides and secure with toothpick inserted through breast. Dip chicken rolls in egg and submerge in 350° oil until brown and crisp. Place all fried chicken rolls on a baking sheet and bake in 350° oven for 15–30 minutes until done.

To prepare sauce: add thyme, dry mustard, salt, pepper, wine, celery, mushrooms, and onion to white sauce. Mix well in a saucepan and heat. Serve over chicken rolls.

Serving suggestion: serve with pilaf or whole red potatoes.

Serves: 4–6

Le Coup de Fusil
New York, New York
Proprietor: Marina de Brantes
Chef: Etienne Lizzi

GATEAU AUX FOIES DE VOLAILLE HOMARDINE (Chicken Mousse with Lobster Sauce)

    5   chicken livers
    1   ounce back fat
  1/2   clove garlic
  1/2   shallot
    2   tablespoons olive oil
    1   pinch *each* salt and pepper
    2   tablespoons port wine
    1   egg yolk
  1/2   cup heavy cream
    1   chopped truffle
        Lobster Sauce (*see recipe below*)
    1   cooked julienne carrot
    1   julienne truffle

To prepare chicken mousse: saute chicken livers, back fat, garlic, and shallot in olive oil for 2 minutes. Transfer to food processor and add salt, pepper, and port. Blend 2–3 minutes. Transfer mixture to a bowl and mix into it the egg yolk, cream, and chopped truffle. Pour mixture into a buttered ramekin and place in a pan with boiling water. (Water should come to half of ramekin.) Put in 400° oven and bake for 20 minutes. When ready, unmold the gateau on a plate, pour lobster sauce over it, and decorate with julienne of carrot and truffle.

                                    Serves: 1

WINE: *Champagne*

Lobster Sauce

    1   2 1/2-pound uncooked lobster, cut
        in chunks
        olive oil, to sauté
  1/2   glass brandy
    2   shallots
    1   garlic
    1   glass dry white wine
    2   tablespoons tomato purée
    2   stalks celery
    1   pinch *each* salt, pepper, and cayenne
        pepper
    2   cups heavy cream

To prepare sauce: sauté the lobster chunks for a few minutes in olive oil, then flambé with brandy. Add shallots, garlic, white wine, tomato purée, celery, salt, pepper, cayenne, and heavy cream. Let simmer for 10 minutes. Remove lobster meat and set aside. Strain balance of mixture to yield a fine sauce. Use lobster chunks as garnish.

                                    Serves: 4

Hotel Quirinale
Rome, Italy

AIGUILLETTES DE CANARD MONTMORENCY

1 duck
  salt and pepper
2 ounces brown sugar
1/2 pint stock (*see index*)
1/2 glass white wine
1 tablespoon arrowroot (or cornstarch)
1 4-ounce can red cherries in juice
1 8-ounce can black cherries in juice
1/2 gill kirsch

Rub duck with salt and pepper. Place in a shallow roasting pan and roast uncovered in a moderate oven for about 2 hours.

To prepare sauce: lightly caramelize brown sugar in saucepan and add stock. Bring to a boil and reduce slightly. Add white wine, juices from cooked duck, and juices from the cherries. Season to taste. Bring to a boil, dilute arrowroot with some water and add to the sauce. Bring to a boil to thicken sauce. Add cherries and kirsch and simmer for 1 minute.

Remove sauce from heat and place in sauce boat. Serve with duck.

Serves: 4

Rheinlander Haus
La Jolla, California
Chef: Erich Roesch

ROAST DUCK

1 duck, 4-6 pounds
  salt and pepper, as needed
2 tablespoons melted butter
1 cup dark beer
1 large onion, chopped and sautéed
2 tablespoons flour
  water, as needed

Wash duck and dry. Rub with salt and pepper, inside and out, and place in roaster, breast up. Brush with melted butter. Roast at 350° for 1 1/2 hours. Baste with dark beer every 15 minutes. Remove duck.

Add browned onions, flour, and water to make a gravy from drippings in pan.

Serving suggestion: serve with baked apples and red cabbage.

Serves: 4

WINE: *Light Burgundy*

Mack's Golden Pheasant
Elmhurst, Illinois
Proprietor: Donald Mack

BOHEMIAN DUCK AND SAUERKRAUT

1 duck, 5 1/2-6 pounds, cleaned and viscerated, with wings and excess fat flaps removed and saved
1 whole garlic clove
  salt, to taste
  caraway seeds, to taste
  sauerkraut (*see recipe below*)

To prepare duck: rub garlic in duck's cavity. Put duck breast side down on fat flaps in roasting pan. Roast for 1 1/2 hours at 325°. Pour off fat and turn duck over (breast up) in pan. Sprinkle on salt and caraway seeds, then roast for an additional 1–1 1/2 hours until done. Quarter and serve with sauerkraut.

Serves: 4

WINE: *Rhine wine*

Sauerkraut

1 pound kraut
1 dash salt
1 teaspoon caraway seeds
1 cup sugar
1 cup cider vinegar
1 grated potato
2 tablespoons chopped onion
water, as needed

To prepare sauerkraut: put all ingredients in a pot. Cover with water and simmer for 2 hours. Serve.

Karl Ratzsch's
Milwaukee, Wisconsin
Proprietor: Karl Ratzsch

ROAST DUCKLING

Celery Stuffing

1 cup chopped celery
1 cup chopped onions
  butter, to sauté
8 cups toasted bread
  water, as needed
2 teaspoons salt
1/2 teaspoon pepper
1 teaspoon MSG
2 teaspoons poultry seasoning
1/4 cup currants
1/4 cup apples (optional)
1 cup cooked duck giblets, ground
1 egg
2 tablespoons chopped parsley

To prepare celery stuffing: sauté celery and onions in butter until tender. Turn into a mixing bowl. Slightly moisten bread with a little water. Add all remaining ingredients and mix well.

Duckling

1 5 1/2-pound duck, cleaned
  salt and freshly ground pepper
  celery stuffing (prepared, *see recipe above*)
  shortening, as needed
2 cups chicken stock (*see index*)

To prepare duckling: season the cavity of the duck with salt and pepper. Stuff duck loosely with celery stuffing. Sew the openings, truss, prick the vent, lower thighs and lower breast with a fork.

Preheat oven to 450°. Melt enough shortening to cover about 1/2″ depth in a shallow roasting pan. When shortening is hot, place the duck, breast side up, in pan. When brown, turn over. When second side has browned, turn over once more. Add 1/2 cup stock and reduce heat to 350° and continue roasting for about 2 1/2–3 hours.

Test for doneness by lifting legs: if the juices that drain from the vent run clear yellow, duck is fully cooked.

Transfer duck to a hot serving platter and keep warm. Pour off all fat in pan and deglaze pan over high heat by scraping bottom and sides with a wooden spoon. Add the remaining stock and reduce to 1 cup over high heat. Correct the seasoning and thicken with a roux made of equal parts flour and duck grease, if desired.

Serves: 4

WINE: *Burgundy*

DUCK À L'APRICOT

    3   ducks
        salt, rosemary, pepper, as needed
    1   cup chopped onions
    1   cup chopped carrots
    1   cup chopped celery
    1   cup tomato purée
    1   pint red wine
    1   gallon chicken stock (*see index*)
  2-3   bay leaves
    1   tablespoon whole rosemary
    1   teaspoon whole black pepper
    2   cups sugar
    1   cup apricot glaze or marmalade
    2   cups canned apricots with syrup (16-
        ounce can)
    1   pint red wine
        arrowroot flour or cornstarch, as
        needed
    1   dash each red wine vinegar, salt,
        white pepper
    1   dash kitchen bouquet (optional)
        glaze (*see recipe below*)
        sherry wine, as needed
        apricot brandy, as needed

To prepare ducks: defrost slowly in refrigerator. Take giblets and livers out. Save giblets and necks. Cut lower part of wings off. Tie wings and legs to body with string. Add salt and rosemary to inside cavity of the ducks. Salt and pepper outside and roast in oven at 475° for 1 hour. (Start the ducks on their backs for 20 minutes, then turn one side for another 20 minutes, drain grease and turn onto the other side for 20 minutes.) Baste occasionally. When ducks are done (nice and brown on all sides) drain all the grease and water from the inside, cut in half, and cool *over night.*

To prepare sauce: roast giblets, necks and lower part of wings in a roasting pan over moderate heat until golden brown. Add chopped onions, carrots, and celery. Roast another 20–30 minutes. Add tomato purée and 1 pint red wine. Cook until almost dry. Then, add about 1 gallon of chicken stock and cook slowly for 2 hours. Add bay leaves, whole rosemary, and black pepper.

After boiling for 2 hours, strain stock. Discard bones and vegetables. Skim off grease.

In a sauce pan, start 2 cups sugar over moderate heat and caramelize. Do not burn. When sugar is caramelized, add 1 cup apricot glaze, canned apricots with syrup, and 1 pint red wine. Cook and reduce 2/3. Then add duck stock, boil for 1/2 hour slowly over moderate heat. Use 3 tablespoons and mix arrowroot flour (or cornstarch) with some red wine and add to sauce. Cook another hour, slowly, stirring occasionally. Season with a dash of vinegar, salt, and white pepper to taste. (Optional: add a dash of kitchen bouquet for color and body.)

Glaze

    1   cup apricot glaze or marmalade
    1   cup honey
    2   cups dry sherry wine
    1   dash ground cinnamon
    1   dash ground cloves
    1   dash ground rosemary
        juice of one lemon

To prepare glaze: in a saucepan, mix together all above ingredients except use only 1 cup sherry wine. Cook slowly approximately 1/2 hour, stirring occasionally. When ready, add one more cup sherry and bring to a boil. Let cool.

On day of serving: reheat ducks, sauce, and glaze. Put ducks on a baking pan with insides down. Add a little sherry. Spread duck glaze generously onto ducks and reheat in oven at 400° for about 10 minutes. Remove from heat. Top each duck half with 2/3 glaze and sprinkle some apricot brandy over them. Serve immediately with sauce on the side.

Serving suggestions: serve with wild rice and French string beans with sliced almonds.

(Leftover ducks and sauces freeze well.)

Serves: 6

WINE: *Chardonnay Reserve Robert Mondavi*

Chef Gregoire
Sherman Oaks, California
Chef: Gregoire Le Balch

CANARD ROTI SAUCE BIGARADE

1   **6-pound duck (ask butcher to remove wishbone)**
    salt
2   **small carrots, chopped finely**
1   **onion, chopped finely**
2   **stalks celery, chopped finely**
    Sauce Bigarade (*see recipe below*)
    orange slices, 16 sections as garnish

Cut off wings and season inside cavity of duck with salt. Shape and tie. Rub outside with salt. Chop the neck and wings and giblets and put them on the bottom of the roasting pan to give the base for the sauce. If you have a rack, put the duck on the rack so it does not stick. If not, place it on top of the bones, etc., on its side in a 450° oven. When it is brown on one side, turn it on the other side. When it is brown on both sides, turn it on its back and lower the temperature to 400°. Total roasting time will be at least 1 1/2 hours or until drumstick is loose in socket.

One-half hour before duck is done, add mirepoix (chopped carrots, onion, and celery). Remove duck to platter after roasting. Keep duck warm while preparing sauce:

Sauce Bigarade

3   **tablespoons sugar**
    water
2   **tablespoons vinegar**
1/2   **lemon**
    juice of 1 orange
2-3   **tablespoons currant jelly**
14-16   **ounces brown sauce (*see index*)**
    red food coloring
3   **tablespoons Grand Marnier**

Pour off the grease in the pan and discard with the bones and giblets. Spray sugar in the pan and add a drop of water (about 1/2 ounce) to make a caramel out of it. When sugar is caramelized, deglaze the pan with vinegar. Squeeze lemon juice and orange juice in the pan. Scrape the pan to blend the flavors. Add currant jelly.

Add brown sauce and cook slowly. When it is almost ready, add a little red food coloring to the sauce. Taste it. If it is not sweet enough, do not add sugar—add currant jelly. Then you may need a little more lemon juice. Strain the sauce. Finish with a little Grand Marnier.

Decorate duck with sections of orange (about 4 sections per person). Coat the sections slightly with Sauce Bigarade. Serve remaining sauce separately.

Serves: 4

Emmett's-Celtic Room
Evanston, Illinois

FAISAN EN ARGILE SOUWAROFF

Stuffing

1/2	cup chicken liver
3	tablespoons cognac
8	ounces pork loin
8	ounces veal
1/4	cup chopped shallots
1	tablespoon butter
6	ounces goose liver
3	ounces diced truffles

To prepare stuffing: marinate chicken liver in cognac for several hours. Using finest blade of meat grinder, grind together chicken livers, pork loin, and veal. Sauté chopped shallots in butter until tender. Add to ground meat mixture and mix well. Cut goose liver and truffles into 1/4"-cubes and add to stuffing. Keep covered in refrigerator until needed.

Pheasant

1	pheasant
	salt and black pepper, to taste
	stuffing, prepared (*see above*)
1	pinch thyme
1/4	cup oil
1/4	cup butter
2	tablespoons cognac
1/4	cup red Burgundy wine
4	tablespoons dry Madeira wine
2	truffles cubed with juice
1	bay leaf
1	small onion
1	medium sliced carrot
	dough (*see below*)

To prepare pheasant: season inside of pheasant with salt, pepper, and herbs. Stuff the cavity with the prepared stuffing. Secure the legs and wings to the body with a string and sew the opening with a trussing needle.

Preheat oven to 375°. Place pheasant in a roasting pan, breast up. Add oil and butter and brown the bird slowly on all sides in the oven. After 15 minutes, remove pheasant from roasting pan and put it in a clay roasting casserole. Add cognac, Burgundy, Madeira, truffle cubes, truffle juice, bay leaf, onion, and sliced carrot. Replace the lid and set aside. Prepare the dough.

Dough

4	cups flour
1	cup water

To prepare dough: place flour in mixing bowl. Add water and mix together. Press dough firmly into a roughly shaped ball. Cover and keep at room temperature. Roll dough between hands into a 1" rope.

To assemble the dish: seal the lid to the casserole by molding the dough rope around the edges. Place sealed casserole in oven and bake at 300° for approximately 1 1/4 hours.

Present casserole at table directly from oven. Open the lid by inserting a knife around the edges. Remove bird to a serving platter and carve it. Serve each guest pheasant, stuffing, and sauce from the casserole.

Serves: 4

Arthur's
Dallas, Texas
Chef: Gerard Vullien

ROAST PHEASANT WITH APPLEJACK AND CREAM SAUCE

4	tablespoons butter
1/4	cup finely chopped onion
2	pheasant livers, coarsely chopped
1 1/2	cups day-old bread, cut in 1/2" cubes
1/2	cup peeled, cored, and diced apple (1/2" cubes)
1	tablespoon parsley
	salt and freshly ground black pepper, to taste
2	tablespoons soft butter
2	drawn pheasants (about 1 pound each)
4	strips bacon, cut in half
1/2	cup applejack
1/2	cup chicken stock (*see index*)
1/4	cup heavy cream

To prepare stuffing: melt 2 tablespoons of butter over moderate heat in an 8"-skillet. When the foam subsides, add chopped onion and pheasant livers. Stirring frequently, cook mixture 2–3 minutes until livers have stiffened slightly. Scrape mixture into a bowl. Add 2 tablespoons butter to sauce skillet and, over high heat, brown the diced bread for 3–4 minutes. Add to the livers in the mixing bowl. Mix in the apples and parsley. Add salt and pepper to taste.

To prepare pheasant: preheat oven to 375°. Rub soft butter (2 tablespoons) into skins of each pheasant and fill cavities with stuffing. Secure opening with skewers or sew with strong white thread. Truss birds by tying legs together with cord. Drape bacon strips over legs and breasts and place them, breast-side up, on a rack in a shallow baking pan just large enough to hold birds comfortably.

Roast undisturbed in center of oven for about 30 minutes. Remove pan from oven and sprinkle birds lightly with salt and pepper.

Heat 1/4 cup applejack in a saucepan. Light with a match and pour it, flaming, over the birds, shaking pan gently until flames die. Baste thoroughly with the accumulated roasting pan juices and return to oven.

Roast for 10–12 minutes, or until the birds are brown, crisp, and tender. Remove to heated platter to make sauce.

To prepare sauce: pour chicken stock and remaining applejack into roasting pan and bring to boil on top of stove, scraping into it any brown bits clinging to bottom and sides of pan. Boil briskly for 2–3 minutes, then stir in the cream. Bring to a boil once more and season to taste.

Pour sauce over pheasants or serve separately in a gravy boat.

Serves: 4

WINE: *Husch Vineyards Chardonnay*

L'Auberge Bretonne
Patterson, New York
Proprietor: Corentin Conan

ROAST PHEASANT

1   2-pound pheasant aged 4 days in refrigerator
    bacon, as needed
    salt and pepper, as needed
    salad oil, as needed
3/4   cup water
3/4   cup chicken stock (*see index*)
    Cointreau
    prunes, as garnish

Preheat oven to 450°.

Cover breast of pheasant with slices of bacon and tie them in place with string. Tie wings and legs close to the body. Sprinkle bird with salt and pepper and rub outside skin with salad oil. Place bird on roasting rack for 15 minutes, basting once. Turn bird on the other side, baste, and roast another 15 minutes. Then, with bird on back, baste again and roast 15 minutes longer or until done. Pour off fat from pan and add water and stock. Simmer until volume is reduced to 1/2 cup. Season with salt, pepper and a touch of Cointreau. Flambé with Cointreau and serve with prunes.

Serves: 2

WINE: *Graves,*
wines of the Côte-de-Beaune

The Palace Arms Inn
The Brown Palace Hotel
Denver, Colorado
Chef: Ira Dole

BREAST OF CAPON, CENTENNIAL, WITH WHISKEY SAUCE

3   capons, 2 3/4 pounds each
    MSG, salt and pepper, to taste
6   thin slices Virginia ham
6   slices bacon
    flour, as needed
2   eggs, beaten
    bread crumbs, as needed
    oil, for frying
    Whiskey Sauce (*see recipe below*)

Use breasts only and remove all bones from breasts. Lay breasts on table with skin down. Season with MSG, salt, and pepper. Place a slice of ham on each breast, then roll breast into a cone shape. Wrap 1 strip bacon around the center of the capon cone, then dip in flour, egg batter, and roll in fresh bread crumbs. Fry in a deep fryer until golden brown. Place on a sheet pan and cook in a slow oven until tender. Serve topped with Whiskey sauce.

Serves: 6

WINE: *Chablis Premier Cru,*
Pinot Chardonnay

Whiskey Sauce

1/2 small onion
1/2 small carrot
1/4 stalk celery
1/2 bay leaf
1/4 teaspoon rosemary leaves
1/4 teaspoon sweet basil leaves
1/4 teaspoon whole black pepper
4 ounces vegetable shortening
4 ounces flour
1 quart chicken stock (*see index*)
1 ounce coffee cream
1 ounce bourbon whiskey
  salt and MSG, to taste

To prepare sauce: braise vegetables and spices in shortening at 300° for 10 minutes. Add flour and mix well. Braise for 3 more minutes, then add chicken stock and simmer for 1 hour. Strain through a fine cheesecloth. Add coffee cream, and whiskey, then salt and MSG to taste. Bring back to boiling point and serve.

Yields: 1 quart

Season with salt and pepper. Roast for 45 minutes or until nicely browned. Drain all grease from pan and set aside.

Turn drumettes over, add apples, onions and bouillon liquid to drumettes. Cover and put back in oven. Roast at 350° for 1 1/2 hours. Remove cover, continue to roast until golden brown and crisp. Strain juice from roast pan into sauce pan.

Place flour in frying pan and brown. Add the goose grease, mix well to a smooth paste. Bring the mixture in the sauce pan to a simmer. Add flour mixture slowly, stirring constantly until desired consistency is obtained. Add red wine and simmer 2 minutes. Pour into sauce boat and serve with the drumettes.

Serving suggestions: serve with red cabbage and potato dumplings.

Serves: 4

WINE: *Zinfandel*

Karl Ratzsch's
Milwaukee, Wisconsin
Proprietor: Karl Ratzsch

ROAST GOOSE DRUMETTES

8 goose drumettes (11-12 ounces each)
1/4 teaspoon salt
1/2 teaspoon pepper
2 apples, quartered
2 medium onions, quartered
4 chicken bouillon cubes dissolved in
  1 1/2 quarts hot water
1/2 cup flour
1/2 cup goose grease
3 ounces red wine

Preheat oven to 350°. Place goose drumettes, fat side down, into roasting pan.

Imperial Palace
San Francisco, California

MINCED SQUAB

    2 tablespoons peanut oil
    2 squabs, skinned, boned, and
       chopped finely
    2 cloves garlic, minced
    2 ginger slices, minced
    8 Chinese mushrooms, washed,
       soaked, and chopped finely
    8 water chestnuts, skinned, washed,
       and chopped finely
 1/4 cup bamboo shoots, chopped finely
 1/4 cup Virginia ham, chopped finely
    1 tablespoon dark soy sauce
    1 tablespoon oyster sauce
 1/2 teaspoon sugar
 1/2 teaspoon salt
    1 teaspoon sesame oil
 1/2 cup chicken stock (*see index*)
    2 stalks scallions, minced
    2 teaspoons cornstarch mixed with 2
       teaspoons water
    8 lettuce leaves
       Hoisin Sauce, prepared

Heat wok and add peanut oil. When oil is hot, add squab, garlic, and ginger and stir-fry for 2 minutes. Add mushrooms, water chestnuts, bamboo shoots, and ham; stir-fry for 1 minute. Add soy sauce, oyster sauce, sugar, salt, and sesame oil; stir-fry for another minute. Add chicken stock and cover for 2 1/2 minutes. Add scallions. Thicken mixture with cornstarch blend. Mix thoroughly.

Spoon 2 tablespoons minced squab onto each lettuce leaf, top with 1 teaspoon Hoisin sauce, roll up like a tortilla, and eat with fingers.

Serves: 4

Seafood Entrées

Barton's
Chicago, Illinois
Proprietor: Luis Azevedo

BARTON'S OWN LOBSTER CURRY

2 1/2	pounds diced lobster meat
1	cup chopped fresh mushrooms
1	medium onion, chopped
5	tablespoons butter
4	tablespoons flour
1 1/2	cups warm milk
	salt and pepper, to taste
	lemon juice, as needed
2	medium apples, grated or chopped in blender
2	tablespoons curry powder

Sauté lobster meat, mushrooms, and onion in 2 tablespoons butter in a large casserole over medium heat until lightly brown.

To prepare sauce: melt 3 tablespoons butter in saucepan. Stir in flour with a wooden spoon over low heat until well blended. Remove from heat. Beat in milk with a wire whip. Beat in salt and pepper. Return to heat and boil slowly about 4 minutes while stirring. Add a few drops of lemon juice to flavor. Blend in apples and curry powder.

Pour sauce slowly into casserole and blend with lobster mixture. Simmer 20 minutes, stirring occasionally.

Serving suggestion: serve hot over bed of fluffy long grain rice

Serves: 6

WINE: *Grao Vasco (Portuguese white Burgundy), Aveleda (Portuguese green wine)*

La Petite Ferme
New York, New York
Proprietor: Charles Chevillot
Chef: Rainer Langbein

POACHED LOBSTER

3	quarts water
4	ounces salt
3	quarts white wine
1	pound minced carrots
1	ounce peppercorns
1	pound minced onions
4	ounces parsley stalk
	small amount thyme
1	bay leaf
2	lobsters, 1 1/4–1 1/2 pounds each

To prepare court bouillon: put water, salt, wine, carrots, peppercorns, onions, parsley, thyme and bay leaf into water. Bring to a boil; allow to simmer for 1/2 hour.

Place lobsters in court bouillon, head-side down. Let boil for 18 minutes. Remove lobsters and put in foil. Let lobsters rest in foil for 5 minutes, on a hot plate, then serve.

Serves: 2

L'Affaire
Mountainside, New Jersey
Proprietor/Chef: Robert. B. Connelly

LOBSTER IN WHISKEY SAUCE, L'AFFAIRE

2	ounces fresh butter
2	cups raw rice
	salt and pepper, to taste
2	bay leaves
3	cups water
2	ounces fresh butter
24	ounces raw lobster meat, drained
1 1/2	ounces whiskey (Seagram's 7 or V.O.)
3	teaspoons fresh herbs (equal parts chopped parsley, dill, chives, and sweet basil)
2	cups fresh heavy cream

To prepare herbed rice: put 2 ounces butter in ovenproof skillet and heat on stove. Add rice, salt and pepper and bay leaves. Sauté 2–3 minutes. Add water and bring to a boil. Cover and put in 400° oven for 20–30 minutes.

To prepare lobster and sauce: put 2 ounces butter in skillet and heat on high heat. Add lobster meat and sauté 2–3 minutes. Remove from heat, add whiskey, return to heat, and flambé. Sauté lobster 1–2 minutes or until flame goes out. Add herbs, salt, pepper, and heavy cream. Bring to a simmer and cook 5 minutes.

Dish out rice in center of a serving plate. Place lobster chunks in center of rice and pour whiskey sauce over the top.

Serves: 4

WINE: *Dry white*

Pano's & Paul's
Atlanta, Georgia

QUENELLES OF LOBSTER AND CRAYFISH WITH SAUCE CARDINAL

11	ounces raw lobster
8	ounces raw crayfish
3/4	cup heavy cream
1	dash salt
1	dash cayenne pepper
1/2	ounce cognac
2	egg whites, stiffly beaten
	fish stock (*see recipe below*)
	Sauce Cardinal (*see recipe below*)
	sliced truffle, to garnish

To prepare quenelles: grind 3 ounces lobster meat and all crayfish very fine in food processor. Add heavy cream, salt, cayenne, and cognac. Fold in beaten egg whites. Let cool in refrigerator 1–2 hours.

Fish Stock

	shells from crayfish
1	branch celery
1	small onion
1	bay leaf
3	quarts water

To prepare fish stock: combine ingredients and simmer for 1/2 hour. Strain and reserve.

Sauce Cardinal

	lobster shells
1	teaspoon shallots
1	teaspoon butter
1/4	cup white wine
1	cup fish stock
1/2	cup heavy cream
1	dash salt
1	dash cayenne pepper
1	ounce cognac

To prepare Sauce Cardinal: put lobster shells, shallots, and butter in a hot skillet and cook for 2 minutes or until lobster shells begin to turn color. Add white wine and fish stock. Cook slowly for 1/2 hour, or until sauce acquires red color. Place in mixer and mix to break up contents. Strain through very fine cheesecloth. Place in pot and add heavy cream. Cook until sauce become creamy. Season with salt and cayenne and add cognac. Stir and remove from heat. (Sauce will be slightly cardinal red.) Reserve.

To assemble dish: place about 2 quarts of fish stock on stove and heat until just before boiling, but *do not boil*. Take a spoon and form quenelles (dumplings) from the cooled fish mixture and stuff them with the remaining diced cooked lobster meat. (Make sure the quenelles are well formed.) Place quenelles in fish stock and cook for 15 minutes. Do not boil.

Remove dumplings and place in casserole, pour over Sauce Cardinal, and place in 300° oven for 15 minutes. (Quenelles will expand.)

Garnish each quenelle with a slice of truffle and serve hot.

Serves: 4

Yesterdays
Ft. Lauderdale, Florida
Proprietor: Peter Goldhahn
Chef: Jean Claude Mille

LOBSTER WHISKEY

        water, as needed
1 3/4   -pound Maine lobster
    2   ounces fresh mushrooms, quartered
        clarified butter, as needed
    3   ounces Canadian whiskey
    3   ounces heavy cream
    4   ounces prepared lobster sauce (or *see index*)
    2   ounces Hollandaise sauce (prepared or *see index*)

Boil lobster, cool, split, and remove meat. Sauté mushrooms in butter, then flambé with whiskey. Add heavy cream and reduce to 1/2. Add lobster sauce. Place lobster meat in sauce and heat to just boiling. Refill shell with mixture, coat with Hollandaise sauce and brown on low flame under broiler.

Serves: 2

Tangier Restaurant & Cabaret
Akron, Ohio
Proprietor: Edward J. George

TANGIER LOBSTER SAVANNAH

    1   small diced red pepper
    1   medium onion, chopped
    1   green pepper, chopped
1/2   cup fresh mushrooms, sliced
    1   pound lobster meat, cooked and chopped
1/4   cup sweet butter
1/2   cup butter
1/2   cup flour
    1   quart scalded milk
    1   dash nutmeg
1/2   cup sherry
    1   handful croutons
1/4   cup grated fresh Parmesan cheese

Cook vegetables and lobster in 1/4 cup butter until tender.

To prepare sauce: melt 1/2 cup butter, add flour, mix thoroughly, and cook over moderate heat for 5 minutes. Add scalded milk and stir constantly for 10 minutes. Add dash of nutmeg and sherry.

Mix vegetables and lobster with sauce and cook 10 minutes. Add croutons, sprinkle with Parmesan cheese and brown in very hot oven.

Serve in casserole or lobster shell.

Serves: 4–6

WINE: *Pinot Chardonnay*

Coral Reef Restaurant
Sacramento, California
Proprietor: Elwood Maleville

LOBSTER TAILS CANTONESE

1/3	cup Chinese black beans
2	cloves garlic
1/4	cup peanut oil
1	teaspoon salt
4	6-8-ounce frozen lobster tails, meat thawed and cut into 1" pieces
1/4	pound ground lean pork
1	onion, cut in 1"-squares
1	green pepper, cut in 1"-squares
1	cup chicken broth
	soy sauce, to taste
1	tablespoon cornstarch mixed with 1 tablespoon water
2	eggs whites, slightly beaten

Soak black beans in warm water for 2 minutes. Rinse several times to remove thin black coating. Mash beans and garlic together and set aside.

Heat oil and salt in large skillet. Add lobster meat and pork and cook on high heat, stirring, for 3 minutes or until lightly browned. Add bean mixture, onion, green pepper, chicken broth and soy sauce, mixing well. Cook for 2 minutes on high heat. Thicken with mixed together cornstarch and water. Slowly add egg white to lobster mixture, stirring constantly.

Serve over steamed rice.

Serves: 4

WINE: *Chablis*

Belle Angeline
St. Louis, Missouri
Proprietor/Chef: Richard Ronzio

LOBSTER IN WHITE WINE AND MUSHROOM SAUCE

24	ounces lobster tail meat
1	stick butter
12	ounces chicken stock (*see index*)
3 1/2	ounces white sauterne
2	ounces lemon juice
1	tablespoon flour
1	cup sliced fresh mushrooms
	salt and white pepper, to taste

Cut lobster in bite-size pieces. Sauté lightly in small amount of butter and set aside.

To prepare sauce: boil chicken stock, sauterne, and lemon juice. Combine remaining butter with flour and add to boiling stock. Whip until sauce tightens.

Add lobster and mushrooms, season to taste, and serve.

Serves: 4

WINE: *Chablis*

Gage & Tollner
Brooklyn, New York
Proprietors: Edward S. Dewey
and John B. Simmons

LOBSTER NEWBURG

2	small live lobsters
4	tablespoons butter
4	tablespoons flour
1	pinch paprika
1	pinch salt
3 1/2	cups heavy cream
3	ounces good dry sherry

Steam and split lobsters. Remove meat in chunks.

Melt butter in heavy saucepan, add flour. Stir and cook together for 2 minutes. Add paprika and salt. Gradually stir in warm heavy cream and simmer, stirring constantly with a wooden spoon or wire whisk, until smooth and creamy.

Add sherry. Add lobster meat and cook gently in the sauce for 1–2 minutes. Serve on toast points.

Serves: 4

WINE: *Burgess Chardonnay, Sonoma County, 1976*

Vargo's
Houston, Texas

SCAMPI DINNER

36	medium-sized shrimp
	salt and pepper, as needed
3/4	cup finely chopped garlic
1	pound butter
1	tablespoon browned bread crumbs
1 1/2	tablespoons lemon juice

Clean shrimp and leave tails. Salt and pepper them. Slit shrimps in half only in the middle, leaving ends together. Pull tail up through slit and open so as to butterfly. Broil under 500° for 5–6 minutes until done. Remove and cover.

To prepare sauce: mix garlic and butter in blender until creamy. Then, combine butter and garlic mixture with remaining ingredients in a deep saucepan. Heat until warm.

Place shrimp in warm shallow bowl and cover with scampi sauce. Serve hot.

Serves: 6

Settlement Inn
San Antonio, Texas
Proprietor/Chef: Michael Pope

BBQ SHRIMP

2	pounds medium-sized shrimp (about 21-24)
1	pound bacon strips
24	ounces catsup
1	tablespoon horseradish
1	dash A.1. Steak Sauce
1	dash tabasco sauce
1/2	cup Worcestershire sauce
1/4	cup vinegar
2	tablespoons brown sugar dissolved in water

Clean and devein shrimp. Cut bacon into 3″ pieces. Wrap each shrimp with one short strip of bacon and skewer to secure. Cook over open fire or broiler until bacon is almost crisp (about 15 minutes).

To prepare sauce: mix together all other ingredients and warm over low heat.

Remove shrimp from skewers and smother with sauce.

Serves: 4

WINE: *Semi-dry white*

The London Chop House
Detroit, Michigan
Proprietor: Lester Gruber
Chef: Jimmy Schmidt

MUSSELS AND SCALLOPS À LA CAMARGE

1	handful seaweed
1	bunch parsley stems
1	onion, coarsely chopped
2	cloves garlic, smashed
4	ounces white wine
4	ounces clam juice
12	hot red peppers
36	blue mussels, cleaned
2	tablespoons finely chopped shallots
1	clove garlic, finely chopped
8	tablespoons sweet butter, to sauté
4	ounces white wine (Pinot Chardonnay grape)
2	ounces clam juice
2	cups heavy cream
1	tablespoon leaf basil
1	pound bay scallops, cleaned
1	pinch saffron
	salt and white pepper, to taste

To prepare mussel court bouillon: combine first 7 ingredients in a stainless steel or enameled cast iron pot. Add the mussels over it. Place over medium heat and cover. Every minute or so, after they come to a simmer, shake the pot to distribute the heat throughout the mussels.

While the mussels are steaming, sauté the shallots and garlic until transparent over medium heat, then boost the heat. Add white wine and clam juice. Reduce by half. Add heavy cream and basil and reduce to sauce consistency.

While sauce is reducing, pull steamed mussels from shells and reserve.

Sauté scallops over high heat. Drain the butter and reserve.

Sauce should now be at proper consistency. Add saffron and season with salt and pepper. Add the mussels and scallops to mixture, return to proper sauce consistency, and serve.

Serves: 4–6

Jimmy's Harborside Restaurant
Boston, Massachusetts
Proprietors: James and Charles Doulos

SHRIMP CHARLES

1	medium onion
2	cloves garlic
12	ounces stewed tomatoes (canned)
2	teaspoons vegetable oil
	salt and pepper, to taste
1	teaspoon chopped parsley
12	large shrimp
1/4	pound Feta cheese

Chop finely both onion and garlic. Open stewed tomatoes and strain the juice (reserve). Chop tomatoes finely and place back into juice. Chop parsley finely. In an oiled skillet, sauté onions and garlic until golden brown. Add tomato mixture, bring to a fast boil and then simmer for 1 hour. Five minutes before removing from heat, add parsley and season to taste. Remove from heat.

Peel shrimp and split from the inside enough to remove intestines. Wash shrimp thoroughly. Cut Feta cheese into pieces 1/2″ × 1 3/4″ and place into the split shrimp. Place the shrimp into a shallow buttered casserole dish, cover them with the tomato sauce, and bake in a 400° oven for 20 minutes.

Serves: 4

WINE: *Pinot Chardonnay*

ARROZ CON MARISCOS

1/2	cup Spanish olive oil
1/2	cup diced onion
1/2	cup diced green pepper
3	cloves garlic
16	ounces peeled, boiled shrimp
16	ounces boiled lobster tail meat, cut in squares
8	oysters or mussels with shells
8	ounces red snapper, cut in small pieces
8	ounces scallops
1	cup dry white wine
1 1/2	cups tomato sauce
2 1/2	cups fish stock or consommé (*see index*)
2	cups white rice (Valencia preferred) laurel, pepper, cumin and salt, to taste
4	red pimientos
4	stone crab claws (or substitute other type crab)
1/2	cup petit pois (peas)

Put olive oil in a large frying pan or paella dish and brown the onions, green peppers and garlic. Add shrimp, lobster, oysters, snapper and scallops. Add white wine and cook for a few minutes. Add the tomato sauce and fish stock. When mixture begins to boil, add the rice, seasonings, and pimientos. Allow it to boil for 5 minutes, then place in a 350° oven for 20 minutes or until the rice is tender.

In a separate pot, boil the stone crab and set it aside.

Serve mixture right from oven decorated with stone crab, pimientos, and peas.

Serves: 6

WINE: *Chablis or Pouilly-Fuissé*

DELICA DI MARE

2	cloves crushed garlic
2	tablespoons olive oil
8	ounces cleaned squid
12	medium shrimp
2	4-6-ounce lobster tails, with shells, cut in half
8	ounces cooked conch
12	littleneck clams
12	fresh mussels
8	ounces tomato purée
1	pinch hot pepper
2	bay leaves (optional)
	teaspoon chopped fresh basil
1	pound uncooked semolina linguine
6	quarts boiling water, lightly salted parsley, to garnish

Sauté garlic in olive oil in large skillet on high heat. Add all seafood and sauté for 10 minutes. Add tomato purée and seasonings and let simmer 15 minutes on low heat. Do not overcook.

Place linguine in large pot of boiling water and cook 7–10 minutes or until desired tenderness. Strain pasta and place on large preheated platter.

Using a slotted spoon, remove seafood from skillet to top of pasta. Ladle 1/2 sauce in skillet over the seafood and remaining 1/2 into a sauce boat. Garnish seafood and linguine with parsley and serve.

Serves: 4–6

WINE: *Red Reserve Chianti or Gattinara*

Smith Bros. Fish Shanty
Los Angeles, California
Chef: Alfonson Ramo

ABALONE STUFFED WITH SHRIMP

6-8	medium cooked shrimp
1	cup Newburg Sauce
1	dash sherry wine
	butter, to saute
2	abalone steaks, tenderized
	flour, as needed
1	egg, beaten

Mix whole shrimps in Newburg sauce. Add sherry and stir until piping hot in top of double boiler. Quickly sauté in butter both abalone steaks which have been dusted with flour and dipped in egg.

Place 1 slice abalone on platter, spoon on 1/2 Newburg and shrimp mixture. Add second slice of abalone and remainder of sauce on top.

Serving suggestion: sprinkle with sliced roasted almonds and add garnish of Broiled Tomatoes Parmesan on the side.

Serves: 2

WINE: *Charles Krug Chenin Blanc*

Sign of the Dove
New York, New York
Chef: Guy Gauthier

BAY SCALLOPS MALGACHE

1	pint chicken stock (*see index*)
	juice of 3 lemons
3	pounds extra white mushrooms
1	pint heavy cream
1/2	ounce green peppercorns (1/2 can)
	salt, to taste
3	pounds fresh bay scallops
2	teaspoons chopped parsley

Place chicken stock, lemon juice, and 1 1/2 pounds of the mushrooms in a pot.

Heat to boiling and let boil for 5 minutes. Strain mushrooms and blend in blender until puréed. Put mixture back into juice and add heavy cream.

Quarter the remaining mushrooms and add to sauce. Let boil 5 minutes.

Add the peppercorns and salt to taste. (For very spicy, add the whole can.) Five minutes before serving, put the scallops into the boiling sauce. As soon as it starts to boil again, remove it from the heat *immediately*. Let stand 3 minutes.

Serve on a bed of rice and sprinkle generously with chopped parsley.

Serves: 6

WINE: *Pouilly Fumé, La Doucette*

Primo's
Arlington, Virginia
Proprietor: Artis Kipsidas
Chef: Thomas Papadopoulos

ZUPPA DEL GOLFO

1	6-ounce can white sauce
2	tablespoons olive oil
2	cloves fresh garlic, slice thinly
2	tablespoons chopped fresh parsley
1/2	teaspoon crushed red pepper
1/2	teaspoon oregano
4	small squids
6	small clams
6	mussels
3	large shrimp
1	cup water

Place all ingredients, except water, in a frying pan. Sauté on high heat until the garlic is brown. Add water to mixture, cover, and lower heat. Allow to simmer until the clams and mussel shells open.

Serving suggestion: serve over linguine or spaghetti.

Serves: 1

WINE: *White*

Michel's at the Colony Surf
Honolulu, Hawaii
Chef: Gordon W. K. Hopkins

BOUILLABAISSE

2	ounces olive oil
1 1/2	pounds celery, cut in 1" squares, no leaves
1 1/2	pounds carrots, cut in 1" cubes
1 1/2	pounds onions, halved
4	whole tomatoes
4	ounces chopped garlic
1/2	ounce caraway seed
1/2	ounce fennel seed
1/2	ounce coriander
26	ounces white wine
2	gallons fish stock (use lobster, mahi-mahi, and opakapaka bones and heads)
30	ounces tomato juice
6	ounces Pernod
5	pinches saffron
1	dash *each*: salt, pepper, thyme, bay leaf, aromat, tabasco
2	chopped peeled tomatoes, sautéed in garlic
2	handfuls julienne carrots, celery, leeks (cut lengthwise)
1	whole lobster
2	crab legs
1	crab claw
1	piece opaka
2	shrimps
3	clams
	any other desired shellfish
	parsley, to garnish

Heat olive oil very hot! Sauté vegetables and tomatoes first. Add garlic and sauté. Add caraway, fennel and coriander. Add white wine and reduce for 3 minutes. Add fish stock, fish bones and heads, tomato juice, Pernod, saffron, and boil gently for 1/2 hour or until reduced by half.

Add dash of salt, pepper, thyme, bay leaf, aromat, and tabasco. Check seasoning and consistency to taste. Strain and set aside.

Add chopped tomatoes and julienne carrots, celery, and leeks.

Just prior to serving, add all shellfish and simmer. Sprinkle with parsley to garnish.

Serves: 8

WINE: *Château du Nozet, La Doucette, Pouilly Blanc Fumé*

The Shadowbrook
Shrewsbury, New Jersey
Proprietor: Robert Zweben
Chef: Andre Cintron

SHELL FISH FRA DIAVOLO

4	South African lobster tails in shell, split lengthwise
12	large white Panamanian prawns, peeled
12	cherrystone clams, in shell
	olive oil, to sauté
4	large cloves garlic, finely chopped
1	pinch *each* oregano, basil, crushed red pepper
	salt, to taste
1	cup dry white wine
8	ripe tomatoes, cored and chopped

Sauté lobster tails, prawns, and clams in a small amount of olive oil in skillet until lightly browned. Add garlic, oregano, basil, and crushed red pepper. Add salt and white wine. Simmer 5 minutes. Add tomatoes. Simmer 10 minutes or until clams open.

Serving suggestion: serve over bed of "al dente" linguine, garnished with parsley and freshly grated Romano cheese.

Serves: 4

WINE: *Batard Montrachet*

ZUPPA DE PESCE

4 cups sliced mixed vegetables
  (potatoes, celery, leeks, onions,
  carrots)
1 pound fillet of cod
1 pound fillet of striped bass
1 pound white fish (Merluzzo)
1 pound red snapper
1 pound pollack
1 pound sea bass
1 pound scallops
8 shrimp
1 pound eels (optional)
1 dozen small clams (littlenecks)
1 dozen fresh mussels
2 small lobsters, cut up
  Court Bouillon (*see recipe below*)
1 pinch *each*: dried basil, thyme, hot
  pepper, parsley

Select a heavy, large deep pot with a tight cover—approximately 12″–14″ in diameter and 4″ high. Place sliced vegetables on bottom of pan and add all fish, then clams and mussels. Add the lobster and pour in Court Bouillon. Sprinkle with herbs and parsley. Bring to a boil, lower heat, and simmer very gently. When fish is flaky, serve in pot on the table. *Do not overcook.*

Court Bouillon

1 cup chopped onion
1 cup chopped leeks
3/4 cup olive oil
6 cups water
2 cups dry white wine
  approximately 2 pounds fish heads,
  bones, and trimmings
2 cups ripe tomatoes, chopped
1 teaspoon chopped fresh garlic
1 bay leaf
2 tablespoons fresh basil (or 1
  teaspoon dried basil)
1/4 teaspoon saffron
  salt and fresh ground black pepper,
  to taste

Bring above ingredients to a boil and simmer slowly, about 30 minutes. Remove from stove, strain to a container, and reserve.

Serves: 8

WINE: *Dry white*

LOUP DE MER

1 head of Florence fennel
2 ounces butter
  salt and pepper, to taste
1 tablespoon Pernod
2 8-ounce fillets of sea bass
1/2 teaspoon ground fennel seed
  flour, as needed
  cooking oil
1 lemon, halved
  parsley, to garnish
  butter sauce (*see recipe below*)

To prepare the fennel: trim off any green fronds and reserve. Cut the fennel in half lengthwise and slice thinly. Melt the butter in a small stew pan and add the fennel. Cook slowly until tender. Season and add a dash of Pernod. Reserve in a serving dish to keep warm.

To cook the bass: season with salt and the ground fennel seed. Coat with flour and brush both sides with cooking oil. Place on a grilling rack and cook under a hot broiler.

Dress the fillets on the bed of fennel and garnish with the fancy cut lemon halves and sprigs of parsley. Add a dash of Pernod and flame when serving. Serve the butter sauce separately in a sauce boat.

Serves: 2

Butter Sauce

1/2 pound butter
1 teaspoon wine vinegar
milled white peppercorns
crushed fennel seed
1 tablespoon Pernod
2 egg yolks
chopped fennel leaves

To prepare butter sauce: place butter in a small sauce pan and melt slowly to clarify. Reduce the wine vinegar, milled pepper, and crushed fennel to half quantity over high heat. Pour into a small mixing bowl with the Pernod. Add the egg yolks. Whisk this mixture in a bain-marie until light and frothy.

Remove from heat. Slowly whisk in the clarified butter, as if making mayonnaise. Add chopped fennel leaves.

The Barbados Hilton
Bridgetown, Barbados

CARIBBEAN FLYING FISH IN CRUST

4 4-ounce fillets of flying fish (or substitute red snapper)
juice of 1 lime
1 tablespoon fresh chopped dill
salt and pepper, as needed
1 tablespoon sweet butter
1/2 cup chopped onions
1/3 cup chopped shallots
1/4 cup chopped leek
1 cup diced mushrooms
1 tablespoon crushed garlic
1 tablespoon fresh chopped parsley
1 cup crabmeat
1 tablespoon dry white wine
bread crumbs, as needed
3/4 pound puff pastry dough (*see index*)
1 egg beaten

Clean the fish, skin and remove bones very carefully. Place on a plate and sprinkle with lime juice, fresh dill, salt and pepper.

To prepare stuffing: sauté butter, onions, shallots, leeks, mushrooms, garlic, parsley, crabmeat and white wine in this order. Season well and blend carefully to maintain lumps of crabmeat. Use bread crumbs for additional binding. Cool well before using.

Wrap each marinated fillet and 4 tablespoons of stuffing into thinly rolled portion of puff pastry. Cut out in the shapes of fish. Brush with egg glaze and bake at 375° for 20–25 minutes; brown.

Serving suggestions: serve with mushrooms filled with broccoli, glazed with Hollandaise sauce, buttered pea pods, and lemon halves.

Serves: 4

Hilton International Mayaguez Hotel
Mayaguez, Puerto Rico
Chef: Dieter Hannig

NAVARIN OF CARIBBEAN SEAFOOD "COQUI"

4 ounces pie crust dough (without sugar)
  pâté à choux
1 ounce red snapper fillet
1 ounce dolfin fillet (dorado)
1 ounce sea bass fillet (grouper)
1 Spanish shrimp
1 fresh water shrimp
1 teaspoon chopped shallots
3 fresh mushrooms, sliced
  salt and pepper, as needed
3 tablespoons dry white wine
3 tablespoons cream
1 teaspoon fresh chopped parsley
2 ounces butter
1 fresh walnut (julienne) or truffle

Roll out the pie crust thinly and cut into a fish shape. Cover the edges of the pie fish with a thin layer of pâté à choux. (During baking, the pâté à choux will rise, giving a nice and thin fish mold.)

Place the seafood in a well-buttered skillet with the shallots. Add sliced mushrooms and sprinkle with salt and pepper. Pour in white wine, cover and poach over low heat. When done, place the fish and shrimps into the preheated fish mold.

Place the skillet (in which the seafood poached) over moderate heat, add cream and parsley. Reduce the sauce, stirring constantly. When sauce is thickened, remove from heat, add butter. Continue stirring without letting the sauce boil. Taste for seasoning.

Pour the sauce over the seafood. Sprinkle julienne of fresh walnut or truffle over it.

Serving suggestions: serve with saffron rice, baby okra, pommes nature (small boiled potatoes in butter and parsley).

Serves: 1

"21" Bayside
Bayonne, New Jersey
Proprietors: Dom Annunziata,
Brian McLoughlin, Rich Massarelli,
and Rick Zaleck
Chef: Ernest Mattei

BAKED FILLET OF SCROD MEDITERRANEAN

4 10-ounce fillets of scrod
1/3 cup peeled, diced lemon
1/4 cup chopped scallion green tops
1/3 cup diced fresh tomatoes
1/4 cup diced black and green olives
4 teaspoons capers
1 1/2 cups Chablis wine
  bread crumbs, as needed
1/2 cup melted butter
  parsley sprigs and lemon wedges, to garnish

Place scrod in ovenproof baking dish. Combine lemon, scallion greens, tomatoes, olives and capers and pour over fillets. Sprinkle wine over all, being careful not to wash off vegetables. Sprinkle bread crumbs sparsely over all and top with melted butter. Bake in 375° oven for about 12 minutes or until scrod flakes when touched with fork. Serve with parsley sprigs and lemon wedges to garnish.

Serves: 4

WINE: *Mountain White Chablis*

The Old Warsaw Restaurant
Dallas, Texas
Chef: Jean La Font

STRIPED BASS

3 striped bass, 2 1/2 pounds each
salt and white pepper, as needed
3 ounces Pernod
2 bunces fresh fennel
9 bay leaf halves, sliced lengthwise
9 thin slices of lemon in halves
1/2 bottle white Burgundy wine
2 ounces chopped shallots
2 pints heavy cream
2 pounds butter
juice of 1/2 lemon

Thoroughly clean and scrape fresh bass. Salt and pepper moderately. Pour small amount of Pernod inside belly and add fennel, pulling through the fish mouth. Make six 2″ lengthwise incisions on top of each fish. Alternate slices of bay leaves and lemon slices in each incision. Marinate in white wine, remaining Pernod, and shallots for 4 hours.

Place fish in pan and cook for 1 hour, constantly basting fish. Reserve the stock.

To prepare Fish Sauce Elysienne: strain fish stock and simmer until reduced. Add heavy cream and simmer again until slightly thickened. Remove pan from heat and add butter, whipping slowly. Add lemon juice and season to taste.

To serve: place fish on platter and garnish with lemon and parsley and a bouquet of fresh vegetables for decoration. Remove skin before serving.

Serves: 6

Wine: *Chassagne-Montrachet,*
Château Moltroye, 1973

Maison Robert
Boston, Massachusetts

MONKS FISH IN MUSCADET WINE

2 finely chopped shallots
butter, as needed
1 sliced white of leek
2 chopped carrots
1 1/2 pounds fresh monks fish cut into 1″ squares
2 cups Muscadet wine
6 ounces whipping cream
skinless white grapes, to garnish (optional)

Pan fry shallots in butter. Add leek whites and stir well. Add chopped carrots and continue to pan fry. Add the monks fish. Toss and mix thoroughly while cooking. Add Muscadet wine and bring almost to a boil. Cover, remove from heat, and allow to sit 5–7 minutes.

With a slotted spoon, remove the fish and vegetables from the liquid. Return liquid to heat and reduce to a glaze. When thick and bubbly, remove from heat. Add a piece of butter and whipping cream. Return to slow heat, but be careful not to allow the mixture to boil.

Add grapes to fish and vegetable mixture if desired. Place in a heated serving dish and cover with the sauce.

Serves: 4–6

Wine: *Muscadet or other dry white wine*

Farfallo
Dallas, Texas
Chef: Cherif Brahmi

SALMON MOUSSE WITH SAUCE VERTE

  2 ounces unsalted butter
  2 large shallots, chopped finely
1/4 teaspoon salt
     pinch of pepper
1 1/2 pounds fresh salmon
3/4 teaspoon salt
1/4 teaspoon white pepper
1/4 teaspoon ground nutmeg
  2 eggs
1 1/2 cups heavy cream
     Sauce Verte (*see recipe below*)

To prepare shallot butter: melt the butter and add shallots, salt and pepper. Let simmer in butter 5–7 minutes over medium heat, stirring occasionally. Do not let butter brown. Strain through a fine sieve, pressing well to extract all juice from shallots. Discard solids and let liquid cool to room temperature.

To prepare salmon mousse: chop or grind salmon in meat grinder as finely as possible. Put in heavy-duty blender or food processor the chopped salmon, shallot butter, and spices. Blend to a smooth even paste. Add the eggs, one at a time. Add cream and blend to a homogeneous texture and color.

Put mixture in a well-buttered mold of any size or shape. Cook in bain-marie (pan inside of pan with water) in 325° oven for 35–45 minutes depending on depth of mold. Mousse is done when knife inserted in center comes out clean. Serve mousse hot after cooling a few minutes or cold from the refrigerator with Sauce Verte ladled over it.

Serves: 2–4

WINE: *Pouilly Fuissé*

Sauce Verte

  2 egg yolks
  1 teaspoon Dijon mustard
     salt and pepper, to taste
  2 cups salad oil
  1 tablespoon tarragon vinegar
  1 handful fresh spinach leaves, chopped finely
  1 tablespoon finely chopped fresh parsley
  1 clove garlic, finely chopped

To prepare sauce: in a medium-sized mixing bowl, combine egg yolks, mustard, pinch of salt and a pinch of pepper. Add oil slowly with a constant and rapid whipping action. Add vinegar to mixture. (This is basic mayonnaise.) Add remaining ingredients and finish to taste. Keep refrigerated.

Steamers Restaurant
Chumaree Rodeway Inn
Portland, Oregon

SALMON CARDENAL

  6 ounces white wine
  2 finely chopped shallots
  1 teaspoon butter
  1 10-ounce salmon fillet
  8 ounces fish velouté (*see index*)
  2 ounces lobster butter
  3 ounces Hollandaise sauce (prepared or *see index*)
  2 ounces whipped cream
     chopped sweet basil, to garnish
     salt and pepper, to taste

In an 8" skillet, bring wine, shallots and butter to a boil. Poach salmon in mixture, covered, until done. Remove salmon from skillet and set aside.

Reduce liquid to half, add fish velouté

and bring to a boil. Remove from heat and add lobster butter, Hollandaise sauce, and cream. Pour sauce over fish. Garnish with chopped basil and season with salt and pepper.

Serves: 2

WINE: *Chablis*

The Selfridge Hotel
London, England
Chef: Erich Himowicz

ROUGET À LA NIÇOISE

8   5-ounce red mullets
    flour, as needed
1/2   pound melted butter
    salt and pepper, to taste
2   finely chopped onions
8   diced tomatoes
1   crushed garlic clove
1   ounce finely chopped parsley
1   teaspoon tomato purée
2   bay leaves
8   anchovy fillets
16   black olives, stoned
2   lemons, halved

Dip red mullets in flour and a little melted butter. Season with salt and pepper and grill until cooked.

Pour some melted butter into a pan and heat. When butter is hot, add chopped onion and fry until golden brown. Add diced tomatoes, crushed garlic, parsley, tomato purée, and bay leaves. Season to taste. Cook for 5 minutes.

Place red mullets on an oval dish and put the anchovy fillets on top in a criss-cross fashion. Pour the sauce around the fish and place black olives on top of sauce. Serve with 1/2 lemon for each portion.

Serves: 4

Le Manouche Cafe Restaurant
Washington, D.C.
Proprietor/Chef: Christian M. Boucheron

FRESH SALMON "A LA NAGE"

6   medium carrots, sliced
2   sliced onions
1   pinch ground coriander
1/2   pinch thyme leaves
3   bay leaves
    salt and pepper, to taste
1 1/4   cup cold water
1/2   quart Chablis wine
2   pounds fresh salmon steak
1/2   quart heavy whipping cream
1/2   pound butter
    fresh chives, to garnish

Put sliced carrots and onions into a saucepan with all the spices. Add water and Chablis and cook for 1 hour. Add salmon to the broth and cook for 10–12 minutes. Remove salmon and vegetables and reduce the broth for 15–20 minutes.

Remove pan from heat. Add whipping cream and butter, very slowly, while stirring.

Serve with vegetables in dish. Garnish with chives.

Serves: 4

WINE: *Chablis*

Le Cirque
New York, New York
Proprietor: Sirio Maccioni
Chef: Alain Sailhac

FEUILLETÉ DE SAUMON AU BEURRE BLANC

2	pounds salmon fillets
1	cup dry white wine
1	cup fish stock (*see index*)
2	bay leaves
2	ounces chopped shallots
1	tablespoon white wine vinegar
	salt and pepper, to taste
1	pound spinach leaves
2	ounces butter
1	dash nutmeg
4	ounches mushroom duxelle (*see index*)
1 1/2	pounds prepared puff pastry
1	egg, beaten
	Beurre Blanc (*see recipe below*)

In a large flat pan, combine and boil for 5 minutes: salmon, white wine, fish stock, bay leaves, chopped shallots, vinegar, salt and pepper. Remove salmon and set aside. Reserve the broth for the sauce.

Chop spinach and sauté with butter and nutmeg in a small pan, then mix with mushroom duxelle.

Knead puff pastry into 1/4"-sheet, then cut in two pieces. Place 1/2 the salmon fillets on one piece of puff pastry, then top it with mixed spinach and mushroom duxelle. Cover with remaining salmon. Cover this with the second layer of puff pastry, glueing it together with beaten egg.

Make a fish scale decoration on top, then glaze with egg. Cook in preheated oven for 30 minutes at 400°. Serve with Beurre Blanc.

Beurre Blanc

	remaining salmon broth, strained
1	cup white wine
1/2	cup chopped shallots
1/2	teaspoon crushed white pepper
1/2	pound soft butter

Heat salmon broth, white wine, shallots, and pepper. Reduce to 1/4 original volume. Remove sauce from heat. Add butter to sauce in small pieces while stirring sauce until thickened. Place sauce on bain-marie to keep warm.

Serves: 4–6

WINE: *Clos des Mouches (white)*

The Panorama Restaurant
The Portland Hilton Hotel
Portland, Oregon
Chef: Larry Button

BROILED FILLET OF SALMON

4	10-ounce Chinook salmon fillets
1	cup white wine
1 1/4	cups white vermouth
	lemon butter, to taste, sufficient for basting
	salt and white pepper, to taste

Marinate fillets for a short while in a mixture of the white wine and 1 cup white vermouth. Place on a charcoal broiler on moderate heat and cook slowly. Baste with lemon butter and remaining white vermouth. Season to taste with salt and white pepper. Cook approximately 4–6 minutes on each side, depending on thickness of fillets. Fish should be moist and flaky when cut into.

Serving suggestion: coat fillets with 2 ounces of Hollandaise sauce and serve with browned rice topped with sour cream on a lettuce leaf with tartare sauce. Garnish with watercress, lemon wedges, and tomato.

Serves: 4

WINE: *Pouilly Fuissé*

Alexis
San Francisco, California
Proprietor: R. E. Lee
Chef: Theodore Gugolz

KOULEBIAKA OF SALMON

24 ounces pâté feuilleté (puff pastry, *see index*)

10 crepes, unsweetened (*see index*)
salt, pepper, parsley, and dill, to taste

12 medium-sized mushrooms, sliced

1 onion, minced
butter

1 cup whipping cream

5 cups pre-cooked rice

8 hard-boiled eggs, sliced

1 pound fresh cooked salmon
beaten egg yolks, as needed

Koulebiaka is a large loaf-shaped pastry enclosing layers of crepes, rice, mushrooms in cream and onions, sliced hard-boiled eggs, cold cooked salmon, and seasonings.

Role out the pâté feuilleté into an oblong shape. Place half of the thin, unsweetened crepes flat in the middle, leaving margins of dough all around. Season with salt, pepper, parsley, and dill.

Sauté the mushroom slices and minced onion in butter. Combine with whipping cream.

Spread a layer of rice on top of the crepes, a layer of sliced hard-boiled eggs, a layer of onions and mushrooms in whipping cream, a layer of cooked salmon in

flakes, another layer of rice, and a final layer of crepes.

Press the filling into an even loaf by folding the ends of the dough up, then folding the long sides over the middle with an overlapping seam. Decorate with the trimmings cut into designs and brush with beaten egg yolks. Let rise for 1/2 hour. Make small slits at each end of the top to allow steam to escape during baking.

Bake in moderate (375°–400°) oven for about 45 minutes. Serve in slices with Smitane Sauce (*see index*) and a cupful of hot consommé.

Serves: 4–6

WINE: *Dry white*

La Scala
Beverly Hills, California
Proprietor: Jean Leon
Chef: Emilio Nunez

FILLET OF SOLE AU CABERNET

1 tablespoon butter

4 Dover sole, skinned and boned
salt and pepper, to taste

2 very finely chopped shallots

8 ounces Cabernet wine

1 cup Hollandaise sauce (prepared or *see index*)

Butter baking pan and arrange sole in pan. Add salt and pepper, shallots, and wine. Cover pan and place in 500° oven for about 10 minutes. Remove sole from pan and arrange on a platter.

Reduce the liquid in the pan until very little is left. To this, add Hollandaise sauce and stir. Strain through a fine sieve and pour over sole.

Serve at once accompanied with fresh asparagus.

Serves: 4

McAteers Restaurant
Somerset, New Jersey
Proprietors: Felix and John Protos

FILLET OF SOLE VLADIMAR

4	5-ounce pieces rolled fillets of lemon sole or flounder
12	ounces boiling water
4	ounces dry white wine or Chablis
8	boiled shrimp
1/3	cup sliced mushrooms
3	tablespoons butter
1 1/2	tablespoons flour
1 1/2	cups hot heavy cream or milk
2	ounches dry white wine
	salt, pepper, and nutmeg, to taste
	steamed mussels or clams
1	teaspoon grated Parmesan cheese

Poach rolled fillets for 5 minutes in boiling water with dry white wine. Add boiled shrimp and sliced mushrooms.

To prepare cream sauce: in a separate saucepan, melt butter, then add flour. While stirring constantly, add hot heavy cream and dry white wine. Add salt, freshly ground pepper, and nutmeg to taste.

Place the poached sole, mushrooms and shrimp into a casserole. Cover with cream sauce. Garnish with steamed mussels or clams. Sprinkle Parmesan cheese over the top and glaze in a 400° oven for 10–15 minutes or until golden brown.

Serves: 2

WINE: *Semi-dry white*

Café Johnell
Ft. Wayne, Indiana
Proprietor: John Spillson
Chef: Nike Spillson

SOLE BONNE FEMME AUX EPINARDS

2	medium carrots, julienne
1	large stalk celery, julienne
1	small Bermuda onion, julienne
	butter, as needed
	water, as needed
4	pounds spinach
	lemon juice, as needed
3	tablespoons butter
4	14-ounce Dover sole, cleaned, skinned, bone in
3	cups fish fumet (*see recipe below*)
3	shallots
1	cup cream
1/2	pound sliced mushrooms
	juice of 1 lemon
	salt and white pepper, to taste
1	stick butter
	sliced lemon, to garnish
2	small bunches watercress, to garnish

Cook until crisp: carrots, celery, and onions in small pot with 1 pat butter and just enough water to cover. Drain, reserve, and keep warm.

Cook spinach, just to wilting, in lemon juice, small amount of butter, and water. Drain, reserve, and keep warm.

Butter a long shallow pan. Place fish in pan, allowing a little room between each. Moisten with 1 cup fish fumet. Cover with foil. Place in 375° oven for about 12 minutes. (Poaching the fish on the bone allows for less shrinkage). Remove fish when done (fillets separate from vertebrae with only gentle pressure).

While fish is poaching, prepare sauce as follows: add shallots to remaining 2 cups of fumet in a saucepan and reduce over high heat to 4/5 its volume or until it makes a syrup. Stir occasionally. When fish is removed from oven, pour the pan liquid into the sauce and reduce sauce again to 4/5 its volume.

Bone fish, reconstruct, and place on a buttered serving platter. Cover and keep warm.

Add cream and sliced mushrooms to sauce reduction and boil for 3 minutes. Add lemon juice and salt and white pepper to taste.

Remove sauce from heat and swirl in 1 stick butter.

Outline the serving platter with a band of spinach. Pour sauce over fillets and sprinkle with vegetables. Decorate platter with lemon slices and watercress. Serve immediately.

Serves: 4

WINE: *Corton Charlemagne, Pinot Chardonnay, Chablis*

Fish Fumet

2 tablespoons butter
1/2 cup chopped carrots
3/4 cup chopped onions
3 chopped shallots
1 pound Dover sole bones
1/2 cup dry white wine
3 cups water or clam juice
1 bouquet garni (small branch celery cut in half and tied together with parsley stalks, bay leaf, and branch thyme)

Melt butter in large shallow pan. Add vegetables when hot. Allow to cook, stirring occasionally, until they wilt without coloring (about 4–5 minutes).

Break or chop each bone into 3 parts, add to pot and cook for 2 minutes, stirring occasionally. Moisten with white wine, bring to boil, lower heat and allow to reduce to 1/2. Add water or clam juice and

bouquet garni. Return to boil, lower heat, and simmer for 20 minutes.

During the cooking time, skim off any gray foam that surfaces. At the end of the cooking time, pass liquid through a chamois or strainer and reserve.

---

*Les Saisons
Dallas, Texas
Chef: Marc Balocco*

FILLET OF SOLE BONNE FEMME

1 glass white wine
3 chopped shallots
4 ounces sliced mushrooms
1 teaspoon finely chopped parsley
2 pinches salt
1 pinch white pepper
2 pounds fillet of sole
1/2 cup heavy cream
    juice of 1/2 lemon
2 egg yolks

Preheat oven to 375°.

Combine wine, shallots, mushrooms, parsley, salt and pepper in a pan. Place sole in this mixture and cook for 10 minutes. Remove sole from pan.

Add the heavy cream to the remaining sauce and continue cooking until the sauce thickens. Stir in the lemon juice and egg yolks.

Place sole on serving dish and pour sauce over it. Place the serving dish under the broiler for 30 seconds until glazed, and serve.

Serves: 4

WINE: *Chablis Grand Cru Les Clos, 1976*

Allgauer's Fireside
Northbrook, Illinois
Proprietor: Frank S. Allgauer
Chef: Jesse Cobb

BAKED DOVER SOLE WITH SALMON MOUSSE FLORENTINE, EN CROÛTE

1	pound salmon fillet (fresh Alaskan Red)
1/4	teaspoon salt
1/8	teaspoon white pepper
1	ounce cognac
2	egg whites
8	ounces cooked spinach
1/4	teaspoon salt
1/8	teaspoon white pepper
1/8	teaspoon nutmeg
2	ounces grated Parmesan cheese
2	egg yolks
2	egg whites
8	6-ounce Dover sole fillets
1	10"×16" sheet prepared puff pastry dough
2	egg yolks, beaten
2	tablespoons water
2	cups basic white sauce, prepared
4	ounces diced mushrooms
3	ounces white wine
4	ounces chopped shrimp

To prepare mousse: combine first 5 ingredients in blender on purée. When mixture is a smooth paste, remove from blender and put aside.

To prepare spinach: combine ingredients 6–11 in blender on chop and chop for 1 minute. Remove from blender. In a separate bowl, whip 2 egg whites stiff and fold into spinach mixture. Put aside.

Place 4 sole fillets on table, spread with 1/2 mousse mixture, cover with spinach mixture, then the balance of mousse mixture. Top with the remaining 4 sole fillets.

Divide puff pastry dough into 4 equal parts and roll out to 1/8" thick. Place fillets in center of dough, fold ends over fillets, and pinch to seal ends. Mix 2 beaten egg yolks with water and brush on dough with pastry brush. Place in 400° oven for 20–25 minutes.

To prepare wine sauce: combine white sauce, diced mushrooms, white wine, and chopped shrimp. Bring to a boil and serve on side or on bottom of baked Dover sole.

Serving suggestion: serve with cauliflower, broccoli, carrots, button mushrooms as garnish.

Serves: 4

WINE: *Château Carbounieux, 1977*

La Folie
New York, New York
Chef: Bernard Norget

LES PAUPIETTES DE SOLE EN CASSEROLETTES CHANTAL

	puff pastry (prepared or *see index*)
8	fillets of sole
	Mousseline of Salmon (*see recipe below*)
	Duxelle of Mushroom (*see recipe below*)
	Special Lobster Sauce (*see recipe below*)
	Glaçage Sauce (*see recipe below*)
4	chopped shallots
1/2	quart white wine
	salt and pepper
4	large mushroom caps

Make casserolettes with puff pastry 3" in diameter and set aside. Slightly flatten fillets by pounding on the outside surface. Place fillets on a sheet-pan and refrigerate.

Mousseline of Salmon

1   **pound fresh fillet of salmon**
1   **egg white**
1/2 **teaspoon salt**
14 **ounces heavy cream**
    touch of freshly ground nutmeg
2   **tablespoons whipped cream**

To prepare Mousseline of Salmon: dice and place salmon fillet in a food processor and add egg white and salt. Process until puréed for approximately 30 seconds. Slowly add heavy cream while blending. Remove Mousseline and pass through a fine sieve. Place Mousseline in a bowl and add ground nutmeg, adjust seasoning. Fold in whipped cream and place Mousseline in the refrigerator.

Duxelle of Mushroom

1   **pound mushrooms, finely chopped**
    juice of 1/2 lemon
1   **teaspoon butter**
4   **shallots, finely chopped**
6   **ounces heavy cream**
1   **egg yolk**
    salt and pepper, to taste

To prepare Duxelle of Mushroom: squeeze the lemon juice over the mushrooms. In a saucepan melt the butter and add chopped shallots. Over a low flame, sweat them for about 30 seconds. Add mushrooms, stir well, and cook until liquid is evaporated. Add heavy cream and cook until thickened. Remove from flame, stir in egg yolk, add salt and pepper to taste, set aside.

Special Lobster Sauce

12 **ounces prepared lobster sauce**
8   **ounces heavy cream**
    salt and pepper

To prepare Special Lobster Sauce: heat prepared lobster sauce. In a separate pan, take heavy cream and reduce in half over a medium flame. Mix cream into lobster sauce, season properly, and set aside.

Glaçage Sauce

2   **egg yolks**
2   **tablespoons whipped cream**
4   **ounces lobster sauce, prepared**

To prepare Glaçage Sauce: whip egg yolks until cold. Add whipped cream and lobster sauce. Set aside.

To prepare Paupiettes: spread a reasonable amount of Mousseline of Salmon on the fillets of sole and roll the fillets, starting from the tail. Fasten them with toothpicks. Place them in a saucepan previously buttered and sprinkled with chopped shallots. Pour in 1/2 quart of white wine and fill the rest with water until the paupiettes are submerged. Add seasoning, cover and bring to a boil. Cook for 5 minutes and drain.

Stuff the bottom of the puff pastry shells with a tablespoon of Duxelle of Mushroom and keep warm. Remove the toothpicks from the paupiettes and dry them with an absorbent towel.

Place the paupiettes on the casserolettes, top with a mushroom cap, and pour 2 tablespoons of Special Lobster Sauce and 1 tablespoon of Glaçage Sauce over each casserolette. Place under a hot salamander, glaze the top, and serve.

Serves: 4

WINE: *White*

Aldo's Restaurant
Sacramento, California
Proprietor: Aldo Bovero
Chef: Paul Coulat

FILLET OF SOLE RIVIERA

1 6-ounce fillet of sole
   milk and flour, as needed
   salt and pepper, to taste
2 eggs, beaten
2 tablespoons butter
4 ounces sliced mushrooms
1 fresh bottom of artichoke
1 teaspoon butter
1 chopped shallot
1 sprig of parsley, chopped
   juice of 1 lemon
2 ounces Chablis wine

Dip fillet of sole in milk, then in flour seasoned with salt and pepper. Then, dip floured sole into beaten eggs. Lightly sauté in hot pan with butter. Remove sole from pan and keep warm.

In same pan, sauté the mushrooms and artichoke bottom to medium doneness, then drain excess juices. Add 1 teaspoon butter to sautéed mixture along with shallot, parsley, lemon juice, and wine. Sauté to desired consistency.

Pour mixture over fillet of sole and serve.

Serves: 1

WINE: *Chablis*

Tom Sarris Orleans House
Arlington, Virginia
Proprietor: Tom Sarris
Chef: Jerry Moutzalias

STUFFED FILLET OF FLOUNDER

3 pounds fresh fillet of flounder
   butter, as needed
3 eggs
1 tablespoon prepared mustard
1 teaspoon salt
1/2 teaspoon white pepper
1/2 teaspoon Old Bay Seasoning
1 teaspoon finely chopped parsley
1 teaspoon finely chopped green
      pepper
1 teaspoon finely chopped pimiento
3 tablespoons mayonnaise
1 pound lump crabmeat
   sauce (*see recipe below*)
   paprika, as needed

Cut 1 1/2 pounds of flounder into 5 equal portions and place into a well-buttered baking pan.

Combine eggs, mustard, seasonings, parsley, green pepper, pimiento, and mayonnaise. Mix well then gently fold in lump crabmeat. Divide mixture into 5 equal portions and top each piece of flounder with crabmeat mixture.

Cut remaining 1 1/2 pounds of flounder into 5 portions and place over mixture. Pour melted butter on each portion. Bake for 20 minutes at 450° and remove from oven.

Sauce

1 pint mayonnaise
4 eggs
2 tablespoons grated cheese
2 tablespoons dry sherry
1 tablespoon lemon juice
1/2 teaspoon salt
1/2 teaspoon white pepper

To prepare sauce: combine all ingredients.

Pour sauce over each serving of flounder. Sprinkle with paprika and place under broiler until lightly brown.

Serves: 5

WINE: *White*

Maxim's
Houston, Texas
Proprietor: Camille Bermann
Chef: Ronnie Bermann

RED FISH COURT BOUILLON À LA LOUISIANE

5-6	pounds red fish (snapper) cut into 3"-pieces
2 1/2	quarts cold water
5	cups white wine
1 1/2	cups wine vinegar
	juice of 2 lemons
12	-ounce can tomato paste
1	bay leaf
3	medium-sized white onions
4	cloves garlic
3	carrots
2	ribs celery
6	strings parsley
2	jalapeno peppers
	salt, pepper, and tabasco sauce

Poach fish in cold water to start. Add wine, vinegar, lemon juice, tomato paste, and bay leaf. Chop finely the onions, garlic, carrots, celery, parsley, and peppers. Put everything together in a large pot. Bring to a rolling boil. Simmer 20 minutes. Salt and pepper and tabasco, to taste (on the spicy side).

Serves: 6

WINE: *Meursault, 1976*

Le New Manoir
New York, New York

ROUGET GRILLE BEURRE NANTAISE (Red Snapper with Butter Nantaise)

1/4	teaspoon salt
	dash pepper
1/4	teaspoon dried thyme
1	small bay leaf, crumbled
1	tablespoon lemon juice
1	3-pound cleaned red snapper
	cooking oil
1/8	teaspoon salt
1/4	teaspoon dried thyme
1/4	cup shallots, chopped
1/4	cup white vinegar
1/4	cup white wine
1 1/2	cups whipping cream

Combine salt, pepper, thyme, bay leaf, and lemon juice. Rub in cavity of fish. Rub outside of fish with a little oil and sprinkle with salt and thyme. Place in greased baking pan. Bake in 350° oven for 45–60 minutes.

To prepare Beurre Nantaise: in a small pan, combine shallots, vinegar, and wine. Bring to a boil and boil until reduced to 3 tablespoons. Discard solids. In a 3-quart saucepan, boil cream until reduced to 3/4 cup. Add strained wine liquid. Serve with the fish.

Serves: 2

WINE: *Chablis*

Joe's Pier 52
New York, New York
Chef: Ernest Donatich

STUFFED FLOUNDER

1 1/2   pounds lump crabmeat
1   pound Alaskan King Crab
3   eggs
1   teaspoon salt
1   teaspoon white pepper
1   teaspoon MSG
1   cup bread crumbs
6   scallions, chopped finely
1   medium-sized onion, chopped finely
1/2   cup sherry wine
2   tablespoons mustard
2   tablespoons A.1. Sauce
1   cup liquid, equal parts water and oil
6   whole flounder fillets, split
  paprika (optional)

Mix well all ingredients, except flounders and paprika. Then, stuff the flounders. Bake for 25 minutes at 350°. If desired, sprinkle with paprika.

Serves: 6

Mr. Angelo's Cape Cod
Garden Grove, California
Chef: Ed Ballestero

ANGELO'S STUFFED TROUT

2   ounces clarified butter
2   tablespoons bell pepper
1/2   medium onion
1   cup ground milk crackers
  juice of 1/2 lemon
  salt and pepper, to taste
2-3   ounces milk
1/2   pound Alaskan King Crab
2   8-ounce boned trout

Sauté the bell pepper in butter, and then add onion and continue to sauté until tender. Add crackers, lemon juice, salt, and pepper. Mix. Add milk and crabmeat. Lay the prepared stuffing on open trout and bake in oven at 400° for 15–20 minutes or until lightly browned.

Serves: 4

WINE: *Wente Brothers Le Blanc de Blancs*

Four Seasons Plaza Nacional Hotel
Anaqua Restaurant
San Antonio, Texas
Proprietors: Pepe and Martha Lucero
Chef: Geoffrey Johnson

PAN FRIED RED SNAPPER

4-6   red snapper fillets, 6 ounces each
  milk, as needed
  flour seasoned with salt and pepper
  soy bean oil, to sauté
  butter, to sauté
16-20   cooked shrimp
1/2   avocado cut in 4 pieces
3   cherry tomatoes
2   ounces white wine
  chopped fresh shallots, to garnish
  chopped fresh parsley, to garnish

Dip snapper into milk, then transfer into seasoned flour. Heat soy bean oil in sauté pan. When oil is hot, shake flour from fish and sauté fish on both sides until golden brown. Put sautéed fish on serving platter.

Drain oil from pan and add whole butter. Sauté shrimp, avocado, and tomatoes. Add white wine. Pour mixture over snapper. Garnish with fresh chopped shallots and parsley and serve.

Serves: 4–6

WINE: *1976 Chassagne Montrachet*

The Loft Restaurant
San Antonio, Texas
Proprietor: Reg Brenner
Chef: Pierre Leclercq

STUFFED FLOUNDER À LA LECLERCQ

4   cups milk
1   teaspoon salt
1/2   teaspoon white pepper
1   teaspoon sugar
1   ounce white wine
1   cup flour
1/4   pound melted butter
1   pound crabmeat
1   cup shredded Swiss cheese
1/4   cup grated Parmesan cheese
2   pounds (8 pieces) fillet of flounder
1/2   cup bread crumbs
   salt and pepper, to taste
2   teaspoons paprika
1/4   pound melted butter

To prepare cream sauce: in a saucepan, scald milk. Add salt, pepper, sugar, and white wine. Make roux in separate pan by combining flour and melted butter. Add roux to scalded milk. Using a whisk, stir until thickened

To assemble the dish: pour cream sauce into either a large 1"-deep pan or into individual casserole dishes. Place crabmeat on top of sauce. Put Swiss cheese and Parmesan cheese on top of crabmeat. Lay flounder fillets on top of cheeses. Sprinkle lightly on top with bread crumbs. Add salt and pepper to taste. Sprinkle with paprika very lightly for color. Drizzle with melted butter. Bake for 20 minutes in 375° oven.

Serves: 4

WINE: *Dry white wine*

Golden Palace Restaurant
San Antonio, Texas
Proprietor: Sheu Gai Lim

STEAMED TROUT

1   tablespoon oil
2   2 1/2-pound fresh trout, cleaned
   water, as needed
1/4   cup light soy sauce
1/2   teaspoon sesame oil
4   black Chinese mushrooms, soaked 5-10 minutes in hot water
5   slices Virginia ham, cut in 3" squares
4   slices slivered ginger
1/4   cup peanut oil
   sliced green onions and cilantro, to garnish

Rub tablespoon of oil over fish.

Fill bottom of wok with 3–4" water. Regulate heat to keep from boiling away too rapidly. (Have another pot of boiling water ready in case wok water evaporates.) Place fish on dish. On top of fish, put soy sauce, sesame oil, mushrooms, ham slices, and ginger. Place dish on top of steaming rack in wok and steam for 20 minutes. Cook fish until firm, moist and tender. (Eyes will be milky white when fish is done.)

While fish is cooking, heat peanut oil in separate pan. When fish is done, pour hot oil over fish and serve, garnished with green onions and fresh cilantro.

Serves: 2–3

WINE: *White*

Dinner Horn Country Inn
Kansas City, Missouri
Proprietor/Chef: Bonnie Kellenberg

BAKED STUFFED RAINBOW TROUT

butter, as needed
salt and pepper, to taste
6   6-ounce rainbow trout
12   fresh mushrooms sliced with stems
1/2   medium yellow onion, chopped
    finely
1/2   green bell pepper, chopped medium
2   pimientos, chopped coarsely
4   ounces Uncle Ben's Wild Rice
    mixture
6   slices of tomato
6   whole mushroom caps
paprika, as needed

Preheat oven to 350°.

Butter a pan to hold 6 trout. Salt and pepper trout and butterfly them so they are open at top with head on.

In a separate pan, combine mushrooms, onions, pimientos, and green peppers. Sauté lightly. Cook rice according to instructions on package, then add sautéed vegetables.

Butter and salt and pepper inside of trout, then place rice mixture inside trout. Top each with a slice of tomato, then with mushroom caps. Sprinkle with butter and paprika.

Bake at 350° for 20 minutes or until trout flakes with a fork.

Serving suggestion: pour a lemon butter sauce over trout before serving.

Serves: 6

WINE: *Mondavi Fumé Blanc*

Vegetable Specialties

Michaels
Sunnyvale, California
Proprietor: Ted Faravelli
Chef: Alfred Saarne

STUFFED BAKED ONIONS

8 large onions, peeled
2-3 slices of ham
2-3 mushrooms
   pepper
   thyme
1 egg, hard-boiled (optional)
   Supreme Sauce (prepared cream
     sauce)
   parsley

Parboil onions in water approximately 10–15 minutes (according to size). Scoop out the insides leaving a 2 to 3 layer shell. Chop the inside onion finely with the slices of ham and mushrooms. Season with pepper and a little powdered thyme. (One hard-boiled egg finely chopped may be added to the mixture.) Pack the onion shells with the stuffing and place them in a pan close together (otherwise, they slide).

Pour a light Supreme sauce over the onions. Bake in 350° oven for about 15–20 minutes. Dust with chopped parsley and serve with any fowl or hen.

Serves: 6–8

Ambrosia
New York, New York
Proprietor: Lyn Goldstein
Chef: William McCann

SPINACH AND JARLSBERG STRUDEL

1 cup minced onions
3 tablespoons butter
4 pounds fresh spinach, blanched and
   chopped
8 whole eggs
2 cups loosely packed grated Jarlsberg
   cheese
1 quart heavy cream
1 teaspoon salt
1/4 teaspoon white pepper
1/4 teaspoon freshly grated nutmeg
4 strudel sheets approximately
   17″ × 23″, prepared

Sauté onions slowly in butter. Blend with all other ingredients and place in lined, buttered baking pan (9″ × 9″ × 2″) over 2 strudel sheets. Fold bottom overlapping strudel sheets over ingredients. Place 2 top sheets over ingredients.

Bake at 350° for 80–90 minutes, then cool slightly. Can be reheated for 10–15 minutes.

Serves: 6 as vegetable,
9 as appetizer

Blackhawk Restaurant
Chicago, Illinois
Proprietor: Don Roth

CREAMED SPINACH

2 1/2 ounces salted pork, ground finely
1 1/2 ounces chopped onion
1 1/2 pounds finely ground spinach
salt and pepper, to taste
1/2 pint cream sauce (prepared or *see index*)

Sauté the ground pork until brown. Add chopped onion and sauté 20–30 minutes. Add ground spinach, salt and pepper to taste, and let come to a boil, stirring occasionally. Add cream sauce and cook about 35 minutes, stirring frequently.

Serves: 8

Karl Ratzsch's
Milwaukee, Wisconsin
Proprietor: Karl Ratzsch

RED CABBAGE

1 small head red cabbage, cut finely
1 apple, chopped finely
1 small onion, chopped finely
1 tablespoon salt
1/4 cup sugar
3/4 cup vinegar
2 cups water
4 strips bacon, minced and fried (use rendered fat)
1 teaspoon mixed spices (cloves, mustard seed, bay leaves, dill seed, cinnamon, red pepper, coriander)

Place all ingredients in kettle and boil until tender.

Serves: 6

Dallas
Alexandria, Virginia
Chef: Ken Kinnaman

SWEET & SOUR PEPPER CABBAGE

1/2 quart cabbage, shredded
3 ounces green pepper, julienne
3 ounces onion, julienne
1/2 cup cider vinegar
1/2 cup sugar
salt, to taste
3/4 teaspoon celery seed
3/4 teaspoon dry mustard
1 dash turmeric

Toss cabbage, green pepper, and onion together. Set aside.

To prepare marinade: mix together remaining ingredients in saucepan. Bring to a boil and boil for 5 minutes.

Pour marinade over cabbage mixture and refrigerate for at least 24 hours. Keeps well up to 6 weeks.

Serves: 6–8

The Continental Ristorante and Teahouse
Brownsville, Texas
Proprietors: Lynn and Walter Rox
Chef: Maurice Hebert

BAKED POTATO CONTINENTAL

2 tablespoons cream cheese
1 ounce fresh cream
1 ounce vodka
1 pinch each salt and white pepper
1 baked potato, cut in half
1 ounce black caviar, to garnish
capers, to garnish

Whip together cream cheese, cream, and vodka until smooth. Add salt and white pepper. Carefully scoop out potato from shells and mix with 1/2 the cheese mixture. Return to shells. Put remaining cheese mixture on top of potato halves and garnish with caviar and surround with capers.

Serves: 1–2

Royal Street Crossing
San Antonio, Texas
Proprietor: William F. Grinnan, Jr.

VEGETABLE CREPE

2   pounds sliced yellow squash
2   pounds sliced zucchini
2   pounds sliced carrots
3   pounds sliced mushrooms
1   sliced medium bell pepper
1   sliced medium yellow onion
1   pound sliced eggplant
    butter, to sauté
3   pounds grated Gruyère cheese
6   crepes (*see index*)
    sliced avocados and sprigs of
        parsley, to garnish

Mix sliced vegetables together. Sauté until tender in butter. Sprinkle 1/2 the Gruyère cheese in crepes and place cooked vegetables in center of each crepe. Fold sides in and sprinkle top with remaining Gruyère. Place slices of avocado and sprigs of parsley on top of crepes to garnish.

Serves: 6

Kutsher's Country Club
Monticello, New York
Chef: Danny Kuen

VEGETABLE CUTLET WITH MUSHROOM SAUCE

1/2   head celery, chopped
1/2   pound onions, chopped
  1   carrot, peeled and chopped
  1   10-ounce package frozen mixed
         vegetables, defrosted
1/4   pound butter
  2   tablespoons flour
  6   eggs, well beaten
         salt and pepper, to taste
         approximately 3 tablespoons
             vegetable oil
  1   medium onion, finely chopped
  2   tablespoons butter
  1   6-ounce can sliced mushrooms,
         drained
  2   tablespoons flour
  1   cup milk

In a large frying pan, sauté chopped celery, onion, carrot and mixed vegetables in butter until soft and golden, but not browned. Add flour and cook for 2 minutes more. Let cool slightly and place in large mixing bowl.

To vegetable mixture in bowl, add beaten eggs and salt and pepper to taste. Shape mixture into 6 oval patties. In frying pan, brown patties in oil until golden on both sides. Place them in a baking dish and bake in 400° oven for 15 minutes.

To prepare mushroom sauce: while cutlets are baking, sauté onion in butter until soft and translucent. Add sliced mushrooms and sauté for 1 minute more. Add flour and cook, stirring, for 2 minutes more. Add milk and cook and stir until thickened. Add salt and pepper to taste.

Serve cutlets with sauce poured over.

Serves: 6

Karl Ratzsch's
Milwaukee, Wisconsin
Proprietor: Karl Ratzsch

POTATO DUMPLINGS

    1   large raw potato, ground
  1/2   small onion, ground
    4   strips bacon, diced and fried
  1/2   cup croutons
    2   eggs
        pinch parsley
    1   cup flour
        pinch salt, pepper, and nutmeg
        salted water
        melted butter

Mix all ingredients thoroughly. Form into balls about the size of an egg and boil in boiling salted water for 30 minutes. Remove dumplings from water, put melted butter on top, and serve immediately.

Yields: 4 dumplings

The Fisherman
Ft. Lauderdale, Florida
Chef: Willie Schlager

RATATOUILLE

      1   medium onion, diced
      1   clove garlic, chopped
    1/4   stick butter
      2   medium zucchini, diced
      2   medium yellow squash, diced
      2   whole tomatoes, diced
      1   12-ounce can stewed tomatoes
      1   dash each salt and pepper
      3   bay leaves
          thyme, to taste
      1   beef bouillon cube
  1 1/2   cups sauterne wine
      2   eggplants, diced

Sauté onion and garlic in butter to a golden brown. Add remaining vegetables, except eggplant. Add seasonings, bouillon cube, and wine. Cover and cook for 5 minutes. Add eggplant, cover, and cook for 5 more minutes. Serve.

Serves: 4

Lafayette Restaurant
Garden Grove, California
Proprietor: Edmond Sarfati
Chef: Pierre Boulenaz

LAFAYETTE FRESH VEGETABLES

    4   small zucchini
    2   green peppers
    1   large onion
    1   head of cauliflower
  1/2   cup olive oil
    4   crushed garlic cloves
    1   pound button mushrooms
    4   ounces pitted green or black olives
    3   bay leaves
    3   cloves
  1/2   cup wine vinegar
    8   ounces chili sauce
        tabasco, to taste
        salt and black pepper, to taste

(All vegetables should be fresh.) Slice zucchini (with skins) 1/3" thick. Chop green peppers and onion. Cut cauliflower buds 2" (coarsely) thick and set aside.

Sauté chopped green pepper and onions in olive oil for about 3 minutes. Do not brown. Add garlic, zucchini, mush-7rooms, olives, bay leaves, cloves, vinegar, chili sauce, tabasco, salt and pepper. Boil together for 5 minutes.

In a separate saucepan, boil cauliflower for 1 minute. Drain and mix into rest of the preparation. Let complete mixture boil together for 1 minute, then let cool.

Serves: 8

Pano's & Paul's
Atlanta, Georgia

VEGETABLES ORIENTAL

3	tomatoes
	salt and pepper, to taste
10	ounces leaf spinach, blanched
2	ounces sautéed pine nuts
	butter, as needed throughout
6	mushroom caps
1	cup pilaf rice
1	teaspoon cumin
2	tablespoons green peppers, diced
2	tablespoons raisins
2	tablespoons small diced cooked lamb or beef
2	medium-sized zucchini
	boiling water, as needed
1	dash saffron
1	dash salt
	pre-cooked artichoke hearts
	freshly chopped dill

To prepare tomato and spinach: cut each tomato in half and gently press centers with thumb to remove seeds. Salt and pepper lightly and stuff each half with blanched leaf spinach and with pine nuts that have been sautéed in clarified butter. Top each tomato half with a mushroom cap, cover and heat in oven until tomatoes are cooked.

To prepare zucchini squash with Oriental rice: combine pilaf rice, cumin, diced green peppers, raisins, and diced lamb or beef. Cut zucchini in 2″-lengths; scoop out centers and blanch in boiling water with saffron and salt added. Remove and chill zucchini. Stuff with Oriental rice, place in buttered pan, cover and heat until squash is cooked.

To prepare artichoke hearts: sauté pre-cooked artichoke hearts in butter; sprinkle liberally with freshly chopped dill.

Place all vegetable preparations on serving platter and serve immediately.

Serves: 6

The Brass Key
Atlanta, Georgia
Proprietors: Michele Fitzgerald
and Heinz Sowinski
Chef: Heinz Sowinski

SPECIAL PEACH-PECAN STUFFING

14	medium-sized day old French rolls, cubed
2-3	cups warmed milk
1	large chopped onion
3	stalks celery, chopped
1/2	cup butter
1	29-ounce can sliced drained peaches
1	cup pecan pieces
3	leaves fresh sage or 1 teaspoon ground sage
1	tablespoon chopped Italian parsley
1	tablespoon fresh thyme
1	tablespoon chopped basil
1/2	tablespoon oregano
1/2	tablespoon fresh mint
	peel of 1 lemon, finely chopped
6	large eggs

Soak bread in large mixing bowl by pouring warm milk over the cubes slowly, just enough to soften bread.

In a skillet, sauté onions and celery in butter until golden (not brown) and tender. Let cool.

Add to bread all ingredients at once and mix gently with a spoon, keeping the stuffing very loose. Place in well-buttered shallow casserole dish. Bake at 400° for 30 minutes.

Serves: 10–14

Golden Temple Concious Cookery
Washington, D.C.
Proprietor: Lehri Singh Khalsa
Chef: Mata Mandir S. Khalsa

WARSAW MUSHROOM CASSEROLE

1/4   pound butter
5   cups diced onions
6   cups sliced mushrooms
2   bunches broccoli flowers cut in bite-size pieces
1   clove garlic, diced
1/2   teaspoon black pepper
1   teaspoon salt
1   tablespoon marjoram
1   pound cream cheese
1   red apple, cut in bite-size wedges
1 1/2   cups walnuts
4   cups grated cheddar cheese
2   cups whole wheat bread crumbs
  Sharp Cheddar Cheese Sauce (*see recipe below*)

Divide butter into 2 woks and sauté onions and mushrooms separately. (Be sure to drain liquid from mushrooms.) Steam broccoli until 3/4 cooked. Add spices to onions and then mix in mushrooms and cream cheese and mix until cheese is thoroughly blended.

Layer a casserole as follows: 1. onion-mushroom-cream cheese mixture on bottom 2. apple, 3. broccoli 4. walnuts 5. cheddar cheese 6. bread crumbs. Bake casserole at 350° for 45 minutes, then serve with sharp cheddar cheese sauce poured over it.

Serves: 5–6

Basic Sharp Cheddar Cheese Sauce

1/2   pound sharp cheddar cheese, broken in pieces
3 1/2   cups milk
1/4   pound butter
1/2   cup whole wheat all-purpose flour
1   teaspoon salt
1/4   teaspoon black pepper

Blend together cheese and milk and heat in a double boiler until hot, stirring occasionally.

In a separate pan, make a roux by melting the butter and slowly adding the flour. Stir constantly for 10–15 minutes on low heat. Add salt and pepper and then combine with milk and cheese mixture. Blend thoroughly to break up any lumps.

Reheat and simmer in a double boiler until thick. Milk may be added if sauce is too thick.

SECTION THREE

Desserts   *Beverages*

Desserts

Pano's & Paul's
Atlanta, Georgia

SUGARBUSH MOUNTAIN MAPLE MOUSSE WITH RUM SAUCE

8	egg yolks
6	ounces sugar
1	ounce gelatin
1	cup hot water
6	ounces corn syrup
2	ounces maple flavoring
1/8	teaspoon salt
8	egg whites
1	quart whipping cream
	Rum Sauce (*see recipe below*)

Mix egg yolks and sugar together on high speed for about 6 minutes until creamy. Dissolve gelatin in hot water and add to the egg yolk mixture. Add corn syrup, maple flavoring, and salt. Mix on medium speed until room temperature. Whip egg whites until very stiff and fold gently into mousse base along with whipped cream. Pour mousse into 9″ spring form pan and chill until firm. Serve with rum sauce on the bottom.

Serves: 8–10

Rum Sauce

6	ounces sugar
1	egg
1/4	pound butter
1/2	cup dark rum

To prepare rum sauce: melt butter in a double boiler. Stir sugar and egg together and add the mixture to the melted butter. Mix for 2–3 minutes until sugar dissolves completely. Remove pan from heat and let sauce cool to room temperature before stirring in the rum.

The Villa Nova
Winter Park, Florida
Proprietor: Jeanne Rodriguez
Chef: Ann Pantilione

CHOCOLATE MOUSSE À LA VILLA NOVA

1/2	cup cocoa powder
3/4	cup sugar
1	teaspoon vanilla
1/4	cup Kahlua liqueur
1	quart prepared whipped topping
1/4	ounce plain gelatin
1/4	cup cold water
1	cup shaved chocolate or jimmies

Mix cocoa, sugar, and vanilla into a large mixing bowl. Add liqueur and topping and whip on medium speed until it becomes firm (about 10 minutes). Mix gelatin in cold water and dissolve by placing in hot water bath or double boiler. Stream into bowl while mixing. Mix thoroughly

Press through pastry bag with large tip and swirl into champagne glasses. Place shaved chocolate on top. Serve cold. (Will keep for 48 hours.)

Serves: 6

Raphael Restaurant
Raphael Hotel
Kansas City, Missouri

CHOCOLATE MOUSSE

8	ounces bitter chocolate
2	ounces cocoa
6	ounces Kahlua
6	ounces Grand Marnier
6	ounces coffee
6	egg yolks
4	quarts heavy cream
20	egg whites

In a double boiler, melt chocolate. When chocolate is melted, add cocoa and stir until cocoa is blended and mixture is smooth. Add Kahlua, Grand Marnier, and coffee. Stir until smooth and free from lumps. Add egg yolks. Whip heavy cream. Add to base and mix well. Beat egg whites and fold into cream and base. Chill for 1–2 hours.

Serves: 10

Bagatelle Restaurant
Dallas, Texas
Proprietor: Leodegar Meier
Chef: Hubert Treiber

TRILBY MOUSSE

1/2	pint whipping cream
2	ounces arrack liquor (or use dark rum)
8	ounces granulated sugar
2	ounces toasted sliced almonds
2	ounces miniature marshmallows
6	ounces fresh strawberries, sliced

Whip cream until stiff. Fold in arrack (or rum), sugar, almonds, and marshmallows.

Pile into champagne glasses and place in freezer.

Before serving, top each glass with sliced fresh strawberries.

Serves: 4

WINE: *Spumante*

Casina Valadier
San Diego, California
Proprietor: Joseph Ferrari
Chef: Josette Ferrari

KAHLUA MOUSSE

2	egg yolks
1/4	cup sugar
	pinch of salt
1/2	teaspoon vanilla
1/4	cup milk
1/4	cup strong coffee
1/2	envelope gelatin
1	teaspoon cold water
1/2	pint heavy cream, whipped
3	egg whites, stiffly whipped
2	ounces Kahlua liqueur

Beat the yolks with sugar until mixture is light yellow. Add small pinch of salt.

In a separate pan, add vanilla to milk and bring to a boil. Add milk mixture and coffee to the beaten yolks, mixing thoroughly. Heat over low heat, stirring constantly, but do not boil.

Soften gelatin in cold water, add to hot mixture, then strain mixture through a fine sieve. Cool on a large bowl of ice, then fold in whipped heavy cream. Fold in stiff egg whites and add Kahlua. Pour into serving bowl or into separate glasses and refrigerate.

Before serving, float a tablespoon or 2 of Kahlua on top of each portion.

Serves: 6

Paradiso Cafe
Detroit, Michigan
Proprietors: Daniel and Marcella Moody

ZABAGLIONE

2   egg yolks
2   teaspoons granulated sugar
2   ounces Coppa Marsala wine

In top of double boiler, beat egg yolks with granulated sugar until they are a light lemon color. Slowly add wine. Set top part of double boiler with combined ingredients over boiling water and beat until mixture foams and thickens. Do not overcook. Serve in a parfait glass.

Serves: 1

Royal's Hearthside Restaurant
Rutland, Vermont
Proprietor: Ernest H. Royal

HEAVENLY PUDDING

4   egg yolks
2   tablespoons sugar
2   cups milk
      lemon extract, to taste
      vanilla extract, to taste
1/2   pound sponge cake or plain day-old
      cake, cut into large cubes
1/2   cup sherry
1/2   pint whipped cream, sweetened

To prepare soft custard: beat egg yolks lightly and stir in 1 tablespoon sugar. Sweeten milk with remaining tablespoon sugar and scald the milk. Slowly beat the hot milk into the egg mixture. Cook the mixture in a double boiler over hot water until it thickens, stirring constantly. Remove from heat and continue to stir occasionally until it cools. Add a few drops of lemon and vanilla extract to taste.

To prepare pudding: place cake in a glass bowl and moisten with sherry. Cover the cake and wine with 3/4 of the soft custard and stir gently. Smooth the remaining custard over the top of the pudding. With a pastry bag or spatula, decorate the top of pudding with whipped cream. Chill 1 hour before serving.

Serves: 6

Gordon
Chicago, Illinois
Proprietor: Gordon Sinclair
Chef: John Terczak

BAVARIAN CREAM

1/2   tablespoon unflavored gelatin
      water, as needed
3   egg yolks
1/3   cup sugar
1   cup scalded milk
      vanilla or liqueur, for flavoring, to
      taste
3/4   cups whipping cream

Dissolve gelatin in cold water. Mix egg yolks and sugar in a mixing bowl and whisk in scalded milk. Put mixture into a saucepan and cook slowly until it coats a wooden spoon. Add the gelatin and strain back into the mixing bowl. Place in ice bath and add flavoring. Whip the cream and fold it into the mixture (crème anglaise) as it begins to set. Pour into a lightly buttered mold and refrigerate until set. To unmold: dip into hot water for a moment and turn out onto a plate.

Serves: 6

BREAD PUDDING WITH RUM SAUCE

4 eggs
1/2 cup sugar
1 quart milk
1 teaspoon vanilla
1/2 stick butter
1 pan of leftover French bread (New Orleans style) broken in bite-size pieces
1 pound raisins
1 pound shredded coconut
Rum Sauce (*see recipe below*)

To prepare pudding: mix eggs, sugar, milk, and vanilla in saucepan and heat until sugar dissolves. Butter baking pan, add bread, raisins, coconut, and mixture from saucepan. Bake in moderate oven until juice is absorbed. When ready to serve, spoon rum sauce over individual portions.

Serves: 6–10

Rum Sauce

1 cup sugar
1/2 cup butter
1 cup coffee cream
4 ounces dark rum

To prepare rum sauce: combine sugar, butter and coffee cream in top of double boiler. Cook for 10 minutes, then stir in rum. Serve warm.

PEAR-ALMOND MOUSSE

2 cups heavy cream
1/2 cup sugar
1 tablespoon unflavored gelatin, softened in 1/2 cup cold water
1/2 cup boiling water
2 egg yolks, beaten
2 tablespoons pear brandy
2 medium-sized fresh pears
1/4 cup sliced almonds
1 cup prepared chocolate sauce

Whip cream with 1/3 cup of the sugar. Dissolve softened gelatin in boiling water. Beat egg yolks with the remaining sugar and the brandy for about 5 minutes. Peel, core and slice pears. Toast sliced almonds. Stir dissolved gelatin into egg mixture, add pears and almonds, and fold into whipped cream.

Pour into a 1 1/2-quart mold and chill for 2 hours.

Just before serving, pour 1 cup warm chocolate sauce over mousse. (For a quick chocolate topping, melt 1 cup of extra-rich chocolate ice cream and pour over mousse just before serving.)

Serves: 6

Joe's Pier 52
New York, New York
Chef: Ernest Donatich

RICE PUDDING

1   gallon milk
2   cups rice
1/2 pound sugar
1/2 cup raisins
1   tablespoon vanilla extract
     pinch of salt
1   tablespoon chopped orange peel
1   teaspoon chopped lemon peel
4   egg yolks

Bring to a boil 3 1/2 quarts of milk, then add rice and simmer for about 20 minutes. Then add the remaining ingredients except for the remaining 1/2 quart milk and the egg yolks. Mix.

Mix together the remaining milk and egg yolks and add slowly to the rice and boiling milk mixture. Cook for another 10 minutes.

For the best results, portion out and refrigerate. Pudding will keep 5 days when refrigerated.

Serves: 20

The Court of Two Sisters
New Orleans, Louisiana
Proprietor: Joe Fein III
Chef: Richard R. Roland

COURTYARD COTTAGE PUDDING

4   cups diced bread
1   cup raisins
8   eggs
4   cups milk
3   ounces bourbon whiskey
2   cups sugar
2   teaspoons nutmeg
2   teaspoons cinnamon

Put bread and raisins in large mixing bowl. In a separate bowl, mix together eggs, milk, bourbon, and all dry ingredients. Pour mixture over bread and raisins, mix lightly. Pour into a large greased casserole dish and bake at 350° for about 45 minutes or until mixture is firm. Cut into squares and serve hot.

Serving suggestion: serve with whipped cream or a liqueur sauce.

Serves: 8–12

Hotel Napoléon
Paris, France
Proprietor: Guy Pierre Baumann

SOUFFLÉ À LA NAPOLÉON

2   cups milk
1/2 teaspoon vanilla extract
6   egg yolks (reserve whites)
1   cup sugar
1/4 cup flour
6   soufflés (*see recipe below*)

To prepare crème pâtissière: boil milk with vanilla; while milk is boiling, mix with a whip the egg yolks, sugar, and flour. While milk is still boiling, add mixture and whip over the heat, mixing it constantly to avoid sticking for 5 minutes.

This recipe makes enough crème for at least 6 individual soufflés. It can also be used for filling eclairs, etc.

Soufflés

36   tablespoons crème pâtissière
12   tablespoons candied fruit
6   tablespoons kirsch
12   egg whites
6   teaspoons sugar
6   soufflé dishes, buttered and sugared

In a bowl, mix crème pâtissière, fruit and kirsch. In a separate bowl, whip egg whites with sugar until thick like whipped cream. Mix slowly with a spoon into the crème mixture. Return back into egg whites and mix gently.

Pour into individual soufflé dishes and bake at 450° for 15 minutes.

Serves: 6

Hotel Quirinale
Rome, Italy

OMELETTES VESUVIENNE

6	bananas
1/2	pint Strega liqueur
12	slices sponge cake, 1 1/2 ounces each
1 3/4	pints vanilla ice cream
14	ounces egg whites
7	ounces cherries in syrup
3 1/2	ounces confectioners' sugar
1/2	pint cognac

Begin preparation 1 day in advance.

Peel and slice bananas and marinate in Strega for about 1 hour. Using 6 bowls, place 1 slice sponge cake into each bowl, removing a little sponge cake from the center. Place alternating layers of ice cream and marinated banana slices over sponge cake in each bowl. Finish layering with 1 slice of remaining sponge cake. Pour equal amounts of marinade over each preparation. Freeze overnight.

Just before serving, whisk egg whites until stiff to make a meringue. Remove bowls from freezer and unmold onto ovenproof dishes. Cover each mound with meringue. Decorate with cherries and sprinkle liberally with sugar. Place in very hot oven just until the meringue turns golden.

Heat cognac and pour a little in center of each mound. Ignite and serve flaming volcanos.

Serves: 6

Ma Bell's Restaurant
New York, New York

ENGLISH TRIFLE

3	ounces strawberry preserves
2	ounces sliced sponge cake
4	ounces custard pudding (*see index*)
2	ounces sliced sponge cake
1 1/2	ounces Special Trifle Sauce (*see recipe below*)
2	ounces fresh whipped cream
1	teaspoon toasted sliced almonds

To prepare trifle: layer a 20-ounce Hoffman stemmed, footed goblet in this order: preserves, 2 ounces sponge cake, custard pudding, 2 ounces sponge cake, and Special Sauce. Top with whipped cream and sliced almonds.

Serves: 1

Special Trifle Sauce

1	tablespoon prepared Melba sauce
5	ounces cranberry cocktail juice
4	ounces sherry

Combine all ingredients and blend well.

Chez Jean Restaurant Francais
Indianapolis, Indiana
Proprietor/Chef: Jean Marc Milesi

GRAND MARNIER SAUCE

1 egg yolk
1 egg
1 cup sugar
5 teaspoons Grand Marnier
3 drops water

Combine all ingredients and place in top of double boiler over medium heat. Beat with wire beater until thickened. Remove from bottom heat and whip until pot is room temperature.

Use sauce over soufflés or over ice cream.

Jimmy's
Beverly Hills, California

KIWI SOUFFLÉ À LA JIMMY'S

3/4 cup milk
3 egg yolks
1/3 cup brown sugar
1/3 cup flour
2 gelatin leaves
3 lime peelings, grated
1/2 cup water
5 mashed kiwis
1 teaspoon amaretto
5 egg whites
   butter
1 teaspoon sugar

Heat milk over low flame. In a small bowl, beat egg yolks lightly. Add sugar and flour and mix well. Combine with milk and cook over low heat until thickened.

In another saucepan, melt gelatin in 1/2 cup water. Mix in lime peelings, kiwis, and amaretto. In a medium-sized bowl, beat egg whites stiff, but not dry. Fold egg whites into gelatin mixture, then combine with milk mixture.

Butter lining of 4 soufflé molds (2 1/2″ diameter) and sprinkle with sugar. Pour soufflé into molds, filling 3/4 of each container. Bake in preheated oven at 450° for 12–15 minutes.

Serve at once with prepared apricot sauce and/or whipped cream.

Serves: 4

La Bourgogne
San Francisco, California

SOUFFLÉ GRAND MARNIER

1/2 cup milk
2 tablespoons sugar
   pinch of salt
2 tablespoons sifted flour
4 ounces Grand Marnier
3 egg yolks
2 teaspoons butter
4 egg whites, stiffly beaten
   powdered sugar

Bring to a boil in a saucepan milk, sugar, and salt. Add sifted flour, previously blended with a little cold milk to make a roux. Add Grand Marnier. Cook, stirring for 2–3 minutes.

Away from the fire, add egg yolks, butter, and at the last moment, 4 stiffly beaten egg whites. Mix quickly and fill the buttered, sugar-coated soufflé dish.

Smooth the surface of the soufflé. Then cook in a moderate oven for about 20 minutes or until nice and golden colored. As soon as cooked, sprinkle with powdered sugar to glaze, serve immediately.

Serves: 2

SOUFFLÉ AU GRAND MARNIER

3 tablespoons sweet butter
4 tablespoons flour
1 cup milk
1/2 cup sugar
  few drops vanilla
4 egg yolks
1/2 ounce Grand Marnier
5 egg whites, firmly beaten
  sweet butter, as needed

Cream the butter and add the flour. Blend to a paste-like consistency (*beurre manié*). In a saucepan, heat the milk, sugar and vanilla together. As it starts to boil, add the beurre manié, stirring constantly. Let boil 1 minute. Remove from heat and immediately add egg yolks, blending into mixture for 30 seconds. Pour the batter into a bowl. Mix in Grand Marnier gently and then add egg whites.

Prepare 4 individual *bols à soufflé* by buttering them slightly inside. Heavily coat the inside edge of each bowl with sweet butter (almost 1/8″ thick). This is very important in allowing soufflé to rise higher and more evenly during baking.

Pour batter into the buttered soufflé bowls and bake in preheated 400° oven for 12–15 minutes.

Serving suggestions: serve with crème anglaise (*see index*), melted ice cream, or melted ice cream mixed with whipped cream. Add a few drops of Grand Marnier to the sauce.

Serves: 4

GRAND MARNIER SOUFFLÉ L'ORANGE

1 1/2 ounces sugar
1 1/2 ounces flour
1 1/2 ounces unsalted butter
1 1/2 pints milk
    4 eggs and 1 egg white
1 1/2 ounces Grand Marnier
1 1/2 ounces sugar
    orange skins, buttered and sugared
    orange segments and strawberries, to garnish.

Blend the first three ingredients into a smooth paste. Bring milk to the scalding point in a sauce pot. Using a French whip, whip in paste. Separate eggs, add liqueur to egg yolks, and blend. Add to milk mixture which is on moderate heat. Whip until it appears to thicken, then shut off heat. Whip egg whites to a soft peak, then add the remaining sugar to them and whip to a stiff froth. Let milk mixture stand to room temperature, then fold the egg whites in the milk mixture gently. Add this to buttered and sugared orange skins. Garnish with orange segments and strawberries.

Serves: 8–10

Ambrosia
Newport Beach, California
Chef: Tarla Fallgatter

SOUFFLÉ CAPPUCCINO AMBROSIA WITH MOCHA CREAM

1/4	pound butter
1/4	pound sugar
2	cups milk
1	pinch salt
3/8	pounds flour
2	tablespoons cocoa powder
8	egg yolks
1/4	cup Kahlua liqueur
2	tablespoons Martell Cognac
10	egg whites
6	ramekins, buttered and sugared
	Mocha Cream Topping (*see recipe below*)

Bring butter, sugar, milk, and salt to a boil. Add flour, cocoa powder and cook 3 minutes until it leaves the side of the pan. Add egg yolks, one at a time, and beat well after each yolk is added. Pour in Kahlua and cognac and mix well.

Beat, in a separate bowl, egg whites until stiff. Fold 1/4 of them well into the mixture and then fold the balance of them gently into the mixture.

Butter and sugar soufflé ramekins, fill with the mixture, and bake in preheated oven at 425° for 20 minutes or until done. Serve immediately with mocha cream topping.

Mocha Cream

1	cup heavy cream
2	tablespoons confectioners' sugar
2	tablespoons Kahlua liqueur
1	tablespoon Martell Cognac.

Beat cream and sugar until soft peaks are formed, then add Kahlua and cognac. Beat until stiff.

Serves: 6

WINE: *Sauterne*

Hilton International Mayaguez Hotel
Mayaguez, Puerto Rico
Chef: Dieter Hannig

RUM RAISIN ICE CREAM

1	fresh vanilla stick
16	ounces fresh milk
1	egg
5	ounces sugar
4	ounces dark rum
6	ounces raisins
4	ounces fresh cream
5	egg whites, stiffly beaten

Slice vanilla stick and remove seeds. Add seeds to the milk in a saucepan and bring to boil.

In a separate bowl, beat the egg with the sugar and add to the milk. Simmer and stir until mixture thickens, but do not allow to boil again. Cool and strain through a cloth before placing in ice cream freezer.

When half set, add the rum, raisins, cream, and egg whites. Return to freezer until set.

Serving suggestion: serve ice cream on half a young coconut.

Serves: 6–8

Charley Magruder's
Atlanta, Georgia
Proprietor: William S. Swearingen
Chef: Hans Bertram

FRESH PINEAPPLE BEIGNETS WITH SAUCE CHAUDEAU

3/4	pounds flour
1	bottle beer
1/2	cup oil
	salt, pepper and sugar, to taste
6	eggs
2	fresh pineapples, cleaned and cut in 6 slices
	oil, for deep frying
3	ounces granulated sugar
1	ounce cinnamon
	Sauce Chaudeau (*see recipe below*)

To prepare beer batter, mix flour, beer, and 1/2 cup oil together slowly. Stir constantly until batter is smooth. Then add salt, pepper, and sugar to taste. Add eggs and mix for 3–4 minutes.

Dip slices of pineapple in beer batter and drop into hot oil. Fry until golden brown. Remove and place on paper towel to dry. Mix sugar with cinnamon and sprinkle over fried pineapple. Place on a plate and cover with Sauce Chaudeau.

Sauce Chaudeau

4	egg yolks
2	whole eggs
3 1/2	ounces sugar
	juice and shaved rind of 1 lemon
1	pint white wine (not too dry)

To prepare sauce: mix together egg yolks and whole eggs. Add sugar, lemon juice and lemon rind. Beat constantly until smooth. Add wine and beat over low heat until mixture begins to thicken. Keep sauce warm in container of hot water until used.

Sauce may be flavored with rum or Grand Marnier. This dish is excellent over vanilla ice cream.

Serves: 6

Le Bon Vivant Cafe
Glenview, Illinois
Proprietor: Jovan Pajich

BANANAS FOSTER À LA JOVAN

4	peeled bananas, halved and sliced diagonally
4	ounces butter
1	cinnamon stick
4	ounces brown sugar
4	ounces chopped pecans
1	ounce banana liqueur
2	ounces Bacardi rum
4	scoops prepared cinnamon ice cream

Sauté bananas in butter over low heat. Turn bananas, making sure both sides are browned slightly. Add cinnamon stick and brown sugar, mix gently. Add pecans, banana liqueur, and rum and flame, pulling pan out of heat slightly tilted. Simmer for 1 1/2–2 minutes and serve on cinnamon ice cream.

Serves: 4

WINE: *Château D'Yquem Sauterne, 1968*

Clarence Foster's
Atlanta, Georgia
Proprietor: William S. Swearingen
Chef: Hans Bertram

CHARLOTTE WILLIAMS WITH CREAM BAVAROISE

1 cup apricot glaze
1 package ladyfingers
4 pears, peeled, cored and cut lengthwise into 8 slices *each*
1 quart water
3 tablespoons sugar
  juice of 1 lemon
3 cloves
  small piece of cinnamon stick
  Cream Bavaroise (*see recipe below*)
  whipped cream, as needed
  shaved chocolate
1 bar semi-sweet chocolate, melted
2 teaspoons Grand Marnier
  slivered toasted almonds, to top

Line a Charlotte mold with apricot glaze and place ladyfingers around the side of mold. Poach pears in water with sugar, lemon juice, cloves, and cinnamon stick. Cool. Arrange some pear slices to make a star design on bottom of mold, and arrange the rest around the ladyfingers. Fill mold with Cream Bavaroise and chill 4–5 hours or overnight.

To serve: unmold by dipping in hot water and turning over onto platter. Garnish with whipped cream rosettes around the platter and sprinkle shaved chocolate on top. Serve with melted warm semi-sweet chocolate, flavored with Grand Marnier, to cover portions slightly. Chocolate will stiffen and should be crunchy. Top with slivered almonds.

Serves: 8–10

Cream Bavaroise

10 egg yolks
9 ounces sugar
1 pint milk
1/2 ounce gelatin
1 quart whipped cream
8 egg whites, beaten
  vanilla or flavored liqueur

Beat egg yolks and sugar until creamy and fluffy. In a separate bowl, heat milk to boiling point. Stir in gelatin. Pour over egg and sugar mixture, a little at a time, while blending. (Bowl should be placed in hot water.) Continue to beat until mixture begins to thicken, then put bowl on ice and stir to cool. Fold in whipped cream and beaten egg whites and vanilla or flavored liqueur. Pour into molds.

The Midnight Sun
Atlanta, Georgia
Proprietor: Stig Jorgensen
Chef: Vagn Nielsen

FLAMED STRAWBERRIES WITH VANILLA MOUSSE

2 cups vanilla ice cream
1/4 cup whipped cream
1/2 cup Grand Marnier
2 pints strawberries

Mix together, on ice, the ice cream, whipped cream and 1/4 cup Grand Marnier. Flame the strawberries in remaining 1/4 cup Grand Marnier and serve all in a glass with strawberries on top.

Serves: 4–6

Mon Petit
Wheat Ridge, Colorado
Proprietor/Chef: Frank Pourdad

PARFAIT AU GRAND MARNIER

- 2 egg yolks
- 1/4 cup sugar
- 4 tablespoons Grand Marnier
- 1/2 pint whipping cream, whipped
- 2 egg whites, beaten
- 1 tablespoon Grand Marnier
  whipped cream and chocolate
  shavings, to garnish

Beat egg yolks and sugar together until lemon-colored. Mix in Grand Marnier. Fold in whipped cream carefully. Fold in egg whites.

Pour into individual dishes. Freeze for at least 4 hours.

Before serving, pour 1 tablespoon Grand Marnier over each parfait. Decorate with whipped cream and chocolate shavings. Serve immediately.

Serves: 4

WINE: *Dry champagne*

Nate's Inner Circle
Beachwood, Ohio
Proprietor: Nate Buckantz

BANANAS FOSTER FLAMBÉ

- 1/4 pound butter
- 4 tablespoons brown sugar
- 1/4 teaspoon cinnamon
- 2 sliced bananas
- 4 tablespoons crème de bananes
  liqueur
- 4 tablespoons plum brandy
- 4 scoops vanilla ice cream

Melt butter in a large frying pan on medium heat. Add brown sugar and melt until smooth. Stir constantly. Add cinnamon and stir. Add sliced bananas and mix well. Add crème de bananes and stir. Turn bananas carefully; do not overcook. Add plum brandy and ignite. Stir and spoon over ice cream.

Serves: 4

Siple's Garden Seat
Clearwater, Florida
Proprietor: Richard B. Siple
Chef: Louis Mantzanas

STRAWBERRIES MARGURITE

- 32-40 strawberries (depending on size)
- 8 meringue shells
- 1/2 pound brown sugar
- 2 cups sour cream
- 2 ounces Cointreau
- 2 ounces curaçao

Wash and hull strawberries.

Prepare the meringue shells in 4 1/2-5" diameter, leaving a depression in the center 2 1/2-3" in diameter.

Prepare the sauce by combining brown sugar, sour cream, Cointreau, and curaçao. Blend thoroughly with a wire whip.

Place 4-5 strawberries around the inside of each meringue shell and add 3 ounces of the sauce over them.

Serves: 8

Hotel Napoléon
Paris, France
Proprietor: Guy Pierre Baumann

ANANAS BEAU HARNAIS
(Raspberries in Pineapple)

1   pineapple
6   cups fresh raspberries
    spun sugar (optional)

Halve pineapple and hollow out both shells. Carefully wash and drain raspberries; arrange in shells. For a festive and edible decoration on a dessert buffet, arrange filled shells on a block of ice and garnish with spun sugar.

Serves: 2

Hotel Napoléon
Paris, France
Proprietor: Guy Pierre Baumann

ANANAS À LA BELLE DE MEAUX
(Pineapple in Kirsch)

1   large pineapple
2   tablespoons kirsch
1/4 cup sugar
1/2 cup heavy cream, whipped
1   cup strawberries
    sponge cake (optional)

Cut pineapple in half, lengthwise. Scoop out fruit, reserving shell, and cut fruit into 1/2"-cubes. To this add kirsch and sugar (sweeten to taste—pineapples vary greatly in sweetness). Replace this mixture in pineapple shell, cover with whipped cream and decorate with strawberries; or serve fruit on a sponge-cake base filled with strawberries, if desired.

Serves: 6

Hotel Dorset
New York, New York
Chef: William J. Spry

COUPE GONZAGA

1   12-ounce can black bing cherries
1   cup Melba Sauce
1   quart vanilla ice cream
1/2 cup chopped walnuts

Chill well 6 dessert dishes (glasses). Drain the liquid from the cherries, add the Melba sauce to the cherries and chill. When ready to serve, place a ball of vanilla ice cream on each dish, top with cherries in sauce, add some chopped walnuts on each, and serve at once. Do not try to prepare this dessert in advance; it has to be assembled at the last moment.

Serves: 6

Clarence Foster's
Atlanta, Georgia
Proprietor: William S. Swearingen
Chef: Hans Bertram

CREPES FITS

1/4 pound bread flour
3   eggs
4   ounces sugar
1/2 quart milk
2   tablespoons melted butter
2   ounces curaçao
1   ounce cream cheese
1/4 ounce sugar
1/2 ounce sour cream
    lemon juice, to taste
6   strawberries
2   ounces raspberry sauce
1   ounce cherry brandy

To prepare crepes: mix bread flour with eggs and sugar. Slowly add milk, melted butter and curaçao. Let rest for at least 2 hours then prepare 2 crepes with batter.

To prepare filling: mix cream cheese with sugar, sour cream and lemon juice for taste.

Fill each crepe with filling. Top each with 3 strawberries and 1 ounce raspberry sauce. Flame with 1/2 ounce each of cherry brandy and serve.

Serves: 2

Mix eggs with flour, sugar and salt. Add milk until batter is the consistency of condensed milk. Beat until smooth.

Heat a 6″ skillet oiled with pastry brush dipped in vegetable oil. Pour about 2 tablespoons of batter into pan, tilting quickly to distribute batter evenly. Cook about 1 minute, until brown, then turn and brown the other side.

Oil pan with brush and repeat. Keep cooked crepes warm in towel.

Yields: 12–15 crepes

Brennan's of Houston
Houston, Texas
Proprietor: Noel A. Hennebery

CREPES FITZGERALD

2	heaping teaspoons cream cheese
2	tablespoons sour cream
2	crepes (*see recipe below*)
1/2	cup strawberries
2	tablespoons sugar
1	tablespoon butter
1	ounce strawberry liqueur
1	ounce kirsch

Mix cream cheese and sour cream together. Divide equally and place in crepes. Roll crepes and put on plate.

In a chafing dish, cook strawberries in sugar and butter. Flame in strawberry liqueur and kirsch and pour over crepes.

Serves: 1

Crepes

2	eggs
3/4	cup sifted flour
1	teaspoon sugar
	pinch of salt
	milk, as needed
	vegetable oil, as needed

McLeod's Restaurant
Sacramento, California
Proprietor: Barry McLeod

STRAWBERRY-CHERRY CREPES

2-3	ounces vanilla ice cream
1	6″- crepe (prepared or *see index*)
1 1/2	ounces frozen strawberries
1 1/2	ounces cherry pie filling
	whipped cream, to top

Place ice cream inside crepe. Fold over to look like taco shell. Mix together strawberries and cherry filling and spoon on crepe. Top with whipped cream.

Serves: 1

Black Forest Inn
Minneapolis, Minnesota
Proprietor: Erich R. Christ
Chef: Brian Gockle

APPLE STRUDEL

3 pounds diced apples
4 ounces raisins
2 ounces blanched almonds
1 tablespoon cinnamon
2/3 cup sugar
    juice and rind of 1 lemon
1 packet fillo leaves
1 cup melted butter
1 cup bread crumbs mixed with 1/3
    cup sugar
    whipped cream (optional)

Mix apples, raisins, almonds, cinnamon, 2/3 cup sugar, juice and lemon rind together. Set aside.

On a very lightly dampened cloth, lay out 1 fillo leaf and overlap with 1 more fillo leaf (overlapping about 2″). Seal leaves together with butter. Spread melted butter over fillo leaves. Repeat procedure until there are 5–6 layers, each layer consisting of 2 fillo leaves overlapped and sealed with butter and spread thinly with butter.

Place apple mixture on edge of dough nearest you in a long strip. Fold extended side of the leaves in and roll gently as for a jelly roll. With the aid of a damp cloth, ease strudel onto a buttered sheet and brush top lightly with melted butter and sprinkle with bread crumb and sugar mixture. Drizzle lightly with melted butter.

Bake at 375° for about 50 minutes or until apples are tender and crust is golden brown. Let cool 15 minutes before cutting into portions. Serve with whipped cream, if desired.

Serves: 10

Maxim's de Paris
Chicago, Illinois
Proprietor: Nancy Goldberg

CRÊPES VEUVE JOYEUSE

1 tablespoon flour
2 eggs
2 teaspoons sugar
1 cup milk
2 ounces melted butter
2 teaspoons flour
2 teaspoons sugar
2 egg yolks
1 cup milk
    zest of 1 lemon and juice
4 egg whites, beaten

To prepare crepes: mix in a bowl the 1 tablespoon flour, 2 eggs, 2 teaspoons sugar, 1 cup milk, and beat. Add melted butter and strain. Cook in a hot skillet for 3 minutes on each side. Be sure the crepes are very thin.

To prepare lemon soufflé filling: place flour, sugar, egg yolks in a bowl and mix. Heat and add the milk. Cook until mixture begins to thicken, then add the lemon zest and juice. Cook for 2 minutes. Add the beaten egg whites and fold in with spatula.

Butter an ovenproof serving tray and place crepes on it. Fill each crepe with soufflé filling and fold in half. Cook in 400–450° oven for 18 minutes. *Serve immediately.*

Serves: 4

Hilton International Mayaguez Hotel
Mayaguez, Puerto Rico
Chef: Dieter Hannig

TROPICAL FRUIT STRUDEL "MAYAGUEZANO"

4	cups flour
1 1/2	cups lukewarm water
1/2	cup oil
1	dash salt
10	ounces peeled and sliced mangoes (a little green)
10	ounces peeled and sliced papaya
10	ounces peeled and sliced pineapple
4	bananas, peeled and sliced
	juice of 4 limes
2	ounces butter
1	cup bread crumbs
1	cup pecan nuts
1	cup shredded coconut
1/2	cup cinnamon sugar

Preheat oven to 385°.

Sift flour into a bowl and add water, oil, and dash of salt. Mix thoroughly for 5 minutes. Cover the dough with a wet cloth and let rest for 20 minutes.

Mix together mangoes, papaya, pineapple, and bananas. Add lime juice to fruit to prevent discoloration.

On a large, floured, tablecloth-covered working surface, roll out the dough about 1/8" thick. Lift the dough and, with floured hands, stretch dough very thin without making any holes. Dough should be at least 25" × 30" after stretching.

Melt butter and brush dough carefully. Sprinkle bread crumbs over dough. Spread the fruit mix over the bread crumbs. Add pecan nuts, coconut, and cinnamon sugar over the fruits.

Fold over left and right side of dough about 3". Lift the tablecloth with both hands and roll strudel to a roulade together.

Move the strudel onto a buttered baking sheet and brush with butter. Bake for about 25–30 minutes.

Serve the strudel warm or at room temperature with Rum Raisin Ice Cream (*see index*).

Serves: 6–8

Marius' Restaurant & Lounge
Lakewood, Ohio
Proprietor/Chef: Marius Eggelmeyer

LEMON CREPES

1	ounce butter
1	ounce white sugar
	rinds of 2 lemons
1/2	ounce Cointreau
4-6	crepes, prepared
1/2	ounce rum

Heat pan until very hot and melt butter. Add sugar and lemon rinds. Let mixture turn slightly brown; pour in Cointreau. Then, place crepes into mixture, one at a time, turning each to cover. Flame with rum. Remove crepes and fold into triangles. Serve with mixture on top.

Serves: 4

Stonehenge
Ridgefield, Connecticut
Proprietors: David Davis & Douglas Seville

STONEHENGE APPLE FRITTERS WITH BAVARIAN SAUCE

4	apples, peeled and cored
	all-purpose flour, to dust
3/4	cup all-purpose flour
1/2	teaspoon paprika
1/4	teaspoon salt
1	dash pepper
3/4	cup beer
	oil for deep frying
1/4	cup sugar
1/4	teaspoon ground cinnamon
	Bavarian Sauce (*see recipe below*)

Slice apples into 1/2" wedges; coat lightly with flour. In bowl, combine the 3/4 cup flour, paprika, salt, and pepper. Add beer and beat smooth. Dip apples into batter. Fry in hot oil (375°) until golden, about 1 minute per side. Drain. Roll in sugar and cinnamon. Spoon about 1/4 cup Bavarian sauce into dish. Arrange fritters in sauce. Serve immediately.

Serves: 4–6

Bavarian Sauce

1 1/2	teaspoons sugar
1 1/2	teaspoons cornstarch
1	cup milk
1	beaten egg
1/4	teaspoon vanilla
2	tablespoons kirschwasser
1/4	cup whipping cream, whipped

To prepare sauce: mix in a 1-quart saucepan the sugar and cornstarch. Stir in milk and egg. Cook and stir over medium-high heat, stirring constantly, for about 9 minutes until mixture thickens and bubbles.

Add vanilla. Cool, then stir in kirschwasser. Fold in whipped cream. Chill.

Yields: 1 1/2 cups

The Farmer's Daughter
Orland Park, Illinois
Proprietor: Kandy Norton–Henely

PEACH COBBLER

2	cups sliced peaches
2	tablespoons flour
1/4	cup sugar
2	tablespoons lemon juice
3/4	cup fruit syrup
1	tablespoon butter
1 1/2	cups sifted all-purpose flour
1/2	teaspoon baking powder
1	tablespoon sugar
1/3	cup margarine
1	egg, beaten
1/2	cup milk
	whipped cream, to top

Arrange fruit in greased round cake pan (8"). Mix flour with sugar and sprinkle over fruit. Add lemon juice and fruit syrup. Dot with butter. Heat in oven at 425° for 10 minutes.

Sift remaining dry ingredients together. Cut in margarine. Mix egg and milk and add to dry ingredients. Stir. Drop dough in 6–8 mounds over fruit. Bake in preheated 425° oven for 30 minutes.

Top with whipped cream before serving.

Best when warm or reheated in 350° oven for 15 minutes.

Serves: 8

PAVLOVA

4   egg whites
2   ounces sugar
1   ounce gelatin, cooked
6   ounces passion fruit pulp
1   ounce brandy
2   ounces pastry cream (*see index*)
4   individual meringue shells
4   ounces whipped cream

Whip egg whites and sugar together. Add cooked gelatin, then lightly spoon in passion fruit pulp.

In separate bowl, fold brandy into pastry cream.

Lightly coat inside bases of meringue shells with cream mixture. Arrange meringue shells on plates and fill with fruit and egg white mixture. Top with whipped cream.

Serves: 4

ALMOND AND PINE NUT TART

1   cup flour
2/3   cup cold butter
1   pinch salt
1/3   cup cold water
1/2   cup orange marmalade
1/2   pound almond paste
3   ounces softened butter
1/3   cup sugar
1/4   teaspoon almond extract
4   eggs
1/4   cup flour
1/2   teaspoon baking powder
1/2   cup pine nuts, shelled

Mix together first 3 ingredients until it resembles meal. Add cold water and mix into dough. Roll the dough into a ball and refrigerate for 1/2 hour. Roll out dough to 1/8″ thickness and fit into 11″ shallow quiche pan with removable ring. (Line shell with waxed paper and fill with dried beans for weight.) Bake at 425° for 10 minutes. (Remove the dried beans) and cool.

Melt orange marmalade over low heat and strain into bowl. Brush shell with strained mixture.

Beat almond paste, butter, sugar and almond extract until smooth. Blend in eggs, one at a time. Add flour and baking powder and beat until smooth. Pour mixture into shell, spread to edges, and top with pine nuts. Bake at 375° for 20 minutes.

Serve warm or cooled with whipped cream.

Serves: 8

Les Tournebroches
New York, New York
Proprietor: Charles Chevillot

RASPBERRY TARTE

17 1/2	ounces flour
8 3/4	ounces sugar
8 3/4	ounces butter
1	lemon rind
1-2	whole eggs
4-6	ounces seedless raspberry jam
4	pints raspberries

To prepare tarte shell: blend together *well* the flour, sugar, butter, lemon rind and eggs. Refrigerate for about 1 hour. Roll out dough to 1/4" thick and place in 9" pie shell.

To prepare filling: heat, but do not boil the jam. Lightly baste tarte shell with jam. Place raspberries in shell, stacking uniformly. Pour remaining jam over top of raspberries, enough to cover.

Refrigerate about 1 hour before serving.

Serves: 6–8

Harold Restaurant
Santa Monica, California
Proprietor: Harold Butler
Chef: Luis Carrido

CHOCOLATE MOCHA ICE CREAM PIE

1	package Nabisco Famous Wafers
4	ounces drawn butter
1	tablespoon granulated sugar
2	cups whipping cream
2	cups homogenized milk
1	cup evaporated milk
2	tablespoons sugar
6	ounces chocolate flavoring
2	tablespoons Kahlua liqueur
2/3	cup walnuts

To prepare crust: grate wafers. Add drawn butter and granulated sugar and mix together thoroughly. Place 2 cups of mixture into a 9" pie tin and press into shape by using a second pie tin. Bake for 5 minutes at 250° and place in freezer for 15 minutes.

To prepare filling: place all remaining ingredients in a mixing bowl and mix *thoroughly*. Pour into an ice cream maker and mix until frozen.

Mold mixture into the chocolate wafer crust and place in freezer until it is frozen solid.

Serving suggestion: cut pie into portions and serve with a rosette of whipped cream and bittersweet chocolate curls.

Serves: 6–8

The Inn at Turtle Creek
San Antonio, Texas
Chef: Jesse Cardanas

TURTLE PIE

1	cup evaporated milk
6	ounces chocolate chips
1	cup miniature marshmallows
1/4	teaspoon salt
1	package chocolate or vanilla wafers, crushed
4	ounces butter
1	quart vanilla ice cream
	whole pecans or walnut halves, as needed

Combine milk, chips, marshmallows, and salt in a 2-quart saucepan and cook over medium heat until mixture begins to simmer. Stir constantly and simmer slowly about 2 minutes until it thickens and coats a spoon. Remove and cool to room temperature.

Moisten wafer crumbs with butter and line bottom of a deep 9" pie plate with crumbs. Place a layer of vanilla ice cream over crumbs, then a layer of chocolate mixture. Carefully place a second layer of ice cream on and then another layer of chocolate mixture. Top with whole pecans or walnut halves. Wrap well and freeze until ready to serve. May be topped with whipped cream if desired.

Serves: 6–8

Gage & Tollner
Brooklyn, New York
Proprietors: Edward S. Dewey
and John B. Simmons

BRANDY ALEXANDER PIE

1/2   cup cold water
  1   envelope unflavored gelatin
2/3   cup sugar
      pinch of salt
  3   eggs, separated
1/4   cup brandy
1/4   cup crème de cacao
  1   cup heavy cream, beaten
  1   9″-graham cracker crust
      whipped cream and shaved
      chocolate, to garnish

Pour water in saucepan and sprinkle gelatin over it. Add 1/3 cup of the sugar, salt and 3 egg yolks. Stir to blend. Place over low heat and cook and stir until gelatin dissolves and mixture thickens. Do not boil. Stir in brandy and crème de cacao. Chill mixture over bowl of ice until mixture mounds slightly. Meanwhile, beat 3 egg whites until foamy. Beat in remaining 1/3 cup sugar until stiff. Fold meringue into thickened mixture. Fold in whipped cream. Spoon into crust and chill several hours.

Garnish chilled pie with additional whipped cream and shaved chocolate.

Serves: 6–8

Spencer's
Atlanta, Georgia
Proprietor: Gerry Weinberg

FRENCH SPONGE CAKE

  6   eggs
  1   cup sugar
  1   teaspoon vanilla
  1   grated lemon rind
  1   cup all-purpose flour
      flour and oil, as needed
      Chantilly Cream (*see recipe below*)

Beat eggs very well until they hold a ribbon and/or double in size. While beating, add sugar 1/3 at a time. Add vanilla and lemon rind.

In a separate bowl, gently combine mixture with flour by adding 1/3 mixture at a time. Pour batter into 2 lightly greased and floured 9″ × 1 1/2″ round cake pans.

Bake at 375° for about 18 minutes or until top lightly browns and edges pull slightly away from side of pan. Turn out immediately to cool on wire rack.

When cooled, spread Chantilly cream over 1 cake layer, then put other layer over cream. Pipe outside as desired to decorate.

(Optional: drop sour cherries into batter just prior to baking, or ring top of cake with cherries during decorating by melting down cherry preserves and pouring carefully into center of top layer. Then pipe Chantilly cream on outside of cherries.)

Chantilly Cream

  1   quart whipping cream
  2   cups confectioners' sugar
  1   teaspoon almond extract

Whip cream until stiff but still smooth. Add sugar slowly. Add almond extract.

The Concord Resort Hotel
Kiamesha Lake, New York
Proprietor: Raymond Parker
Chef: Bob Martin

BANANA BREAD CAKE

1/2	pound butter
1 1/2	pounds sugar
6	whole eggs
1 3/4	pounds mashed bananas
1/4	pounds bread flour
1/2	ounce baking powder
1/2	ounce baking soda
1/4	ounce salt
1	teaspoon vanilla flavoring
1 1/2	pounds diced walnuts

Cream together the butter and sugar, briefly. Mix together all ingredients. Bake at 360°–375° in 2 pans until done. Bread is done when finger pressed on top bounces back.

Yields: 2 large loaves

The Mansion
Atlanta, Georgia
Proprietor: William S. Swearingen
Chef: Hans Bertram

BLACK FOREST CAKE

1	cup cherry juice
3	tablespoons cornstarch
1 1/2	pounds sugar
1/2	cup kirsch
1/4	pound melted butter
4	ounces plain gelatin
	water, as needed
1	quart whipped cream
3	10″-layers chocolate cake prepared from package
1	quart large black cherries
1	ounce chocolate chips
	grated chocolate, to garnish

Boil cherry juice, then add cornstarch. Remove from heat and add sugar, kirsch, and melted butter. Put aside.

Melt gelatin in water and mix together with whipped cream.

In a 10″ cake pan (high), put one layer of cake on the bottom, spread whipped cream mixture over this layer and put a layer of cherries in the center. Put a second layer of cake on top of this and press down. Mix the remaining whipped cream mixture with chocolate chips and put on top of second layer. Add the third layer of cake, press down, and refrigerate overnight.

Cover with cherry butter mixture, decorate with cherries and grated chocolate.

Stonehenge
Ridgefield, Connecticut
Proprietors: David Davis & Douglas Seville

STONEHENGE CHOCOLATE WHISKEY CAKE

	flour and butter, as needed
1/4	cup raisins
1/3	cup whiskey
7	ounces bittersweet chocolate
3	tablespoons water
1/2	cup softened butter
3	egg yolks
2/3	cup granulated sugar
4 1/2	tablespoons all-purpose flour
2/3	cup blanched almonds, ground
3	egg whites
	icing (*see recipe below*)

Cover the base of a 9″ spring form cake pan with waxed paper. Enclose in the spring form and butter the paper and sides of the pan. Flour thoroughly.

Steep raisins in whiskey. Set aside.

Melt the chocolate, in small pieces, in the top of a double boiler with water. Stir until smooth. Remove from heat and stir in the butter, small pieces at a time.

Beat egg yolks with sugar until white and creamy. Beat in chocolate and then stir in flour and almonds. Stir in raisins and whiskey.

Whip egg whites until peaks hold. Stir 1/3 into chocolate mix, then fold in remaining egg whites.

Pour mixture into cake pan. Bake for 20 minutes at 375°.

Allow cake to cool in pan for 15–20 minutes. Turn onto cake rack and allow to rest overnight. (Cake may be refrigerated or frozen at this stage.)

Icing

3 ounces bitter chocolate
3 ounces melted butter
  pistachios or sliced, blanched
    almonds, to garnish

Prepare icing just prior to serving. Melt chocolate, in small pieces, in top of double boiler. Remove from heat and stir in butter thoroughly. Spread over top and sides of cake using spatula. Sprinkle top and sides of cake with nuts.

The Farmer's Daughter
Orland Park, Illinois
Proprietor: Kandy Norton-Henely

SPANISH BRANDY CHEESE CAKE

1 1/3 cups sifted confectioners' sugar
1/4 cup brandy
2 cups cream cheese at room
    temperature
1 teaspoon unflavored gelatin
1/2 cup cold water
2 cups heavy cream, whipped
1 graham cracker pie shell (8" or 9")

Whip sugar, brandy, and cream cheese until blended. Soften gelatin in cold water. Melt over hot water. Add gelatin to the cream cheese mixture and continue to whip. Fold in whipped cream and pour into pie shell. Chill until firm.

Serves: 8

Arnaud's
New Orleans, Louisiana
Proprietor: Archie Casbarian
Chef: Claude Aubert

CHEESECAKE ROYALE

1 pound graham cracker crumbs
1 3/4 pounds melted butter
3 ounces toasted, coarsely chopped
    almonds
2 pounds 6 ounces cream cheese
3 1/2 pounds sour cream
8 whole eggs
9 egg yolks
1 1/2 pounds sugar
3 tablespoons vanilla
1 1/2 ounces curaçao
    zest and juice from 1 lemon
    zest and juice from 1 orange

To prepare crust: mix by hand the graham cracker crumbs, butter, and almonds. Press into a large spring form pan, bottom first, then sides, until 3/8" thick.

To prepare filling: combine cream cheese, sour cream, and all eggs. Soften by hand for a few minutes, then add sugar, vanilla, curaçao and all lemon and orange items. Finish mixing in blender for a few seconds until creamy and without lumps.

Pour filling slowly into crust until full. Bake at 250° for 2 1/2 hours. Serve chilled, topped as desired.

Serves: 18

WINE: *Perrier-Jouet "Fleur de France"*

Guido's Italian Cuisine
Los Angeles, California
Proprietor: Guido Perri
Chefs: Guido and Karin Perri

CHEESECAKE

6	ounces graham crackers, finely crumbled (3/4 cup)
2	tablespoons sugar
1/2	cup sliced walnuts
6	tablespoons unsalted butter, melted
2	tablespoons soft butter
3	8-ounce packages cream cheese, softened
1 1/4	cups sugar
6	egg yolks
1	pint sour cream
3	tablespoons all-purpose flour
2	teaspoons vanilla
1	tablespoon lemon juice
1	tablespoon finely grated lemon rind
6	egg whites
2	tablespoons confectioners' sugar

To prepare crust: in a mixing bowl, with a large spoon, combine graham cracker crumbs, sugar, and walnuts. Stir melted butter into crumbs until they are well saturated. Heavily butter a 9"-inch round, 3" deep, spring form pan with soft butter. Pat an even layer of cracker crumb mixture on the bottom and sides of pan. Refrigerate while preparing the filling.

To prepare filling: cream the softened cream cheese by beating it with a mixer until smooth. Then beat in sugar. Beat in egg yolks, one at a time, and continue to beat until all ingredients are well combined. Stir in sour cream, flour, vanilla, lemon juice and lemon rind.

In a separate bowl, beat egg whites until stiff enough to form unwavering peaks on the beater when it is lifted out of the bowl. With a rubber spatula, fold egg whites into the cream cheese mixture.

Pour the filling into the graham cracker crust and bake in the middle of preheated 350° oven for 1 hour.

Turn off oven and, with oven door left open, let cake rest on oven shelf for 15 minutes. Remove and let cool. Before serving, sprinkle with confectioners' sugar.

Henry VIII
Bridgeton, Missouri
Proprietor: Pat Hanon
Chef: Anthony Danner

HENRY VIII BANANA SPLIT CAKE

3	sticks butter
2	cups crushed graham cracker crumbs
2	eggs
2	cups powdered sugar
5	bananas
1	#2 can crushed pineapple, drained
1	large or 2 small containers prepared whipped cream topping (Pet Whip, Cool Whip, Dream Whip)
1/2-1	cup chopped pecans
8-10	chopped maraschino cherries

To prepare crust: melt 1 stick butter in a pan and mix thoroughly with graham cracker crumbs. Spread on bottom of 13" × 9" pan. Set crust aside.

Combine eggs, 2 sticks butter, and powdered sugar in a mixer bowl and beat for 15 minutes. Spread over crust. Slice bananas and place over mixture. Spread drained pineapple over bananas. Cover with whipped cream, add nuts and cherries, and refrigerate overnight.

Serves: 8–16

MELOMAKARONA

2	sticks softened butter
1	cup Wesson oil
2	tablespoons Crisco shortening
1	egg
2/3	cup sugar, or as needed
1	jigger whiskey or cognac
1/3	cup orange juice
1	teaspoon baking soda
2	teaspoons baking powder
2	pounds flour
1	cup water
1 1/2	cups sugar
1	cup honey
1/4	cup lemon juice
1/2	cup chopped pecans or walnuts

Place butter in bowl and beat. Add oil and shortening and beat very well. Add egg, sugar and whiskey, beating well.

Mix 1/2 the orange juice with baking soda and 1/2 the orange juice with baking powder in separate bowls. Add both orange juice mixtures to warm butter mixture. Gradually add flour (about 1/2) then remove beaters and add remaining flour until dough is pliable.

Shape dough into cookie shapes and bake at 350° for 20 minutes. (To shape, take small pieces of dough, shape into 3" rolls, and press fork down on each.) Cool cookies before dipping in syrup.

To prepare syrup: combine water, sugar, honey and lemon juice in saucepan and bring to a boil. Lower heat and simmer.

Dip each cooled cookie in syrup, covering each one well. Remove and place on serving plate. Sprinkle coated cookies with chopped pecans or walnuts.

Beverages

Toots Shor Restaurant
New York, New York

IRISH COFFEE

1 slice fresh orange
3/4 teaspoon superfine sugar
7 ounces strong black coffee
2 ounces Irish whiskey
1 ounce fresh whipped cream
1/8 ounce green crème de menthe

Wet rim of an 8-ounce stemmed, footed wine goblet with orange slice. Turn goblet over and dip rim in 1/4 teaspoon sugar. Add remaining sugar, coffee, and whiskey to goblet. Top with whipped cream and garnish with crème de menthe.

Serves: 1

Kona-Kai
Chicago Marriott–O'Hare
Chicago, Illinois
Proprietor: Don Sit

KONA GROG

1 dash Angostura bitters
1 ounce lemon juice
1 ounce passion fruit nectar
1 ounce unsweetened pineapple juice
2 ounces Jamaica rum

Combine all ingredients and pour into a Hurricane Squall glass. Decorate with paddle, cherry, and a fresh mint.

Serves: 1

Siple's Garden Seat
Clearwater, Florida
Proprietor: Richard B. Siple
Chef: Louis Mantzanas

THE RUMACADO

1 ounce peeled, ripened avocado
1 1/2 ounces light rum
1 1/2 ounces sweet & sour mix (see instructions)
1 tablespoon crushed ice

(Sweet & sour mix can be prepared by using equal parts lime and lemon juice and simple syrup [*see index*] with 2 egg whites to the gallon.)

Combine all ingredients in blender and buzz until smooth and slightly slushy. Serve in a cocktail glass.

Serves: 1

Cafe Graphics
Schiller Park, Illinois
Proprietor: Wally Kosch

INSTANT HOTEL

1 ounce strawberry liqueur
1 ounce vodka
1 dash lime juice
1 ounce Southern Comfort

Combine ingredients in blender cup with ice. Shake to chill. Serve over ice.

Serves: 2

Campbell House Inn
Lexington, Kentucky
Chef: George Kiser

CAMPBELL HOUSE MINT JULEP

```
7-8  mint sprigs
     cracked ice
  1  lump granulated sugar
1 1/2  ounces Kentucky sipping bourbon
     cool spring water
```

In a silver julep cup or a 14-ounce frosted glass, muddle 2 or 3 mint sprigs all around inside of glass then discard. Using cracked ice, pack glass 3/4 full. Place one lump of granulated sugar on ice. Finish packing glass with ice.

Slowly pour bourbon over the ice and sugar lump. Fill glass with cool spring water and one large sprig of mint (cutting the end to bleed). Insert to bottom of glass. Dust remaining mint leaves with powdered sugar, place on top of drink. Set glass in refrigerator and try to wait 30 minutes before sipping.

Serves: 1

Cafe Graphics
Schiller Park, Illinois
Proprietor: Wally Kosch

BETWEEN THE SHEETS

```
  3/4  ounce rum
  3/4  ounce brandy
1 1/2  ounces sweet & sour mix
  1/2  ounce triple sec
```

Blend and strain into chilled highball glass.

Serves: 1

Trader Frank's Restaurant
Tiki Gardens
Indian Shores, Florida
Proprietor: Frank Byars
Chef: Holum Lee

BANANA DELIGHT

```
2  bananas
5  ounces banana cordial
   sweet & sour mix (see index)
```

Blend bananas in blender. Add liqueur. Pour into 10-ounce glass. Add sweet & sour mix to 2" from top of glass. Blend well.

Serves: 1

Milo's
Dallas, Texas
Proprietor/Chef: Milo Fares

ACAPULCO DREAM

```
  1  ounce amaretto liqueur
1/4  cup fresh orange juice
  2  scoops French vanilla ice cream
```

Blend together all ingredients and serve immediately.

Serves: 1

Trader Vic's at the Shamrock Hilton
Houston, Texas
Manager: Eric Denk
Chef: Victor Bergeron

SCORPION

3 ounces orgeat syrup
6 ounces lemon juice
8 ounces orange juice
8 ounces light rum
4 ounces brandy

Combine and add 4 scoops of crushed ice and blend well.

Serves: 4

Michael's of Ridgefield
Ridgefield, Connecticut
Proprietor/Chef: Michael L. Collins

CAPPUCCINO ROYALE

3 ounces Kahlua liqueur
3 ounces brandy
1 ounce anisette
1 ounce Tuaca
1 ounce Galliano liqueur
2 cups espresso
2 cups hot chocolate
2 cups milk
1/2 pint whipping cream
6 tablespoons sugar
1/8 teaspoon vanilla extract

Blend together all ingedients and garnish each serving with shaved chocolate.

Serves: 4

Carlos 'N' Charlie's
Hollywood, California
Proprietor: Chuck Novak

CHARLIE'S FREEZE

3/4 ounce Mexican coffee liqueur
3/4 ounce California brandy
5 ounces vanilla ice cream
   whipped cream
   ground nutmeg

Place liqueur, brandy, and ice cream in blender and blend until thick. Pour into a 9-ounce wine glass. Top with a swirl of whipped cream and garnish with nutmeg.

Serves: 1

Fifth Avenue Restaurant
South Miami, Florida
Proprietor: Stephen Hill
Chef: Manny Garcia

WHITE FOX

1 shot vodka
1/2 shot dark crème de cacao
1/2 shot crème de noyaux
   whipping cream
   ground nutmeg

Place vodka, crème de cacao and crème de noyaux in glass. Add whipping cream, shake, and top with nutmeg.

Serves: 1

Gordon
Chicago, Illinois
Proprietor: Gordon Sinclair
Chef: John Terczak

KIR

1   splash cassis
6   ounces Cantera (dry white wine)
    twist of lemon

Combine cassis and wine in a glass. Add twist of lemon, but do not rim.

Serves: 1

India House
San Francisco, California
Proprietor: Sarwan S. Gill
Chef: Raminder Sekhon

MAHARAJAH BURRA PEG

1   sugar cube soaked in Angostura
      bitters
1   split of champagne
1   shot brandy
      float of Cointreau
      lemon twist
      cherry

Put all ingredients into a large, brass, ice cube-filled goblet in the order in which they appear above. Serve with 2 straws.

Serves: 1

House of Kwong
Woodland Hills, California
Proprietor: E. Kwong

COCO BALL

1   part lemon juice
2   parts pineapple juice
1   part vodka
1   part rum
1   teaspoon fine granulated sugar or
      sweetener
1   heaping teaspoon coconut powder

In a 10-ounce Collins glass, pour together all the ingredients. Insert a straw and garnish with a fruit brochette.

Serves: 1

Hyatt Kuilima Resort
Kuilima Room
Kahuku, Oahu, Hawaii
Chef: Jerry Westenhaver

BRANDY ICE HOUSE

1 1/4   ounces Scotch
  3/4   ounce brandy
  3/4   ounce amaretto liqueur
    4   ounces (or 2 scoops) vanilla ice
        cream
        ground nutmeg, to top

Blend together Scotch, brandy, amaretto and ice cream. Top with nutmeg. Ice is optional.

Serves: 1

Chez Dante of Newport Beach
Newport Beach, California
Proprietors: Sidney J. Kosloy
and Mary Jane Russo
Chef: Ernesto "Jessie" Pinedo

POUSSE CAFE

grenadine syrup
Kahlua
anisette
Crème de Yuette
crème de bananes
blue curaçao
Sambuca Rumania
orange curaçao
blackberry-flavored brandy
Grand Marnier
green Chartreuse
Metaxa-7 Stars
Bacardi-151-proof rum

Pour in a tall liqueur or 6″ bud base glass equal parts of the ingredients in the given order. Flame top layer to serve.

Serves: 1

Hotel Dorset
New York, New York
Chef: William J. Spry

DORSET CHAMPAGNE COCKTAIL

6 fresh strawberries
   Galliano
   champagne

Chill well 6 champagne glasses. Soak the strawberries in Galliano liqueur and chill until time to serve.
Place one strawberry in each glass and pour over with champagne.

Serves: 6

The Farmer's Daughter
Orland Park, Illinois
Proprietor: Kandy Norton-Henely

SANGRIA

1 bottle (fifth) good dry red wine
1 pint club soda
1/4 cup lemon juice
1/4 cup orange juice
1 ounce cognac
4 slices lemon
4 slices orange
1/4 cup simple syrup (*see recipe below*)
2 cinnamon sticks
8 ice cubes

Mix all ingredients together. Pour into a clear glass pitcher.

Serves: 6–8

Simple Syrup

2 1/2 cups sugar
1 1/4 cups water

Combine ingredients in saucepan. Stir over low heat until sugar is dissolved. Cover pan and simmer 2 minutes. Cool. Store in jar and refrigerate.

The Farmer's Daughter
Orland Park, Illinois
Proprietor: Kandy Norton-Henely

DELUXE EGGNOG

6   eggs, separated
2/3 cup sugar
1   quart coffee cream
1   pint heavy cream, whipped

Leave eggs at room temperature for 1 hour. Beat whites until fluffy. Add 1/3 cup sugar and continue beating until stiff but not dry. Beat yolks and 1/3 cup sugar until light and lemon-colored. Stir into the separated yolks and whites 1 pint of coffee cream to each. Fold whipped cream into yolks. Combine yolks and whites together until well mixed. Refrigerate until ready to use.

Yields: 1 1/2 quarts

Hotel Andalucia Plaza
Marbella, Spain

WHITE SANGRIA

1   fresh peach, sliced
1   apple, sliced
1   banana, sliced
3   tablespoons Cointreau
3   tablespoons cognac
1   bottle white wine, cold
1   cup soda water, cold
    spiraled peel of 1 lemon

Marinate fruit slices in liqueur and brandy for 3 hours before serving. Combine with cold white wine and soda water in a pitcher. Garnish with spiraled lemon rind, removed in one piece.

Serves: 4–6

INDEX OF RECIPES

INDEX OF RESTAURANTS, LOCATIONS, AND CHEFS